# SHALL WE LOOK FOR ANOTHER?

# The Bible & Liberation

## An Orbis Series in Biblical Studies

*Norman K. Gottwald and Richard A. Horsley,*
*General Editors*

The Bible & Liberation Series focuses on the emerging range of political, social, and contextual hermeneutics that are changing the face of biblical interpretation today. It brings to light the social struggles behind the biblical texts. At the same time it explores the ways that a "liberated Bible" may offer resources in the contemporary struggle for a more human world.

Already published:

The Bible & Liberation Series

# SHALL WE LOOK FOR ANOTHER?

*A Feminist Rereading of the Matthean Jesus*

## Elaine M. Wainwright

ORBIS BOOKS

Maryknoll, New York 10545

The Catholic Foreign Mission Society of America (Maryknoll) recruits and trains people for overseas missionary service. Through Orbis Books, Maryknoll aims to foster the international dialogue that is essential to mission. The books published, however, reflect the opinions of their authors and are not meant to represent the official position of the society.

Published by Orbis Books, Maryknoll, NY 10545-0308
Manufactured in the United States of America
Copy editing and typesetting by Joan Weber Laflamme

Scripture quotations are from the New Revised Standard Version Bible, copyright © 1989, by the Division of Christian Education of the National Council of the Churches of Christ in the United States of America.

**Library of Congress Cataloging-in-Publication Data**

Wainwright, Elaine Mary, 1948–
    Shall we look for another? : a feminist reading of the Matthean Jesus / Elaine M. Wainwright.
        p.   cm. — (Bible & liberation series)
    Includes bibliographical references and index.
    ISBN 1-57075-184-6 (pbk.)
    1. Jesus Christ—Person and offices.  2. Bible.  N.T.  Matthew—Feminist criticism.  I. Title.  II. Series.
BT202.W28   1998
226.2'06'082—dc21                                              97-50272
                                                                 CIP

*For my sisters—Bernadette, Carmel, and Loretto*
*and my brothers—Gerard and Paul*
*with and among whom I have learned to celebrate difference*

# Contents

# Acknowledgments

A flash of imagination, a creative insight, a new and challenging question—who knows just where they are born! So too with this book. It would be difficult to locate its point of origin. One significant source, however, for the many questions it seeks to address surely has been the years of work with a small core group of women—Therese D'Arcy, Jill Gowdie, June McNamara, and Marilyn Tutt—committed to rendering the language of the biblical and liturgical texts used in our Sunday eucharistic celebrations inclusive. For fidelity to this task and for the questions it has evoked, which have made the completion of this book more urgent, I thank each one of them.

A sabbatical during the academic year of 1993-94 as visiting scholar at Harvard Divinity School provided me with the library facilities, a community of scholars, and the much-needed freedom from regular academic commitments to begin this research in earnest. Residency at the neighboring Episcopal Divinity School extended these facilities even further. I would like to thank the faculty and students of both institutions for their personal and academic hospitality during those nine months. During that time Elisabeth Schüssler Fiorenza, Carter Heyward, Joanna Dewey, Satoko Yamaguchi, Regula Strobel, and Doris Strahm read early drafts of a developing theoretical framework, and their comments encouraged me to continue. I am particularly grateful for the friendships with these and many other women developed during this time and throughout my academic career; these sustain my commitment to feminist theological research.

At the end of the sabbatical Sean Freyne read a draft of my work-in-progress and warned me that I was writing two books, something with which I have grappled throughout the process. In bringing the work to conclusion, I realize that I still want to address the two issues of creating a map for a feminist reading of the Jesus of the gospels, as well as actually beginning such a reading. I would like to thank Sean not only for his helpful critique but also for introducing me to Susan Perry, my editor at Orbis Books. I am most grateful to Susan for her editorial assistance and to Orbis Books for publishing the work.

A large number of my Australian colleagues have contributed to the writing of this book in ways they will never know. I am particularly grateful to those who offered critical insights that proved most helpful at both the international SBL meeting in Melbourne in 1992, at which I first tested my initial tentative ideas for this research, and at subsequent Catholic Biblical Association of Australia meetings, at which I have explored them further. Veronica Lawson, in particular, has been colleague and friend throughout all the stages of the book's journey. A continued shared commitment to feminist theology in Australia is my gift of gratitude to her.

Faculty and students in the Brisbane College of Theology have likewise contributed significantly. My special thanks go to the women who constitute the feminist postgraduate colloquium. The creativity and variety of their feminist theological research sustain and challenge mine, and our gatherings have provided an arena in which my ideas could be tested. Anne Musso, Anita Munro, and Kath Rushton read drafts of chapters or the completed manuscript; the critical comments of many helped the final title to take shape. My colleagues in Christian Testament studies—Ray Barraclough and James Haire—have read the final draft. And finally, a very sincere thanks to Carolyn Willadsen, librarian at the Catholic campus of the Brisbane College of Theology, who not only painstakingly proofread this text but also provided a professional expertise that facilitated my research.

The writing of this book has been another significant step in my own personal journey in fidelity to the liberating spark in the Christian tradition that has enflamed my life. That flame was enkindled and nurtured in my family, to whom I owe the deepest debt of gratitude. Over the years we have learned together new ways in which that tradition we share can find different expression in our lives.

# Abbreviations

| | |
|---|---|
| AARAS | American Academy of Religion Academy Series |
| Ant | Jewish Antiquities (Josephus) |
| BEThL | Bibliotheca ephemeridum theologicarum lovaniensium |
| *BibT* | *The Bible Today* |
| *BTB* | *Biblical Theology Bulletin* |
| *BZNW* | *Beihefte zur Zeitschrift für die neutestamentliche Wissenchaft* |
| *CBQ* | *Catholic Biblical Quarterly* |
| *CurTM* | *Currents in Theology and Mission* |
| *EvT* | *Evangelische Theologie* |
| *HTR* | *Harvard Theological Review* |
| HTS | Harvard Theological Studies |
| *Int* | *Interpretation* |
| *IBS* | *Irish Biblical Studies* |
| *IEJ* | *Israel Exploration Journal* |
| *JBL* | *Journal of Biblical Literature* |
| *JES* | *Journal of Ecumenical Studies* |
| *JETS* | *Journal of the Evangelical Theological Society* |
| *JSNT* | *Journal for the Study of the New Testament* |
| *JSNTSS* | *Journal for the Study of the New Testament Supplement Series* |
| JSOT | Journal for the Study of the Old Testament |
| *JSOTSS* | *Journal for the Study of the Old Testament Supplement Series* |
| *JTS* | *Journal of Theological Studies* |
| LAB | Liber Antiquitatum Biblicarum (Pseudo-Philo) |
| LXX | Septuagint |
| MT | Masoretic Text |
| *NovT* | *Novum Testamentum* |
| *NTS* | *New Testament Studies* |
| OBO | Orbis biblicus et orientalis |
| *RevQ* | *Revue de Qumran* |

| *RSR* | *Religious Studies Review* |
|---|---|
| SBL | Society of Biblical Literature |
| SBLDS | Society of Biblical Literature Dissertation Series |
| SBLSP | Society of Biblical Literature Seminar Papers |
| SNTSMS | Society for New Testament Studies Monograph Series |
| *ST* | *Studia Theologica* |
| Tg. Ps.-J. | Targum Pseudo-Jonathan |

# Introduction

*I feel a real urgency to elaborate alternative accounts, to learn to think differently about the subject, to invent new frameworks, new images, new modes of thought.*

—Rosi Braidotti

There is, at present, an urgency among many women "to think differently" not only about "the subject" as female and feminist subjectivity[1] but also about many "subjects." The "subject" of this book is the Jesus of the Matthean gospel narrative. Recent feminist critical theology and praxis—the experience and critical reflection of feminist Christian women in both the academy and in communities of faith and resistance—have brought to light a crisis. Images and modes of thought that gave meaning to Jesus in the context of Christian community in the past—Lord, Son of God, Son of Man—are no longer functioning in the same way for women who are moving toward new female/feminist subjectivities. Jesus, as refracted through the lens of centuries of androcentric and patriarchal theology and ideology, is proving a stumbling block.

Women are recognizing that within the history of Christianity the maleness of Jesus has been and continues to be used to exclude the female from the symbolic universe of theology and to limit or exclude women's participation within various public ministries in the churches. Also, around the world and in a variety of cultures, women are saying clearly that some aspects of the gospel story in which Jesus is "re-membered"[2] have held women within patriarchal bonds for centuries and continue to oppress and confine them. The biblical question "Shall we look for another?" (Mt 11:3) is both urgent and real in the lives of Christian women. Women need another way of reading foundational stories so that they yield life-giving not death-dealing meaning, another representation of divinity beyond male symbolization. In fact, this crisis in historical narrative is not confined to Christianity. Donna Haraway suggests that "historical narratives are in crisis now, across the political spectrum, around the world. These are the moments when something powerful—and dangerous—is happening . . . resetting the stage for possible pasts and futures."[3] I will begin, therefore, with a brief analysis of this crisis in historical narrative in terms of the theology of Jesus, or what has traditionally become known as *christology,* particularly from a feminist perspective. This will constitute the first chapter of Part I, "Preparing to Read."

The feminism that characterizes this book is located within the variety of feminisms that have emerged in recent years. The debate of essentialism or constructionism,[4] of gender or difference as key feminist analytical categories, need not concern us here.[5] Rather, I simply locate the position taken in this study among those types of feminisms distinguished by their political or liberationist stance.[6]

Political feminism has as its goal a movement out of patriarchy or a transformation of society, and of church or religious institutions within that society, beyond patriarchy. This rereading of Jesus takes its place within the movement toward such a vision. It will, therefore, be a critical reading as the movement itself is critical, and the focus of the critique will be patriarchy as a multidimensional system of oppressive structures, or "interlocking structures of domination," as Elisabeth Schüssler Fiorenza names it. She also supplements the notion of patriarchy (the rule of the fathers) with that of "kyriarchy" (the rule of elite males).[7] Current insights from ecofeminism and the ecological movement indicate further that patriarchy linked to twentieth-century capitalism underpins the current crisis situation of the entire planet. Patriarchy considered as a multidimensional system must be understood, therefore, to include humanity's domination of the universe.

Awareness of the multidimensional nature of patri/kyriarchal oppression, which finds expression in forms of domination based on race, class, ethnicity, sexual-orientation, and religious affiliation as well as gender, has brought many feminists, especially those who are white and within the Western tradition, to a recognition of their own embeddedness within patriarchy and its power dynamics.[8] The new vision, therefore, toward which the journey that characterizes today's feminisms leads, is a female subjectivity that must likewise be characterized as multidimensional and political. Such characterization is particularly evident in the work of Teresa de Lauretis and Rosi Braidotti, who both recognize that women are situated within the ideology supporting patriarchy and yet are aware that women's analyses of patriarchy place them on the edge, seeking to move beyond patriarchy toward the subjectivity of the feminist female.[9]

As Haraway suggests, the crisis of historical narrative as it is articulated within contemporary feminisms is not an end but a beginning. Some Christian women do not wish to abandon their tradition because they find in it the seeds of liberating praxis and profound meaning-making potential. They are voicing a need for new frameworks, new images, and new modes of thought that will enable a reading of Jesus in the gospel story that will create both possible pasts and possible futures, especially for women. For biblical scholars and biblical Christians this means new readings of familiar texts, new storytelling, and new maps to guide such reading and storytelling. The second chapter of this study will address such constructions. It will draw on the feminist critical *principle of difference* as a key to creating such a framework.

The principle of difference as it will influence this study has been explored most fully by Braidotti. In her essay "Sexual Difference as a Nomadic Political Project," she highlights three aspects of difference—difference *between* women and men; difference *among* women in their cultural, racial, class, religious and gender specificities; and difference *within* each woman.[10] She envisages feminist projects as epistemological and political movements in which differing social locations will focus these aspects of difference in varied ways, both deconstructively and reconstructively. She concludes her essay with the hope that "our differences can engender embodied, situated forms of accountability, of story-telling, of map-reading."[11]

The importance I give to constructing new maps and guides for reading/hearing the gospel story of Jesus within contemporary communities arises first from my own experience in theological, liturgical, and personal faith contexts. I hear the same need being articulated by others in both similar and different contexts. What I seek to offer here is one possible map with some significant pointers to ways of rereading. Feminist theologians have been seeking to articulate new christologies during recent decades (a dialogue with aspects of their work will be undertaken in chapter 1). My concern, however, is with ways of reading/hearing the gospel story in a way that new meaning-making in relation to Jesus can take place. This, it seems to me, is the task of the biblical scholar.

Feminist biblical scholarship has over the last two decades focused most particularly on the female characters in the biblical narrative and women in the biblical world, providing new ways of reading the texts and reconstructing or reimaging women in the world in which the texts were constructed. A wide range of scholars has begun the task of shaping female genealogies for women within Judaism and Christianity.[12] There has been little focus, however, on how feminist readers read the stories of male characters within biblical narratives in general and the Jesus character in the gospel stories in particular.[13] An exception to this is the work of Elisabeth Schüssler Fiorenza. While a rereading of Jesus was not the focus of *In Memory of Her*, her ground-breaking feminist study of early Christianity, she did provide some hints toward such a rereading or re-theologizing.[14] Recently she has addressed critical and methodological issues in relation to feminist christology in the New Testament much more extensively and explicitly.[15]

Marianne Sawicki draws attention to a traditional aspect of meaning-making, which she names *poiesis,* in her study of early Christian practices that "see" Jesus as the Risen One. She recognizes the interaction of three epistemic modes involved in this process of "seeing" or meaning-making. *Theoria* is the detached viewpoint that can very readily separate the knower from what is known. *Praxis* enables the practical and repetitious tasks nec-

essary to achieve one's goal. *Poiesis* is the creative and imaginative bringing to birth of a work.[16] It is this third aspect of meaning-making that will
particularly concern us here.

Early Christian *poiesis* or creative meaning-making in relation to Jesus
and to the reign of God movement[17] was accomplished over time and
through various stages of reading/writing, with each new performance
being a "writing" of a new text.[18] The focus here is the reading/writing of
the Matthean gospel text as reception of a written text in the Matthean
social location toward the end of the first century. A brief study of that
social location constitutes chapter 3 in Part II, "Identifying the Voices,"
since social location and the subject positions of the Matthean households
as reading communities are constitutive elements in the process of *poiesis*.
The Matthean community will be considered in its diversity and multiplicity, with particular attention given to those differences in relation to gender,
status and ethnicity that are significant for a feminist reading.

The difference that the principle of difference brings to the telling of
the Matthean story of Jesus is significant. I will consider women as diverse
characters within the gospel story in terms of how their presence shapes
the characterization of Jesus. Jesus will not be read as the lone hero of the
narrative but always in relationship to other characters. A consideration of
the re-membering of Jesus among women within the Matthean communities of reception will give new shape to the story. Women's experience
within Judaism or the religions of the Greco-Roman world will account
for different reading potentialities. Finally, the images, symbols, and metaphors used in the proclamation of Jesus, whether they are male or female
images, have been articulated in a male voice. I will explore the differences
when such images are refracted through a female lens and in a female
voice, not just as a reversal strategy substituting the female for the male
but within the context of a feminist rhetorical reading. The context for
such considerations will be an exploration of the diverse households within
the Matthean community in which such readings were possible.

Guided by the new maps constructed within the first three chapters of
this study, a number of rereadings of the Jesus of Matthew's gospel will be
undertaken. I have called these *soundings*, because it is impossible within
the confines of this study to read the entire story of Jesus in the Matthean
narrative. I use key texts, therefore, to demonstrate the feminist rereading
that is possible using the new maps. They constitute Part III, "Attending
to the Soundings." It is my hope that these soundings will stimulate further readings by others in relation to those parts of the narrative not explored
in this study.

The opening of a narrative establishes the reading process by way of
both textual and rhetorical features inscribed in the text. The first sounding, therefore, will be taken in Matthew 1–2, the gospel prologue. Since
most scholars recognize Matthew 11 as a turning point in the gospel,
drawing together the threads of the narrative to that point and beginning

to unravel those threads that will stretch through the remainder of the text, that text will provide fruit for a second sounding. The Petrine confession of Matthew 16:13-20 is often considered central to the Matthean *poiesis* of Jesus. Rarely, however, is the same attention given to the confession of the Canaanite woman (Mt 15:21-28) in the same narrative context. In the third sounding these two texts will be studied together to determine their contribution to our feminist re-reading of Jesus. In conclusion, I will give brief attention to the climax of the story, the crucifixion of Jesus and the subsequent resurrection narrative (Mt 27:32–28:20).

Such readings participate in the search for "another." It cannot be otherwise when reading is understood as ongoing *poiesis* and when the task of those who have continued the reign of God movement is seen as meaning-making in relation to Jesus in contemporary contexts. The feminist perspective that informs this work will result in a particular contemporary *poiesis*, and the ethics of reading that accompanies it will seek to evaluate its liberating potential for Christian women and men in diverse situations in today's church and world. This re-membering of Jesus, this telling of the Christian story anew, will construct new identities and new subject positions that will not be an end to the journey but the shaping of a possible past that will enable us to envision new and different futures.

*Part I*

# Preparing to Read

# 1

# "Who Do *You* Say That I Am?"—
# Listening to the Questions

The question "Who do *you* say that I am?" has echoed from the gospel text (Mt 16:15//Mk 8:29//Lk 9:20) across the history of Christian theologizing. It has received myriad answers depending on the social location of the various respondents and the way each has interpreted the question and/or the gospel text in which it is embedded. That these responses have been exceedingly varied alerts us to the fragmentary nature of any attempt to answer the question, not only because of the complexity of the question itself and its implication with rhetorical, theological, and ideological goals, but also because of the nature of the interpretive process, a point that has often been ignored.[1]

The interpretive process is not one way; it takes place in the interstices between questions brought to the text and those the text asks of the reader. And, as Sandra Schneiders suggests, "The interpretive project begins with the proper formulation of the questions one wishes to ask of the text."[2] At present women are raising very serious questions about meaning-making in relation to Jesus within Christian churches and theology. Life experiences and critical analyses of these experiences by women around the globe have led to the recognition of the constructed nature of textual interpretation and meaning generally.[3] No longer, therefore, can the Christian Testament or the christological discourses that have characterized Christian tradition be considered universal and value neutral. They are being seen instead as socio-rhetorical practices of particular readers in particular social locations.

Jacquelyn Grant, Kwok Pui-lan, Virginia Fabella, Chung Hyun Kyung, Anne Pattel-Gray,[4] and many other women of color from a number of nations have highlighted the significance of social location for any reading of Jesus. They challenge those articulations of women's experience that are white, middle-class, and particular to a limited and somewhat privileged group of women. Listening to the voices and experiences of women from different races, classes, and ethnic and economic backgrounds will ensure that an analysis of these experiences is not undertaken simply on the basis of gender but rather on the basis of patriarchy as a multidimensional form of oppression.[5]

Questions and issues arising from women's experience of christological formulations and readings of the Jesus story need to be brought into dialogue with contemporary feminist critical theory. It is not simply women's experience within cultural patriarchy but rather women's experience critically analyzed within the systematic and critical evaluation of patriarchy from a feminist perspective that forms the starting point for feminist theology.[6] These critical evaluations of patriarchy will come not only from white middle-class feminists, but from the voices of women of color and their critique of patriarchy will continually inform this analysis.[7]

Because only some aspects of christological meaning productions or practices can be highlighted here, particular attention will be given to those crises in historical christological narratives that need to be problematized within the framework of a feminist rereading of Jesus.[8]

## "ECCE HOMO!"—BEHOLD THE MAN

The most resounding critique of traditional christology is the centrality given to the maleness of Jesus, an issue that is at the heart of the feminist critique. This in no way suggests that the actual Jesus of Galilee was not biologically male.[9] Indeed, his biological maleness was a constitutive element of his identity, part of the "perfection and limitation of his historical contingency," as Elizabeth Johnson notes.[10] She goes on to say that "it is as intrinsic to his historical person as his familial, ethnic, religious, linguistic, and cultural particularity, his Galilean village roots and so forth." Schüssler Fiorenza has pointed out, however, that to make this claim immediately implicates both writer and reader in the socio-cultural construction of the sex/gender system within Western first-century and twentieth-century thought.[11] The problem is exacerbated when the maleness of Jesus is theologized in a way that diminishes women or renders the female invisible, constructing a theological universe that is androcentric and that supports ecclesial and socio-cultural practices that are exclusionary. As the opening paragraph of the 1987 Conference of Asian Women Doing Theology states:

> The classical ecclesiastic view is of God as male and of the Christ as the male image of God. In this traditional view, Jesus is a triumphal king and an authoritative High Priest. This traditional Christology has served to support a patriarchal religious consciousness in the Church and in theology. Traditional theology has justified and guaranteed male dominance over women and the subordinate status of the female.[12]

Significantly, within this statement there is a critique of the hierarchical images of triumphal king and high priest not just as male images underpinning patriarchy but as images that support the understanding of power as domination in a way that has led to class and race hierarchies within the patriarchal system of Christianity. A particular aspect of this systemic structuring has been made explicit by Choi Man Ja in her essay "Feminist Christology." She says that "the problem of feminist Christology is that Jesus has been confessed as Messiah and Lord, terms that symbolize male patriarchal dominance."[13]

Another significant nuance to the critique of those theologies that focus on the maleness of Jesus is offered by Monica Melanchthon. She emphasizes the possibility of God's being with us in concrete particularities in history but demonstrates the irony in the fact that Jesus' maleness is given universal significance while other particularities of his life are ignored:

> But neither the Jewishness of Jesus, or his physical presence in the first century community is particularized. His maleness is understood to be his humanity. His maleness is therefore particularised and emphasized to keep women away from ordination and meaningful participation in the life of the Church and community.[14]

Melancthon's insight sounds a warning note that in giving attention to gender in a feminist reading of the Jesus character in the gospel story, care be taken that such a reading not separate the maleness of Jesus from his Jewishness and the many other aspects of his first-century context in a way that would continue the focus on that maleness. Judith Butler in her discussion of gender likewise draws attention to the danger of giving "ontological integrity" to gender terminology while ignoring its cultural and political construction.[15] It is, however, Donna Haraway's description of the figure of Jesus as "complex and ambiguous from the start, enmeshed in translation, staging, miming, disguises, and evasions"[16] that shifts attention from the generic figure. Gender, therefore, cannot be simply accepted as one cultural given among others but must be treated as a cultural construct to be deconstructed within a feminist reading of the characterization of Jesus.

Feminist critical theory has defined gender as an either-or distinction that has been socially constructed and has functioned to maintain patriarchal and kyriarchal domination.[17] A critical reading of the gospel text must, therefore, uncover how this binary distinction, together with other binary oppositions that accompany it (such as Jew/gentile, divine/human), operates textually not only to support the exaltation of the male Jesus and masculine power that he represents symbolically but to effect power relationships and to structure gendered meanings and identities. These must not be taken as givens to be either accepted or rejected, an approach that leaves intact the gender binary system that supports patriarchy. To read these oppositions as they have been inscribed into the patriarchal and androcentric narrative is to re-inscribe them into the new texts.[18] Gender, therefore, will not be the single determinant of analysis but will stand as one aspect of the multidimensional personality of Jesus and of those characterized in interaction with him textually as well as in the telling and receiving of the story. The rhetorical effect of gender as inscribed in the ancient text and the rhetorical effect of gender in the rereading of the Jesus character need to be considered against the backdrop of an anthropology that affirms diversity and multiplicity both among and within.[19]

Androcentric anthropology with its inherent dualism has been extremely influential in christological formulations. Johnson and others recognize that even new symbols and images in the interpretation of Jesus will remain "enmeshed in an androcentric framework"[20] unless an alternative anthropology is developed. For her own rereading of Jesus, Johnson therefore proposes a different anthropological model, a "multiple-term schema":

> One human nature instantiated in a multiplicity of differences moves beyond the contrasting models of sex dualism versus the sameness of abstract individuals toward the celebration of diversity as entirely normal.[21]

In addition to the above, this critique of an undue focus on the maleness of Jesus has found expression in a variety of ways in different contexts.[22] It has also been closely linked to a critique of the images, symbols, metaphors, and language that developed in the ongoing meaning productions and practices of Christianity.

## "LORD! TO WHOM SHALL WE GO?"— IMAGES, SYMBOLS, METAPHORS AND LANGUAGE

There is a growing awareness among women that many of the titles[23] and images that developed in the proclamation of the Jesus story were embedded within patriarchal, familial, or imperial structures. The title *Kyrios* or Lord (see Mt 8:2, 6, 8, 21; 9:28; 12:8; 14:28-30 and 15:22, 25, 27) carries with it what Johnson calls the "assumed contours of the male head of household or the imperial ruler."[24] Rita Nakashima Brock emphasizes even more strongly the problems and the abuse that have ensued not only for women but also for children as a result of the assumption within early Christianity of the patriarchal family structure as the source of foundational metaphors and images not only for Jesus but also for the believing community. This structure was not only hierarchical but also gave ultimate power, which could be used as domination, to the male heads of households both symbolically and actually. Brock concludes one such critical analysis with the statement: "Hence, I believe such Christological doc-trines reflect views of divine power that sanction child abuse on a cosmic scale and sustain benign paternalism."[25]

Some women argue that the lordship of Jesus—for instance, as depicted in the gospel story and as experienced by them—is not that of the domi-nant patriarchal ruler.[26] The radical critique that has been made of the functioning of this and other related images within the history of Chris-tianity provides, however, a very timely and serious warning. As long as an image has the potential to function oppressively within patriarchy and when it has been demonstrated that it has so functioned structurally over gen-erations, centuries, and cultures, there is a danger in reclaiming such an image too readily while still seeking to move beyond patriarchy. This study will examine these images to determine whether they have been deconstructed within the gospel narrative in such a way that the gospel can function as one more source of critique for the use of oppressive titles and images for Jesus in contemporary Christian communities.

On the other hand, in relation to the title Lord, Susan Brooks Thistlethwaite has drawn attention to the fact that for many African-Ameri-can Christian women this title is central to their experience of Jesus and to their spirituality.[27] Jacquelyn Grant recognizes this and similar trends among her black sisters—"Black women have been able to transcend some of the oppressive tendencies of White male . . . articulated theologies"—but she nevertheless proposes that "womanists must investigate the relationship between the oppression of women and theological symbolism."[28]

Like to the title Lord, the image of Suffering Servant is two-edged. It is claimed by many women who suffer profoundly in order to give meaning to their suffering[29]; it is the image that is central for those who stand in solidarity with people who suffer under the weight of extraordinary op-pression. Chung, however, identifies the danger inherent in this image when she writes: "Making meaning out of suffering is a dangerous busi-ness. It can be both a seed of liberation and an opium for the oppression of Asian women."[30]

One critique offered by women in relation to the image of the suffering central to Christianity is that it has been used to render women subservi-ent to various modes of domination and to keep them in this position.

Closely associated with the image of suffering is the metaphoric lan-guage of redemption and more particularly atonement central to some forms of traditional christology. One of the most radical critiques of this aspect of christology comes from Joanne Carlson Brown and Rebecca Parker,[31] who point out that their critique is not unique but is shared by "many theologians of the modern and post-modern period."[32] Given the embeddedness of redemption and atonement in Christianity's historical narrative, it is not surprising that there are many who consider these theo-logical categories essential to Christianity and, therefore, able to be reinterpreted or better understood.[33] Perhaps Luce Irigaray leaves us with the most challenging question: "Must the individual be immolated if unity with God is to be achieved once more?"[34]

The feminist critical analysis of the images of Suffering Servant and redemptive atonement highlights the double-edged function of images and metaphors generally. It points to the need to establish a theoretical basis for dealing with metaphor and its rhetorical effect within a hermeneutical framework for reading the story of Jesus. It will be necessary to theorize the heterogeneous nature of meaning-making and metaphor within a *poiesis* that acknowledges the agency of women even while they are embedded in pervasive patriarchal structures and ideology.[35]

Other images, metaphors and titles such as Son of Man (for example, Mt 9:6; 11:19; 12:8; 17:12; 24:27), Son of God (for example, Mt 4:3, 6; 8:29; 14:32; 16:16), King (Mt 2:2; 27:11, 29,37, 42), and even Shepherd function with those already examined, both within the gospel text and ongoing Christian tradition, to construct a symbolic universe that is gendered and that excludes female metaphors and images. The rhetorical effect over centuries has been devastating in terms of female subjectivity within a constructed male-centered universe. The exclusion of female representation of the divine has likewise been formative of humanity's sense of power over the entire universe. Mary Gerhart argues, however, that many of our Christian metaphors have been "assimilated into the network of everyday meanings which support the cognitive status quo."[36] As a result, in many instances they have lost their metaphoric and symbolic qualities, failing to capture and expand the Christian imagination to a new *poiesis* of Jesus suitable to these times. They could be described as "dead metaphors"; within a gendered culture, however, they still function to maintain that system, the status quo.

While recognizing the problems associated with the symbolic world of traditional christology, feminist critical theologians have sought those images from the tradition that resound significantly in women's experience as they seek liberation from patriarchy. The one that has emerged most consistently is that of Jesus as liberator. It is the fundamental image for Nelly Ritchie, speaking from the context of Latin America.[37] For Chung, it is the first of the new emerging images among Korean women, and she links it with images of the revolutionary and the political martyr.[38] It is also the image proposed by Rosemary Radford Ruether.[39]

## "AND THE EYES OF ALL WERE FIXED ON HIM" —ISOLATED FOCUS ON JESUS

As women have sought to re-member Jesus and to re-member their foresisters and themselves at the center of the reign of God movement, they have in various ways critiqued those aspects of traditional christologies that make universal claims for Jesus as the Christ, that separate him from his revelatory work of proclaiming the liberating reign of God, and that separate him and his work from the community gathered around him and his memory. Such tendencies have also separated Jesus from communities of believers who have proclaimed his liberating message down through the ages.

The most radical of these critiques, and perhaps the earliest, came from Mary Daly, who claimed idolatry[40] in those christological formulas that isolate Jesus from humanity:

> It will, I think, become increasingly evident that exclusively mascu-
> line symbols for the ideal of "incarnation" or for the ideal of the
> human search for fulfillment will not do. As a uniquely masculine
> image and language for divinity loses credibility, so also the idea of a
> single divine incarnation in a human being of the male sex may give
> way in the religious consciousness to an increased awareness of the
> power of Being in all persons.[41]

Daphne Hampson addresses the problem differently. She asks whether there is a way of speaking of Christ's uniqueness that is not incompatible with feminism. After examining a variety of feminist responses, she concludes that such an approach is not possible and hence that Christianity, with its claims to uniqueness, is in fact incompatible with feminism and must be abandoned by those who wish to remain feminists. The Enlightenment categories Hampson adopts offer her no way of separating uniqueness from masculinity, and it is this that causes her to consider feminism and Christianity incompatible.[42]

Others, however, have addressed differently what Hampson constructs as an impasse. Brock and Heyward see the limitations of the historical particularities of both Jesus in his earthly life and the early theological claims about Jesus as challenges to absolute or universal claims. Heyward states: "Christological truth is neither unchanging nor universally applicable. It is created in the social, historical, personal praxis of right relation, which is always normative, or central, in Christology."[43] Brock, in a similar way, identifies the political and cultural limitations of theological claims but sees the absolutizing of these into either/or choices within the construct of a dualistic world view. She identifies such a world view as one of the most dangerous legacies of patriarchy, a warning that will need to be borne in mind in any rereading of the gospel story. "Of the life of Jesus we are only allowed shadowy glimpses, veiled in New Testament theological claims full of early church social-political agendas, agendas including the patriarchal demand to make absolute either/or choices on the basis of the 'ideal' divine incarnation."[44]

Ruether bases her critique of the once-and-for-all claims regarding Jesus on their lack of a fundamental basis in the life of Jesus. She says that "Jesus does not think of himself as the 'last word of God' but points beyond himself to 'One who will come.'"[45] The gospel stories likewise point beyond, especially the close of the Matthean gospel (Mt 28:18-20). At the same time, we need to ask whether the seeds of the universalizing tendencies are not already there within that text. This alerts us once again to the socio-rhetorical effects of particular texts as well as particular theological and christological formulations and of the need to examine the effects of these formulations not only in their communities of origin but in today's believing communities. While a text may have functioned in a particular way in one socio-cultural context, it may function very differently in another.

As women in Christian communities become aware of the ways in which christological formulations have been used to support a patriarchal world view, one that has been sacralized because of its link to Christianity, so too feminist philosophers and critical theorists, especially in Western traditions, have recognized that many of the universal theories that have governed ways of knowing and of being in the West have likewise supported and maintained patriarchy.[46] Braidotti, like Brock, has highlighted the inherent dualism within the "universalistic stance" of Western patriarchy, and she explores metaphors like the "web" of power-relations and "nomadism" to characterize the journey toward feminism and away from patriarchy.[47]

While many women have not entered into this theological and philosophical discussion at the theoretical level, they have begun to articulate their own understanding of Jesus, re-membering Jesus in a way that renders their lives and their experience central to their shaping of a new understanding of Jesus. Park Soon Kyung, a Korean woman, names Jesus as the "woman Messiah," as liberator of women's oppression, while Choi Man Ja identifies "Korean women's historical struggle for liberation with 'the praxis of messiahship.'"[48] For Korean women, Jesus is also a priest in the *han* tradition, thus related to an image that carries more female than male symbolism. Elizabeth Amoah and Mercy Oduyoye likewise point out that Christ is being perceived in a variety of contemporary images emerging from African women's experience of being woman and being African.[49] For these women, experience not only shapes their imaging of Jesus but inhabits it. Such reimaging highlights the extent to which male experience has inhabited traditional images of Jesus. The reimaging considered here breaks the hold of claims to unique masculinity and its relation to divinity in the lives of many women.

The reimaging of Jesus experienced in women's new theological discourse is also taking place even more dramatically in the visual arts. The figure of "The Crucified Woman," which hung in the Bloor Street United Church in Toronto and now stands in the garden of Emmanuel College, has called forth celebration and controversy, as has "The Christa" in the

Church of St. John the Divine in New York.[50] Less controversial but equally evocative of new understandings of Jesus beyond traditional iconography is Arthur Boyd's "Crucifixion, Shoalhaven."[51] Maybe one of the most expressive depictions of Jesus' embeddedness within the human context is "The Pregnant Mary," a sculpture in wood and ochre by Australian aboriginal George Mung, in which an adult Jesus is visible in the open womb of Mary.[52]

Other women are looking toward the embeddedness of Jesus and the Jesus story within a community context as it is refracted in the biblical text. D'Angelo and Schüssler Fiorenza, both scholars of the Christian Testament, explicitly focus their interpretations in this way. For D'Angelo, "the first shift to be made in imagining the context of Jesus' life is from the person of Jesus to the movement in which he acted."[53] Schüssler Fiorenza questions whether "the historical man Jesus of Nazareth can be a role model for contemporary women,"[54] and she directs attention more specifically to the Jesus movement with its focus on the proclamation of the *basileia* of God as a renewal movement within Judaism.[55] Ruether, a historical theologian, sees the mission of Christ continued in the Christian community;[56] and Elizabeth Moltmann-Wendel examines "Beziehung" or "inter-connectedness" as the forgotten dimension of christology.[57]

Theologians Johnson and Brock likewise shift the focus from the individual Christ to the community. Johnson takes up the image of "the body of Christ" to demonstrate that "the beloved community shares in this Christhood, participates in the living and dying and rising of Christ."[58] Brock speaks of "Christa/Community" and characterizes it by erotic power within connectedness. This Christa community is linked to Jesus in his lifetime, so that he is not considered apart from it, but it is not limited to that period of time. It continues on as "an ocean which is the whole and compassionate being, including ourselves."[59] The voices of women from across the globe are joining with these voices claiming Jesus within the liberating process in which they are participants.[60]

Women—out of the experience of claiming agency within the theological process that characterizes their lives as members of believing and praxis- and *poiesis*-oriented Christian communities—have demonstrated that christological formulations are not universal truths of once-and-for-all validity but are partial truths carrying with them the historical context and ideological particularities of those who constructed them. In this they share in what has been articulated theoretically by Haraway, who has coined the phrase "situated knowledges" to argue for "politics and epistemologies of location, positioning, and situating, where partiality and not universality is the condition of being heard to make rational knowledge claims."[61] These "situated knowledges" are, she suggests, "about communities, not about isolated individuals. The only way to find a larger vision is to be somewhere in particular."[62]

## CONCLUSION

It is from this particularity of women's experience, refracted through the lens of feminist critical analysis, that a feminist biblical hermeneutic for the analysis of the gospel text can be established and a feminist reading of the gospel story undertaken. This must also be extended to include a theoretical framework of feminist rhetorics, if we are to take account of the effect of the text in its historical context and the effect of any new interpretation in the context of a "yearning" toward feminism or feminisms in worlds that are still predominantly patriarchal.[63]

# 2

# What You See and Hear—
# Engendering Reading

*What seems to be at stake in this aspect of feminist reflection is the re-
reading of the grand narrative of rationality, and of the history of
thought, in order to inscribe in it the living presence of women in their
multiplicity . . . any labour of feminist reflection is above all creative
labour. Women's thinking is always oriented towards creation, in sev-
eral ways at once: whether it looks to the past, to recover cultural
traditions and ways of knowing by women that have not been preserved
by mainstream culture, or whether it aims at illuminating a present
that women often experience as conflictual and contradictory, in feminist thought critique and invention progress together.*

—Rosi Braidotti[1]

This feminist critical rereading of the Matthean story of Jesus takes its
place within the larger rereading that Braidotti advocates, especially given
the profound influence of the gospel story and of Christianity not only on
Western thought but on cultures globally. A *hermeneutics of suspicion* will
therefore be employed in relation to the Matthean text, to its rhetorical
effects, and to its contextualization, both ancient and contemporary. It
will give rise to questions regarding the way in which patriarchy and
androcentrism are inscribed in the text's characterization of Jesus as well
as in the context from which it arose and the way the text functioned to
support or to subvert social structures and ideologies embodying patri/
kyriarchy as a system of multiple oppressions. Representative interpretations of the Matthean story of Jesus likewise will be examined from within
this perspective, and even the proposed rereading will need to be tested to
determine whether it is in fact liberating and for whom.

The Matthean gospel story has not been and is not limited to the production or reproduction of ideologically bound meaning. For those who
stand within the context of liberating Christian *poiesis* and praxis the text
has been and can continue to be read in a way that is creative of new

meaning, meaning in front of the text that can begin the process of shaping a world that radically differs from that of patriarchy. This is not an attempt to rescue Jesus or the gospel text for biblical feminism but a recognition of the polyvalence of language and of text, of those ranges of meanings as yet unspoken but able to be brought to light when feminist reading subjects interact with the text.[2] A feminist rereading of the Matthean story of Jesus and of the Matthean women's telling and retelling of that story is also an act of revisioning, of re-membering, of reimaging. This reconstructive and creative task will, therefore, be placed under the rubrics of a *hermeneutics of creative imagination*.[3] This calls for a seeing of Jesus with new eyes, of piecing together from the gospel those images, stories, metaphors, and symbols that will enable a retelling of the Jesus story so that it can be liberating and transformative for women and men in situations of oppression and provide sustenance for the journey out of patriarchy for those along this road.

The methods that will be employed to best accomplish both this critique and creativity can be placed under the umbrella title *socio-rhetorical*. This is an approach that incorporates narrative critical and reader-response approaches that recognize the formal literary elements encoded in the text as well as the interaction between these formal elements and the first- and twentieth-century readers responsible for production of meaning. This approach, however, is not content with an investigation of the formal literary devices as ends in themselves but interrogates the persuasive effect of the text. These combined approaches might best be named *literary/rhetorical*, but to avoid an awkward designation, the term *rhetorical* has been used to incorporate both the literary and rhetorical aspects. The extension *socio-rhetorical* indicates that account will be taken of the socio-cultural context of reading and meaning production. In this respect, literary and rhetorical methods will be combined with socio-cultural and historical investigations in order that both text and context may be scrutinized under a feminist lens to discover both their oppressive and liberating perspectives and visions within first-century Judaism and Christianity and within contemporary Christian communities.[4]

The Jesus of this study is mediated to the contemporary reader by way of the text interpreted within a reading/interpretive community, just as the Jesus of the Matthean community was mediated to that community by way of text or story within an interpretive community or communities. Theoretical consideration will be given, therefore, to text, reader/hearer/community, and context in an interactive movement that will produce the approach particular to this study. Feminist critical questions and concerns will characterize this entire interpretive movement through what I have called the *poetics*, the *rhetorics*, and the *politics* of engendered reading. I use the term *engendered* because it is evocative of the twofold aspect of the reading being undertaken. It incorporates the word *gender*, that aspect of text, reader, and context that a feminist reading seeks to decenter and to deconstruct. Gender in this respect can function symbolically for multidimensional patri/kyriarchy. The immersion of the word itself into the term *engender* can evoke this deconstruction. The term *engender*, which carries the sense of "bringing into being" or "creating," points toward readings as productive of new meaning. Such new meaning engenders the feminist subject in the multidimensionality of sex, race, class, religious affiliation, and those other dimensions that constitute subjectivity. This subjectivity is social, constituted by society, but at the same time struggles against those socio-cultural representations that are recognized as oppressive.[5]

## THE *POETICS* OF ENGENDERED READING

Within the feminist paradigm as interactive, the gospel *text* is not seen as a fixed object in dualistic opposition to reader/interpreter or to social context. Rather, it is "actor and agent" in acts of meaning construction that constitute a dialogical process.[6] It encodes a network of connections that link it to an entire socio-symbolic system. A feminist reading that brings new questions to the text and to its construction of Jesus informed by the feminist critique of christology is able to expose aspects of this socio-symbolic system that have been constructed by and have constructed and supported patriarchy.

It is then possible for a "hidden wisdom," a "deeper lode" to be explored and to be freed to find a voice in the narrative. This is the underside of the narrative—those perspectives that the female characters and other "nonpersons" provide when the focus shifts from the male hero and male images of that hero to other images, symbols, and metaphors, such as that of Sophia, which are submerged by dominant male images.[7] It is in this interactive process that seeks particularly to uncover those riches, visions, and new textual perspectives that will be liberating for women that the gospel can function as revelatory of God's dreaming with humanity within the context of the *ekklesia* as site of liberating *poiesis* and praxis.[8]

The Matthean story of Jesus and of the reign of God movement is created by the reader in the act of reading a literary text. There are multiple ways in which this creative act takes place. I have chosen to focus on three elements of the literary text—genre, character, and metaphor—as key elements of the story's construction of Jesus. While they are treated separately here for purposes of analysis, they are in fact interactive in the text and in the art of interpretation.

### Genre

Every genre is a code according to which the material to be recounted is embodied. This code affects the account in profound ways. Casting one of the characters as hero, part of the event as climax, or a particular item as an obstacle to the hero's project not only involves interpretive judgments about the original experience but affects the meaning of every element in the account.[9]

Schneiders addresses here the significance of genre from the perspective of the author and the text in the creation of meaning, a perspective familiar within traditional biblical and gospel studies.[10] Recent insights into the narrative or discursive aspect of gospel texts have, on the other hand, demonstrated the significance of the reader. Thus Gerhart can suggest that genres persist before and after authors as well as before and after readers' reconception of them and that one way in which meaning is constituted is by means of the genre lens through which the text is read.[11] While both Schneiders and Gerhart make clear that genre is significant for interpretation and the production of meaning in texts, Gerhart's focus on the significant role of the reader is particularly helpful in this study, whose axes are text, reader, and context.[12]

Gerhart indicates that the narrative genre is an overarching one within which various sub-genres or even other genres can be contained, indicating that the "genric 'parentage' of any specific text is often mixed and multiple"[13] and that the testing of genre is therefore significant. She emphasizes that "reading is always *reading as,*"[14] which means that different readers of the same text may constitute the different genre pointers or narrative motifs in different ways. As a result, the same segment of a text may be understood differently and may function rhetorically in quite a different fashion according to the different constructions of genre within a diverse audience.[15] In the subsequent analysis of the Matthean text, attention will be given to the different genre competencies and hence readings of the Matthean gospel that would have functioned within different subgroups of the gospel's audience or reading community.[16] This will demonstrate Gerhart's claim that "the Scriptures as multiple genres find new readings in the lives of Christic persons."[17]

The reader/hearer's genre choices, however, may be in tension with the power of genre to construct culture and cultural particularities.[18] In this project the constructive aspect of genre will be studied in relation not only to gender but also to race and class, ethnicity, religious affiliation, and a whole range of religious and socio-cultural particularities. How Jesus as character is located in relation to these constructions will be established. Since, however, certain genres also have the capacity to "subvert the worlds of meanings that produce them,"[19] this study will explore alternative possibilities to the dominant reading genre in which the character of Jesus as well as gender, class, and ethnicity may have been constructed differently. This is to imagine the gospel functioning as foundational narrative for communities of resistance within the Matthean reading context.

Considering only the literary aspect of the Matthean text in context could result in what Botha calls "a completely disproportionate impression of an extremely small group of Christians."[20] These will be the very small percentage who were literate and, in particular, those who were able to read, a group from whom women would be almost entirely excluded.[21] Rather, consideration will need to be given to the intimate interaction between the oral and the written productions of a text as a "collective cultural enterprise"[22] involving not the private, selective, and silent activity often imagined but rather the interaction between the audience and the performative producer of text in the form of living speech. In such a context the reception by the readers/hearers would have determined the shape of a text as much as the creative activity of the writer/teller: "Genre is doubly bound: to the reality in which it is performed, heard, read, and to the aspects of reality it controls."[23] Throughout this study I will, for ease of expression, generally use the designation *readers* when referring to those who received the Matthean gospel, but the referent of this term in relation to the first century will be to the entire receptive and interpretive community, most of whom would have heard the story rather than have read it. Their reception and meaning-making, however, is to read/write the text anew.

That variant or multiple readings may have been generated as a result of different reading competencies in the Matthean community of reception will be tested, therefore, in the soundings that follow. Questions will also be raised as to the construction of gender, class, and race as a result of genre choices and the effect of these on interpretations of Jesus. In the process attention will be given to the ways in which the choice of a particular genre lens has contributed to a specific interpretation of Jesus in contemporary studies of Matthew's gospel.

### *Characterization*

While characterization has always been a significant element of narrative and literary critical theory, it has received more focused attention in recent years.[24] It is generally agreed that a character within a narrative is a literary construct, resulting from literary techniques together with "modes and degrees of representation." David Fishelov has developed this understanding further by distinguishing between the textual level of characterization and what he calls the "constructed level."[25] He says of this latter level that it "is a product of various complex constructing and integrating activities that involve the reader's experience and knowledge of the world."[26] In a similar way to Gerhart's theory of the reader's construction of genre, so too the reader and the reader's frame of reference contribute to the construction of character.[27] On the other hand, the reader is also shaped by the rhetorical construction of character in the text.[28]

There is a variety of both narrative and text indicators that will guide a study of the characterization of Jesus that I will note here but not develop in detail as this has been done in numerous literary and narrative critical studies both in general and in relation to biblical studies. First, character is intimately connected to plot and plot sequence. Hence, the cumulative nature of character development from the opening reference to Jesus (Mt 1:1) through the various plot movements to the close in 28:20 will be significant. In this way, careful attention can be given to the narrative, and those theological and ideological claims that often belong to a subsequent era will not be allowed to dominate interpretation.[29] Setting also shapes characterization, as do text indicators that both *show* and *tell* the particular character. These include what the narrator says about the character, what the character under investigation says and does, descriptions used, and, in particular, interaction with other characters by way of speech and action.

It is this last aspect that deserves further attention. Character cannot be studied alone; it is developed in the complex interaction of characters and characterization that is specific to a particular narrative work.[30] David McCracken highlights the boundary points between one character and another, points that create what he calls a "threshold" or potential turning point, "that moment [which] is eternal time, when they face a question of ultimate importance."[31] He goes on to conclude that such a dialogic notion of character is essential for understanding the gospel narrative in which the advent of Jesus and the reign of God movement and proclamation continually confront any notion of a stable and fixed identity and world that is not according to God's visioning among humanity. Focus on the historical Jesus as literary construct will not, therefore, be limited to a male hero-figure but will also be on the complex interaction of characters in the text who may represent for the reader the intricate web of human interaction that would have shaped the actual Jesus.

Schneiders nuances the above understanding of character as construct within the gospel narratives, especially in relation to Jesus, in a way that is significant for this study. She notes that in the gospel text we encounter "the literary construct concerning the actual earthly Jesus as that account mediates to us the properly historical dimension of his career," and she designates this construct the "historical Jesus."[32] This mediation occurs by way of the literary techniques of characterization already noted. The gospel text also functions mimetically in that it seeks to image the "actual Jesus" as first-century Galilean[33]; but such mimesis is limited in terms of the literary and rhetorical choices of the author, the persuasive purpose of the text, the shaping of the story during the period of oral and written transmission, as well as the socio-cultural location of its inception and reception. From this point it is possible for investigation of the Jesus character to proceed in two directions. On the one hand, scholars can follow the route suggested by the word *historical,* investigating to what degree those elements of the narrative that purport to have taken place in space and time did characterize the life of the actual Jesus of Galilee.[34] On the other hand, focus on character as construct and the historical as always narrative-laden can direct scholarly attention to the text and the way character is constructed by and constructs its readers. Characterization is, therefore, closely linked to context. It is the second approach that will be taken in this study.

Within the confines of a literary approach to characterization, Margolin points out that literary characters are what he calls "ontologically thin" and are not subject to definite predications.

> This radical closure or limitation of information about literary characters also means that they are available to us only as radically incomplete entities and that many predications which can be made about them will get the truth value "indeterminate" or "undecidable."[35]

Mieke Bal considers such limitations traditionally or ideologically determined and hence subject to change, at least in the way in which they are read from a different frame of reference than that constructed by the dominant narrative.[36] It is important, therefore, to determine which limitations belong to the art of storytelling and which result from cultural tradition. In relation to the character of Jesus within the context of a first-century gospel text, some of the limitations of the literary construct are overcome by way of metaphorical and symbolic presentation that engages the reader's imagination and faith beyond the limitations of the storytelling and also beyond the limitations of the actual first-century individual. It is in this regard that Schneiders's understanding of the "proclaimed Jesus" as "the construct of the paschal (i.e., Christian theological/spiritual) imagination construing the actual (both earthly and glorified) Jesus as the Christ and presenting that image in literary-historical form in order to elicit the faith response of the hearer/reader" becomes significant.[37] From within a different discipline Haraway offers a similar perspective when she considers the Jesus of our historical narratives as trickster:

> This figure of the Incarnation can never be other than a trickster, a check on the arrogances of a reason that would uncover all disguises and force correct vision of a recalcitrant nature in her most secret places.[38]

It is at this level of the "proclaimed Jesus" that metaphor and symbol operate most particularly, and they will be given particular attention in the next section. Genre, characterization, and metaphor have been separated for purposes of analysis, but they cannot be separated in the interpretation of the character Jesus of the Matthean gospel. A reader's genre choices or genre testing will influence interpretation of character, and characterization is inseparable from those metaphors and symbols both explicit in the text and shaped by the very narrative and reading process.

Reader and context are of central importance in the process of constructing character. This is particularly so in relation to the character Jesus, because each reader brings to the text knowledge about Jesus and his con-text gained from a wide variety of sources. This knowledge, together with the theo-ideological perspective of the reader, will guide the judgments, the selections made about the way the character Jesus is described. In this work the feminist perspective that informs the reading will function in this way together with other theo-ideological factors of which I am not aware and the sources of knowledge on which I choose to draw. First-century readers are likewise constructed, together with the potential knowledge, perspectives, and reading competencies claimed for them. As a result, par-ticular readings of the Jesus character will emerge that will have their own rhetorical function at this point in the history of Christian interpretation of the classical story, the gospel.

### Metaphor

The Jesus of Matthew's gospel is a literary construct to mediate certain historical aspects of the life of Jesus of Nazareth. Even the most cursory contact with the gospel text, however, alerts the reader to what might be called the transhistorical or the theological by way of metaphors, images, symbols, and titles: Christ, Son of God, Son of Man, Lord, Emmanuel, Sophia. This metaphoric process enabled the early communities of believ-ers to express their experience of hearing the story of Jesus and of having their lives shaped by the presence and power of Jesus, whom they believed to be still among them. But this metaphoric process, which can provide Christian understandings of Jesus beyond those available through liter-ary/historical construction of Jesus, can also limit or deflect understanding and be unfaithful to the actual and historical Jesus because of prejudices and purposes that influenced developing proclamation.

Establishing a theory of metaphor is a complex process, as recent books on the subject indicate.[39] I simply draw upon this theory as it is relevant to the shaping of a methodological framework of analysis for the current project.

Janet Martin Soskice provides what she calls a simple working defini-tion of metaphor: "Metaphor is that figure of speech whereby we speak about one thing in terms which are seen to be suggestive of another."[40] From this definition, however, some significant deductions can be made. On the one hand and perhaps fundamentally, metaphor functions to cre-ate new meaning, meaning that can be produced in no other way than by speaking about one thing in terms of another.[41] Therefore, the metaphors and images used to proclaim Jesus in fact give new meaning to the Jesus character and the Jesus story or to what Schneiders calls the "Jesus-im-age."[42] On the other hand, this last claim makes clear that metaphors function not just in the conjunction or combination of two terms but as a whole utterance that itself has a context; namely, the discourse that in our case is the gospel story.[43] For Soskice, context is not limited to the linguistic or textual elements but is extended to include the recognition by the reader of the metaphoric process as well as the functioning of the linguistic references within a socio-cultural context.[44]

One of the shared perspectives that will be helpful in a feminist analysis of metaphors used in the Matthean gospel is that of the *tensive,* or what Patricia Parker calls the "transgressive" nature of metaphor.[45] The combining of two terms, and hence two fields of meaning, creates a tension or disjunction; it is only in the maintenance of this tension or transgression that new meaning is possible and that future meanings will be created as metaphor is interpreted in the unfolding of that process. Many explain this tension in terms of Ricoeur's description of the "is" and "is not" of metaphor.[46] Soskice, however, critiques Ricoeur's understanding in terms of the "split reference" he creates in order to explain his theory together with his emphasis on "redescription." For her, metaphor does not re-describe, especially in its initial creation, but describes for the first time.[47] Such a description functions in a "context of investigation" or a "linguistic community."[48] Sheila Davaney likewise offers a criticism of McFague's appeal to critical realism and her use of the "is/is not" formulation in a theological context, a criticism that is developed by Claudia Camp to emphasize the constructed nature of our knowing, even our knowing about God and the proclaimed Jesus of Christian theology by way of metaphor.[49] Both Soskice and Camp return us to the position of the linguistic and hence metaphoric structure of the reality that we live by, that we live in, and from which and within which we construct metaphors and are constructed as subjects. Bal takes this even further. She indicates that "metaphor is . . . a key to an understanding of language—including itself—as a form of struggle." From this struggle emerges metaphor perceived as a "normal" expression but one that carries the "traces" of what has been repressed. It is this sublimation or "what it makes impossible to say" that Bal sees as the key to metaphor.[50] Rather than engaging with the seemingly literal "is" and "is not" nature of metaphor, our investigation will focus more on metaphor functioning in the early faith communities that initially produced and/or used metaphor not only to construct a world but also to suppress another.

The approach to metaphor to be taken in this study is one that gives significant attention to the function of metaphor within the total symbolic order that the text creates and as product of and for a linguistic community within a socio-cultural context. Hence, no metaphor for Jesus will be considered in isolation; rather, the interconnection of the various metaphors within the narrative and symbolic world will be considered significant. Just as the metaphor father for God has become a model or God-image according to which so many other metaphors and images are weighed, so we need to ask whether the son metaphor for Jesus has likewise become such a model and to test the differences in the symbolic universe created by the text if the central Jesus-image is linked to the subversive elements of the reign of God rather than Son of God metaphoric world.[51] Within such an alternate modeling, the metaphor of Jesus-Sophia (Mt 11:19), an early layer of Christian traditioning, may be significant.[52]

This raises the question of the possibility of new metaphors, of new ways of relating metaphors within a narrative world, and of the ways new readings of narratives might participate in the metaphoric process. It asks how the metaphoric process constructs patriarchal ideology as well as male and female, racial, and class subjectivities. It questions the links between dominant metaphors in a text and power relations in the socio-cultural context of that text. How might the metaphors used in relation to Jesus have subverted socially constructed concepts of gender, race, class and religion as well as participated in their construction? The Matthean community of construction cannot be homogenized. Rather, the question needs to be asked as to how gender, race, and class metaphors may have functioned differently for women and men and for women of different racial and class origins. Finally, there is the possibility that the kyriarchal symbols and metaphors used within the gospel may construct a reality that has little to do with patriarchy, its structures, and its values.[53]

## THE *RHETORICS* OF ENGENDERED READING

The creative power of the *reader* has already been hinted at above in establishing the constructive power of the text. In this section the focus will be on the reader who both constructs and is constructed by the text within a particular rhetorical context. Consideration of reader and rhetorics stands, therefore, between and in creative tension with the understanding of text that has preceded this section and the development of an approach to context that will follow. This very positioning suggests that the approach to reading utilized in this project will be interactive.

The literary and rhetorical features in the text, as well as those socio-cultural norms and values that it encodes, function to shape and to persuade a first- or a twenty-first-century reader in particular ways.[54] Together these textual features, engaged by the reader in the reading process, construct a narrative world. The reading process, however, whether in the Matthean community that produced the gospel or in a community of liberating Christian *poiesis* and praxis today, clearly does not take place in a vacuum. Readers from both these socio-cultural contexts did not and do not perfectly fulfill the task of being ideal readers according to the constructions within the text. Hence multiple factors in the reader's social context shape the reading and its rhetorical and persuasive effects. This work is concerned with actual first- and twenty-first-century readers while recognizing, however, that they are, as posited in this work, the construct of the critic.

The Matthean text cannot and does not characterize Jesus with a single voice when considered from the perspectives of its readers. It is dialogical in its rhetorics as it was in its poetics. It is in this respect that the literary approach of intertextuality can provide a suitable framework for listening to some of the multiple voices or multiple readings.

Mikhail Bakhtin has pointed out that each utterance or word is related to other utterances or words in a relationship that he has called "dialogism."[55] Julia Kristeva developed Bakhtin's insights to claim that "each word (text) is an intersection of words (texts) where at least one other word (text) can be read."[56] This means that the text's rhetorical effect can no longer be seen as "single, complete" but as always "plural, shattered."[57] Fulkerson likewise invites interpreters of a text to "recognize the existence of many texts as they appear from multiple subject positions."[58] Intertextuality, therefore, will be considered in this study from a textual/rhetorical, cultural, and ideological perspective. The socio-cultural aspect will be developed in the subsequent chapter. The ideological is of particular significance to a feminist reading that seeks to attend to difference in the text and its context where many manifestations have been covered over by monological and ideologically bound readings. Gary Phillips suggests that the ruptures, fissures, or gaps that emerge when account is taken of difference "become occasions for observing dynamic, dialogical semiotic processes at work in writing and reading. . . . This is a process which is ongoing at the time of the original production of the text as well as at later times."[59]

The rhetorics of an engendered reading, particularly from a feminist perspective, is intimately connected to the ethics of such a reading. The role of the reader, selecting and ordering the many codes and conventions offered by the text, is significant in building the narrative and constructing the character of Jesus. In constructing a first-century reader, the contemporary reader/critic also selects and orders both literary and socio-cultural indicators, filling in the existing gaps from his or her own imaginative perspective. A feminist reading makes these choices from the perspectives outlined above constitutive of the particular approach that is named feminist.[60] In this way a feminist reading of the Matthean story of Jesus will emerge that will be, as John Darr suggests of contemporary critical readings generally, "no less rhetorical than the text itself."[61] Of course, such a reading will need to be tested to determine whether it can function to shape a world that can be liberating and for whom, and whether it can construct feminist subjectivities for liberating political action toward the elimination of patriarchy by way of its particular reading of Jesus.[62] Both the academy and the *ekklesia* of women can be sites for such testing. Awareness of the ways in which theologies have shaped kyriarchal consciousness in the past will enable members of both communities to question in different ways whether new Christian *poiesis* is allowing for the full subjectivity of participants in relation to gender, ethnicity, race, class, religious affiliation, and other categories of understanding.

Finally, the rhetorics of an engendered reading must not limit itself to the text as de-historicized but rather must give attention to the rhetorical effect of the history of interpretation of the text. In any one project it is impossible, of course, to give attention to this entire history.[63] Representative examples will be drawn especially from those contemporary interpreters who focus on the character Jesus. The readings they propose will be examined for their possible rhetorical effects—do they continue to isolate and dogmatize Jesus; do they provide contemporary underpinning for patriarchy both within the academy and the churches where such readings function; do they open up possibilities for the subversion of patriarchal structures within church and academy? It also will be important to determine whether the reading results from the proposal of an ideal reader or redactor or from the embodied position of a human community of readers living in the extraordinarily complex religio-political context of the Matthean community or the socio-cultural diversity of the present. As Fernando Segovia suggests, we need not only a literary, rhetorical, and political reading of the text and its context but also a literary, rhetorical, and political reading of ourselves as readers/interpreters and of our context at the end of the twentieth century.[64]

## THE *POLITICS* OF ENGENDERED READING

A consideration of the rhetorics of engendered reading in the first and twenty-first century necessitates finally an examination of the *context* that shapes and is shaped by the text. This section will take account, therefore, of the context that produced the Matthean text or what is often referred to as the "world behind the text" as well as the reality-shaping function of the present interpretive undertaking, namely the "world in front of the text." The interaction between the two and their significance politically is stressed by Elisabeth Schüssler Fiorenza:

> Our search for history and roots is neither antiquarian nor nostalgic: it is political. It is political because our understanding of the present shapes our reconstructions of the past, while our reconstructions of the past shape present and future reality.[65]

### The World behind the Text

In order to understand the way the Matthean story of Jesus functioned rhetorically or persuasively, both theologically and ideologically for a first-century Christian community, it is necessary to reconstruct that community and its hearers/readers of the Jesus story. Not only data encoded in the text but also other available literary and nonliterary sources, as well as a developing knowledge of socio-cultural codes that were effective in first-century Mediterranean society, will serve such a reconstruction. The contemporary critic orders this material as well as fills in the gaps the data fail to provide according to the creative and imaginative perspective brought to the entire interpretive process.[66] A feminist reconstruction of the Matthean community will not assume that male experience, which dominates most available records and reconstructions of both historical events and socio-cultural structuring of the context, is descriptive.[67] Rather, it will question both data and reconstruction from the perspective of those not represented or barely represented because of race or class, namely, women and others considered to be non-persons.

The tools for such investigation will be historical critical as well as social scientific, and both will be informed by a feminist critique.[68] Using patri/kyriarchy as an analytical category, questions will be raised regarding differences among women and between certain groups of women and men.[69] Literary and nonliterary data together with reconstructions of the experience of Jewish, Christian, and gentile women in the Greco-Roman world give rise to new questions regarding women's role in the development of the Jesus tradition within the Matthean community as well as in the socio-cultural, theological, and liturgical life of the community. Such investigation provides new ground for questioning the way the Matthean story of Jesus may have functioned within the various Matthean reading communities to either support or to challenge both their world view and hence their activities.[70] According to such an analysis, patriarchy as ideology will not be considered a closed, static, and monolithic system; the ways in which it may have been more unstable and permeable than many of the historical and social scientific reconstructions allow will be examined.[71]

A feminist reconstruction that allows for women's agency even within oppressive patriarchy—women's power within familial, kinship, and religious structures—opens the way for a significantly different understanding of the rhetorical effects of the androcentric Matthean text. This text, however, like the society, is not monolithic but has within it the whispers of alternative voices.

### The World in Front of the Text

These faint whispers and alternative voices create what Ricoeur refers to as the world "in front of the text."[72] Schüssler Fiorenza, on the other hand, has emphasized in recent works the rhetorical effect of interpretations of biblical texts.[73] The way we tell the Jesus story; image Jesus according to male-specific or multidimensional categories; locate the Jesus proclamation within the patriarchal tradition of the maleness of Jesus or within the Jewish emancipatory tradition of the female gestalt of God, Sophia; isolate Jesus as hero within a narrative in which other characters are merely support roles; or proclaim the reign of God movement as shaped by a community of which Jesus was a member—all of these and many other alternatives are and will be significant for both female and male participants in the *ekklesia* of women and other communities of liberating Christian praxis.

Just as patriarchal and androcentric texts and interpretations function to shape gendered, class, and racial subjectivities, to construct the world according to the organizing structures of patriarchy, and then to guide praxis so that socio-cultural codes and organizations are conformed accordingly, so too can alternative interpretations of texts shape and construct alternative world views and so effect changes in society and church. A feminist reading of the Jesus character of Matthew's gospel will take account of the feminist critique of traditional christologies, will bring a hermeneutics of suspicion to an initial reading of the text, deconstructing those aspects of the characterization of Jesus—both the historical and the proclaimed Jesus—that underpin patriarchal and kyriocentric readings of the text and traditional dogmatic formulations. It will bring to light new perspectives that highlight and creatively weave together aspects of the text and its subtext that have been neglected, silenced, or forgotten during centuries of patriarchal Christianity. Such a reading will, therefore, create a new symbolic universe that can shape the reader and according to which a new view of the world can be created.

Imaging Jesus within the context of the reign of God movement as an inclusive and emancipatory movement for women and men, focusing on the Sophia imagery as a decentering of the exclusively male symbolization of both Jesus and God, and configuring Jesus in relation to female characters and female memory and traditioning is profoundly political, especially when situated within the emancipatory struggles within church and society. As such, it participates in what Schüssler Fiorenza calls the "logic of democracy,"[74] it engenders new feminist subjectivity,[75] and it is also genealogical, providing new links with our "sisters in spirit" of the early Christian era.


## CONCLUSION

I have developed this map for reading at length in order that those reading the subsequent soundings, especially those readers who may not wish to navigate little charted and seemingly dangerous terrain,[76] may be provided with a guide to their steps. I hope that others will take up this map and undertake further engendered readings of Jesus, not only in the remaining segments of the Matthean gospel but in other gospels also. Before undertaking the four soundings that will test the map and determine its potential in this study, it is necessary first to offer a feminist reconstruction of the Matthean social location and its diverse households of reception of the gospel text, the context in which multiple voices of interpretation of Jesus might be heard.

*Part II*

# Identifying the Voices

# 3

# "From Galilee and the Decapolis"— A Context for Reading

*There is a sharp and categorical boundary line between the actual world as source of representation and the world represented in the work. We must never forget this, we must never confuse—as has been done up to now and as is still often done—the represented world with the world outside the text. . . . However forcefully the real and the represented world resist fusion, however immutable the presence of that categorical boundary line between them they are nevertheless indissolubly tied up with each other and find themselves in continual mutual interaction. . . . The work and the world represented in it enter the real world and enrich it, and the real world enters the work and its world as part of the process of its creation, as well as part of its subsequent life, in a continual renewing of the work through the creative perception of listeners and readers.*
—Mikhail Bakhtin[1]

Since the focus of this project is on the reading or reception of the Matthean story of Jesus and the reign of God movement, it would seem appropriate to begin this chapter with the development of that aspect of the interpretive project with which the theoretical model of the previous chapter closed, namely, a reconstruction of the socio-cultural and religious worlds in which the story was both formed and received.[2] Such a task of "reading a text in order to understand the group and social situation underlying it is a difficult and treacherous procedure," Anthony Saldarini indicates.[3]

Biblical scholarship has grappled with this difficult task in a variety of ways in recent decades. Schüssler Fiorenza categorizes the different approaches in terms of an "antiquated positivism" that believes that it can discover accurate and value-neutral data about the past; a literary formalism that separates the narrative and symbolic world of the text from any historical eventuality; and a "postmodern constructionism" that is textual and ahistorical.[4] Her development of a model for feminist historiography

in the face of these approaches underscores the integral relationship between text and reality, as did the words of Bakhtin at the head of this
chapter. My own theoretical model established in the previous chapter
likewise indicated the importance of context in a work concerned with the
politics of engendered reading as well as the inseparability of text, reader,
and context. With Schüssler Fiorenza, therefore, as well as Bernadette Brooten
and other feminist scholars of early Christianity, I recognize the need for a
multidisciplinary approach, an integration of literary, socio-historical, and
ideological criticisms in order that the community of reception of the
Matthean gospel might be reconstructed in a way that is not monolithic.[5]
This feminist reconstruction will seek to render visible/audible those persons, groups, and voices that traditional reconstructions have either ignored
or relegated to the margins in order to offer a multidimensional perspective on this particular community within early Christianity.

It has already been stated that one of the significant feminist principles
guiding this study is recognition of difference. This feminist reconstruction will take account of significant differences within the audience in
relation to gender, ethnicity, class, and religious affiliation. Such an approach seems particularly appropriate to a study of the Matthean context
since it has long been recognized by scholars that there are tensions within
the text in relation to a number of key issues—ethnicity, gender, and leadership, to name but a few.[6] Indeed, the gospel itself is often characterized
under the banner of Matthew 13:52, the bringing together of what is new
and what is old, an act that is bound to result in tensions. Unfortunately,
scholarly readings of the text and its context are prone toward coherence
rather than tension and difference. In this reading, however, the way the
Matthean gospel story may have been developed and the way it functioned
will be considered within the diversity that characterized its social location. Into this feminist paradigm of socio-cultural reconstruction, two other
theoretical perspectives will be incorporated to facilitate the project.

First, Bakhtin's notion of a dialogic, whether it is within the literary
world of a text or within the world where text and context intersect, provides a theoretical foundation for the recognition of different voices,
different languages, within any given text, the gospel of Matthew being
one such text. While Bakhtin's major emphasis is on the novel as the finest
expression of multiple voices or heteroglossia, he recognizes that such
polyglossia has always existed and is perhaps more ancient than "pure,
canonic monoglossia."[7] Indeed, he postulates that one of Hellenism's greatest gifts to Europe was a "radical polyglossia."[8] On the other hand, for the
sake of this study, in turning our attention eastward it is clear that the
languages and literatures of Greece, Rome, and a number of indigenous
peoples including the Jewish people intersect in any new piece of literature produced in that context at the beginning of the Common Era. It is
a new reading of many voices. For Bakhtin, these languages are not only
literary but also socio-cultural; the line between the literary and the social

is transmutable, while needing to be profoundly respected. Since the interest of this project is the continual renewing of the work through the creative *poiesis* of listeners and readers, this chapter will establish those different listeners and readers whose voices, whose language, is perceptible in the text and who are being constructed by the text as they construct it in their reading process.

Bakhtin provides a theoretical framework for different voices, but he fails to take account of gender as a significant category of difference. In relation to his theory, however, that lacuna has begun to be addressed by the collection of essays entitled *Feminism, Bakhtin, and the Dialogic*, edited by Dale M. Bauer and S. Jaret McKinstry.[9] These essays demonstrate in relation to contemporary novels how Bakhtin's theories, especially that of the dialogic between different voices, when infused with a recognition of different power perspectives encoded in language, allow us to "pinpoint and foreground the moments when the patriarchal work and the persuasive resistance to it come into conflict."[10] Thus, within this reconstruction of the Matthean community, the dominant voices and language, the centripetal force that strains toward unity, will intersect with those voices contributing toward the centrifugal force offering "persuasive resistance" to monological unity.

Intimately connected to the above is a second dialogic perspective significant for this reconstruction. It is that of Foucault, whose "political vision of intertextuality had become a crucial premise for those critics who wanted to focus on the ways that the social saturates the literary object."[11] His theory is also dialogical but in a manner different from that of Bakhtin. Clayton and Rothstein note that Foucault insists that we must analyze not only "the role of power in the production of textuality" but also the power "of textuality in the production of power."[12] This dialogic recognizes the pervasive notion of power and the production not only of discourse or text but also of counter-discourse. As Foucault indicates:

> Where there is power, there is resistance, and yet, or rather consequently, this resistance is never in a position of exteriority in relation to power. Should it be said that one is always "inside" power, there is no "escaping" it, there is no absolute outside where it is concerned.[13]

In seeking to reconstruct perspectives on the Matthean community of reception, not only the dominant group, whose voices are heard most clearly in the narrative, but more particularly resistant voices, whose counter-story continually challenges claims to a monological voice, will be heard.[14] These will not be categorized as dominant/normative and resistant/aberrant. Rather, the many voices and their socio-cultural contextualization will be heard as heteroglossal, recognizing that the variety of voices may not be easily genderized. Some women may well have collaborated with patriarchal power while some resisted; likewise, there may have been men among those house-churches that were the locations of resistant voices. Marianne Sawicki notes the following in relation to first-century colonized Galilee, the context at least for the oral traditioning if not writing of the Matthean gospel:

> Colonized people devise various strategies of resistance, ranging from outright avoidance, to restrictive regulation, to incorporation of the new features into an updated version of traditional spatial management systems. Moreover, colonized people don't always resist; they also collaborate to some extent with the colonial power.[15]

For the purposes of this project the listening for various voices will be accomplished by way of a feminist critical analysis of some representative recent proposals regarding the Matthean audience in dialogue with the multiple disciplines operative in such reconstructions likewise analyzed from a feminist perspective. From such an analysis some of the different voices characterizing different house-church communities within the Matthean context will be able to be heard and different reading communities of the Matthean Jesus established.

My general characterization of the overall Matthean reading community as constituted by a number of house-churches was formulated as a result of my study of the traditioning process in relation to the stories of female characters contained in the gospel.[16] In that study significant attention was directed to the difference gender made. This study will extend the analysis beyond gender to include class, ethnicity, and religious affiliation as a result of current feminist recognitions of the interaction between these socio-cultural constructs in the lives of individuals and groups within a given society and the possibility of oppression and marginalization occurring across those categories. Resistance may likewise arise as a result of social location determined by such categories.

A number of scholars have noted the presence of diverse groups within the Matthean community of reception. Wayne Meeks said of this context:

> There may have been many small household groups of Christians in Antioch at that time, however, and quite likely there was a certain diversity among them. Not all may have shared the history and perspectives that Matthew assumes.[17]

Michael Crosby also notes that large numbers of converts would have meant that there had to be more than one "church."[18] Most interpretations of the Matthean gospel have, however, focused on the writer of the gospel and assumed that the context of inception was equally the context of reception. The analysis below will demonstrate that such an assumption is fundamentally flawed in relation to the first century.

## CLASS[19] AS A CONTEXT FOR VOICE

I choose to begin with this category of analysis because it opens into an exploration of the relationship between the aural/oral culture of the first-century Matthean community and the initial writing of the Matthean story of Jesus.[20] Although biblical studies have always recognized the significant oral stages of tradition, it is only in recent years in the study of the Christian Testament that attention has been given to the close relationship between orality and the writing of the gospel stories.[21]

It is generally assumed by scholars that the Matthean gospel was first committed to writing sometime within the last two decades of the first century of the Common Era. Prior to that time, and given the aural/oral nature of the society,[22] it can be assumed that members of the Matthean community had received the gospel traditions orally. Even if written collections of miracle stories, sayings of Jesus, and/or the gospel of Mark were functioning in the community, these very traditions generally would have been performed in an aural/oral context and possibly changed in the very performance as a result of audience participation. At times such performances or storytelling may have been undertaken by authorized proclaimers,[23] perhaps even those itinerant missionaries who moved from Galilee to Syria, which may have been the provenance of the Matthean gospel traditions.[24] At other times significant stories of Jesus would have been told by skilled although not necessarily professional storytellers in gatherings such as house-church meetings, work places, and gatherings of women and men in public squares.[25]

It is in such contexts of the Matthean storytelling that two aspects must be noted. On the one hand, storytellers were important in both spreading and maintaining dominant traditions.[26] In the Matthean storytelling the dominant tradition is patriarchal. It opens the narration with the patrilineage, limits discipleship to males, and evokes more consistently the emerging titles for Jesus such as Son of God, Son of Man, and Lord. On the other hand, because oral storytelling crossed boundaries of gender, class, wealth, and literacy, it was also a means of resistance to the dominant tradition. Hence, it may have been in women's storytelling circles that the account of the healing of Peter's mother-in-law (8:14-15) was preserved as a vocation story, contrary to the dominant tradition of male discipleship.[27] The popular appeal of the authority of the house-church (18:18-20) rather than the single male leader (16:18-19) may have ensured the retention of this tradition, which is particular to the Matthean community, among a number of its households. Also, in public storytelling contexts the listeners may have interjected words and lines reflecting their own particular socio-cultural situation, which may have been incorporated into the Matthean community's version of the story. Hence, the oral storytelling stages in the Matthean community would have allowed the voices of both the literate and nonliterate to be heard, the voices of women as well as men, and the voices of the poor among the community, whether slave or freed, as well as those of the more wealthy, who would have been much fewer in number.[28]

The consigning of the story to writing, whether as a dictation of an oral performance or a collecting of diverse story traditions from among the house-churches, gave prominence to an elite voice and most likely a male voice. That the voice was elite can be presupposed on the basis of the cost of writing material in the first century.[29] *Elite* in the Matthean context may not have meant extremely wealthy or belonging to the approximately 2 to 5 percent who held power within the Empire. It may have been that a member or members of the scribal class were commissioned with or undertook the task, supported financially by the Matthean house-churches.[30] That this scribal voice is more likely male has been argued in my previous work.[31] This does not mean, however, that first-century Jewish, Christian, or Greco-Roman women were not literate. Indeed, women among the elite were able to read and write as were women in some occupations.[32] The Matthean text, however, suggests that the writer is an educated male.[33]

While, in the early stages of the written text within a predominantly aural/oral milieu there is often a privileging of the oral by way of storyteller or teacher; as time goes on the written becomes the canonical basis of oral instruction and storytelling dies.[34] Writing also results in the privileging of certain perspectives. The stories of women and other marginalized groups who were often in the company of Jesus in the reign of God movement (lepers, demoniacs, the blind and lame) are told from the point of view of the elite male writer and the voice and perspective of the poor are silenced or hidden.[35] The perspectives of the popular audience, for whom Jesus was a popular teacher and perhaps even a folk hero and messianic figure,[36] become refracted through the lens of the scribe, who proclaims Jesus as the authoritative teacher or interpreter of the law (Mt 5-7; 15:1-20; 21:23-27). Given, however, that this early written text still functioned in a predominantly oral context, its reception would have been in those house-churches of the Matthean context where poor and rich, literate and nonliterate, women and men came together and received the text according to their social status, gender, and literacy.[37] In some house-churches or contexts of gospel performance there may have been a predominance of one particular group so that their reception may have been governed more specifically by their socio-cultural or economic status. This may have been especially so when the gospel was performed in a public setting and hence open to larger numbers of the poor and nonliterate at a particular performance or reception. As this study progresses, these various receptions of the Jesus story in different locations and group compositions will be examined, and it will become clear that in the early stages of inception and reception of the Matthean gospel the Jesus character of this story was interpreted in a variety of ways.

## ETHNIC AND RELIGIOUS VOICES

At present, one of the most generally accepted tenets in Matthean scholarship is that the "palette"—to borrow an image from F. Gerald
Downing—from which the dominant color of the narrative is drawn is
that of Jewish tradition, especially its scriptural or religious heritage.[38] The
gospel opens with a patrilineage constructed from Israel's sacred story (1:1-
17). The early chapters are characterized by the fulfillment formula
(1:22-23; 2:5-6, 15, 17-18, 23; cf. also 4:14; 8:17; 12:17; 13:35; 21:4;
26:54, 56; 27:9). The Jewish law is evoked repeatedly, especially in the
Sermon on the Mount, and patterns and paradigms from the Jewish scriptures shape the storytelling.[39] Recent scholarship has, therefore, tended to
focus more specifically on the Jewish characteristics of the social world of
the Matthean community.[40] The archeological finds that have informed
the reconstruction of first-century Judaism during the latter half of this
century, together with literary and sociological studies, have made it emi-
nently clear that those located within Judaism in the Greco-Roman world
did not belong to a monolithic religious and ethnic group but to groups
whose religious and socio-political lives found a variety of expressions.[41]

For Saldarini, the Matthean group, as he calls the community or communities of reception and inception, stands within this variety of expressions
of first-century Judaism, but it functions deviantly, constructing a new
symbolic universe with Jesus and the story of Jesus at the center.[42]

> Matthew's community engages in many of the functions of a deviant
> association. It recruits members, develops a coherent world view and
> belief system, articulates an ideology and rhetoric to sustain its be-
> havior, and attacks competing social institutions and groups. . . . All
> of these activities are carried out in the narrative through the ser-
> mons and teachings of Jesus.[43]

Saldarini's contribution to an understanding of the Matthean communities of reception is his identification of the Jewish character of at least a
significant group who shaped the gospel traditions. This group or these
house-churches would, in their turn, have received the narrative from within
their particular socio-cultural and religious world view, especially that of
Jesus as the authoritative interpreter of the law and the one who stands in
a unique relationship with God imaged as Father.[44] Their reception, their
reading of the complex of traditions and voices in the final narrative, would
have given it coherence according to their dominant belief, as does
Saldarini's analysis.

Underlying this analysis, it would seem, is the assumption that the
Matthean group, while deviant or sectarian within first-century Judaism,
functioned as a cohesive group with a developing coherent world view

and ideology that was that of the dominant narrative. Saldarini's social scientific model of deviance, however, does not allow him to listen for the voices of resistance within the developing coherence. The voices silenced by this attempt to create a coherent narrative and context may not have been only within the opponent Jewish group or from an earlier stage of traditioning, as is often argued, but also within the house-churches of the Matthean group.

This study will also explore the interpretation of Jesus and the gospel story by those house-churches whose interpretive Jewish framework was more predominantly that of wisdom, an aspect of Jewish tradition that Saldarini virtually ignores. Wisdom rather than interpretation of the law is an alternative lens for the reading of the Sermon on the Mount.[45] Even in the writing of the gospel, Jesus is recognized as both Sophia and Christos (11:2, 19), speaking the language of Sophia (11:28-30) in a way that suggests a strong and developed wisdom tradition in some house-churches.[46]

Likewise, the prophetic tradition highlighted by the claim to its fulfillment and the presence of prophets within the community, even though some are recognized as "false" (7:15), suggest that this tradition also be considered as a significant interpretive lens within some Jewish house-churches. Saldarini, in a carefully nuanced discussion of the difficulty of accurately characterizing what was understood by the term *prophet* in a Matthean context, points out that conflict may have arisen in the community because of "teachers like Matthew, who emphasized the more 'scholarly' interpretation of Scripture and of Jesus' teachings, and the charismatic prophets and healers who stressed the palpable power of God experienced by emissary and recipient."[47] The possibility of itinerant missionaries moving across the arc of Matthean provenance, as suggested earlier, and the large numbers of recipients in various house-churches, whose interpretative matrix in relation to prophecy would more likely be that of popular prophetic and messianic movements rather than a scholarly interpretation, suggest that an interpretation of the reception of the prophetic layers of the tradition will need to be heteroglossal rather than simply that of the scholarly or scribal written voice.

The continued presence of these and other traditions points to the complex web of Jewish traditions within various house-churches of the Matthean group. The Matthean reading community will not be seen as one coherent Jewish group among the variety of first-century Judaisms, but it will be seen to have some of this variety within its own constitutive house-churches. The cultural voices and languages within the Matthean narrative are heteroglossal rather than monoglossal, and it can be assumed that this heteroglossia was evoked within the complex Matthean "reading community."[48] Likewise, if, as Saldarini suggests, the Matthean story of Jesus within a deviant Jewish group functioned to create group identity,[49] then, according to Foucault's recognition that "power grips us at the point where our desires and our very sense of the possibilities for self-definition are constituted,"[50] resistance to such power and knowledge formations might also be detected at such a point.[51] A listening to those readings that are possible in the ruptures, the discontinuities, and the fissures in the narrative, the traces of the less dominant socio-cultural and religious voices, will enable us to hear not only the dominant reading community's voice but also the voices of alternative or resistant communities of reading.

Overman[52] and Segal,[53] like Saldarini, characterize the Matthean community of inception and reception as religious sectarian within the context of what Overman designated "Formative Judaism." Overman speaks of "Matthean Judaism"[54] and characterizes its concerns as predominantly internal religious concerns: leadership, law and legal interpretation, community order and structure, identity and crisis about the future.[55] Like Saldarini, he characterizes the Matthean community of reception as a coherent unity over against its rival sibling, Formative or Rabbinic Judaism. Segal, on the other hand, while recognizing the rising conflict between the Matthean community and Pharisaism,[56] also suggests that "Christian Pharisaism" might be a competing voice within the Matthean context.[57] This suggestion corresponds to the claims made previously regarding the variety of Jewish contexts of reception within the Matthean reading community and the presence of their perspective even when the text is opposed to it.

Amy-Jill Levine, in *The Social and Ethnic Dimensions of Matthean Salvation History,*[58] constructs a literary coherence within which the Matthean gospel can be read rather than a socio-religious one, as do the previously considered studies. She argues that the temporal axis of the narrative allows for a reading of the Jesus mission that includes both Jewish and gentile respondents to the message of Jesus without a favoring of one or the other. A reading of the social axis of the gospel narrative, however, "transcends the religious as well as the ethnic implications of this temporal distinction."[59] She illustrates how faithfulness crosses ethnic and religious boundaries as well as deconstructs religious and social centers.[60] While her analysis is primarily literary, she does venture to suggest that the community consisted of both ethnic Jews as well as gentiles, but that the terms were no longer operative within the *ekklesia*. In relation to this study, therefore, and in particular to this reconstruction of the Matthean community of reception, her work points to the presence of both Jewish and gentile house-churches that may have shared interpretations of Jesus and the gospel story that were egalitarian rather than hierarchical and inclusive with regard to ethnicity and social class. Given the history of reception of this gospel, however, and the anti-Judaism as well as the hierarchical structuring that it has constructed, it seems unlikely that such an "ideal" reading community constituted the entire Matthean context. Rather, I argue that it was communities of difference and of resistance, who read not only with but against the grain of the text, that enabled a reading to emerge that pointed toward the egalitarianism and inclusivity that Levine suggests.

Indeed, her reading within contemporary contexts of interpretation demonstrates this very point as she allows the voices of gender, ethnicity, and class—and the differences they make—to shape a reading that challenges both Jews and Christians today to a "breakdown of patriarchal viewpoints."[61]

The work of David Sim likewise acknowledges the positive characterization of both Jewish and gentile figures in the Matthean gospel.[62] He, however, virtually silences the gentile voice in favor of a Jewish (and Christian) apocalyptic coherence in the gospel and its context. While recognizing that he provides a very plausible account of the Matthean apocalyptic voice, it should be noted that his claim to coherence around this point, both narratively and contextually, silences some voices while privileging others. Here I will particularly address his perspective on the gentile world.[63]

Sim rightly recognizes the positive portrayal of certain gentile characters, especially the Magi (2:1-12), the Roman centurion (8:5-13), and the Canaanite woman (15:21-28). To distinguish their faith, which is praised by Jesus, from discipleship of Jesus is, however, a failure to take account of the temporal axis that Levine highlights.[64] His analysis therefore minimizes the gentile recognition of Jesus' authority and power. Likewise, he offers a minimalist interpretation of 28:19, the gentile mission command, which does not give due recognition to its key position at the close of the gospel and its place among the final words of the risen Jesus. Textually, this minimalist interpretation of 28:19 appears disproportionate to the significant weight given to what are called the "anti-gentile statements" (5:46-47; 6:7-8; 6:31-32; and 18:15-17).[65]

Each of these "anti-gentile" sayings is in the context of an antithesis between the ethics of the Matthean community and other behavioral ethics. In an agonistic society, in which name-calling was the means of legitimating one's world view in the face of conflicting claims to loyalty,[66] one might well agree with Levine that these sayings are not necessarily a sign of "ethnic bigotry."[67] The very general statement of 6:31-32 regarding what one eats, drinks, or wears may be simply contrasting ordinary human concerns with a Christian response, in which case *ethne* may well be translated as the nations generally rather than having a specific ethnic designation. Each of the other three statements makes use of the term *ethnikos/ethnikoi*, the only times this term is used in the gospel, indeed in the entire Christian Testament apart from 3 John 7.[68] In light of the agonistic context one could argue that this may well have been a derisive term in a context of boundary-setting and not necessarily a depiction of an entire world outside Judaism or a rejection of all those who would be so designated ethnically. Furthermore, in two of the texts (5:46-47 and 18:15-17), the *ethnikoi* are linked with tax-collectors, another group who were used in the war of words that characterized an agonistic society.[69]

That such terminology in the teaching of Jesus is not characteristic of his actions or indeed of the gospel as a whole is demonstrated by Jesus' sitting at table with tax-collectors and sinners (9:10-13); tax-collectors believing the message of John (21:32); and a tax-collector being included among the disciples of Jesus (9:9). Jesus is also portrayed as the fulfillment of the Isaian prophecy of justice being proclaimed to the gentiles who will hope in the name of Jesus (12:18-21). In the face of such evidence, Sim's claim that the "Gentile world is for Matthew a godless place whose practices are not to be imitated by the readers of the Gospel . . . [and] that the Matthean community largely avoided contact with its gentile neighbours"[70] would seem to be too strong a statement in the face of the evidence. Its effect is to silence the voice of the gentile house-churches or the gentile members of mixed house-churches whose mission to their brothers and sisters of other ethnic backgrounds was founded in the stories that may have been shaped, preserved, and been the site of conflict in their midst—stories of the Magi, the Roman centurion, and the Canaanite woman and the memory of a significant commissioning of disciples by Jesus to a universal mission.[71]

In establishing both ethnic and religious diversity within the Matthean house-churches, it has been difficult to draw a distinction between these two categories. Indeed, Malina claims that "there was no freestanding social institution recognized as 'religion,' no discernible separation of church and state or church and family, even if one wished to make such a separation."[72] Membership of a household based on kinship and hence ethnic solidarity or of a *collegia* grounded in a new fictive kinship that may have crossed ethnic lines was foundational to the emerging *ekklesia*, grounded in the story of Jesus and the reign of God movement. It is not surprising that the voice of the writer sought to unify diverse ethnic and religious voices. The very presence of diversity among the contexts of reading/ performance ensured that the new and the old were not merged into a single voice but that heteroglossia shaped interpretation.

## GENDERED VOICES

It has already been established in relation to the stories of female characters in the Matthean gospel that the traditioning or storytelling process in the Matthean community involved women.[73] In this section I will not repeat but extend this analysis by way of a critical dialogue with the articles of Stuart Love, which have appeared since the publication of my own work and which rely heavily on what he terms a "macrosociological view,"[74] as well as an integration of other recent feminist analyses that have addressed the genderization of the Matthean social context.[75] It will be claimed that women's storytelling and prophetic voices were not confined only to traditions in which women featured prominently but that in those communities in which their leadership was significant or their voices were most resistant, they participated with the men of their house-churches in the interpretation of the entire gospel story and its characterization of Jesus.[76]

Stuart Love's two articles belong to a growing body of significant literature in biblical scholarship that makes use of sociological and cultural anthropological models to understand first-century Palestine and/or Asia Minor as the context for the development of those traditions that finally formed the Christian Testament. The macrosociological model employed by both Love and Wire is that of "advanced agrarian" society, which has been designated by sociologists as the most applicable to the Roman Empire of the first century of the Common Era.[77] Love outlines key aspects of this society and in particular its genderization. In both articles he draws upon a static model of gender within an equally static and indeed monolithic model of society. The Matthean textual world examined from the point of view of gender is that of the writer whose perspective, we have already established, is male and elite. Indeed, in the second article,[78] the genderization of the advanced agrarian model is compared to that of the Mishnah without sufficient recognition that its world too is the construct of elite males. The results drawn by Love from both analyses could be summarized by his conclusion to the first. While he recognizes "incongruities" in the constructed world of the Matthean text by comparison with those other worlds, which are assumed to be the actual world of women's and men's experience, these incongruities, he claims, "seem to be idiosyncratic and apparently do not break the boundaries of everyday existence."[79]

My first critical response to Love's and Wire's analyses draws upon and shares with that of other feminist scholars, particularly anthropologists and sociologists in relation to both gender and social models. Marianne Sawicki raises critical questions in relation to biblical scholarship's use of the overall model "Mediterranean society," and the "advanced agrarian" description of this entire society comes under a similar critique, namely, that societies at both a macro- and micro-level are not "monolithic structures" but rather "games presenting numerous options . . . whose rules we must discern."[80] Similarly, Judith Shapiro points out in relation to ethnographic studies what could equally apply to sociological models, that "different pictures of the same society can emerge depending on whether one sees that society through the eyes of its male or its female members."[81] I would add to such a claim that a recognition of women's agency rather than their place in a constructed model provides the starting point for a very different study.

Love's gender model is indeed static with deviations from the model named "incongruities." Theoretically, Conkey and Gero critique this notion with their claim that gender, like society, is not a static phenomenon to be neatly defined as norm and deviation but rather is a process "constructed as a relationship or set of relationships" that is "embedded within other cultural and historical institutions and ideologies such as status, class, ethnicity, and race."[82] Practically, the research of a wide variety of feminist historians and biblical scholars has demonstrated that within the first century and across the Greco-Roman world, gender relationships were being constructed in different ways according to location,[83] social status or class,[84] ethnicity, and religious affiliation.[85] Testing appropriate elements of such data within a more flexible and process-oriented understanding of gender in the provenance suggested for the Matthean gospel would yield a much richer analysis of gender both within the gospel text and context, but this is a study that still remains to be undertaken.

The foundational unit of the Matthean community is indeed the house-hold, but Matthean households may be both kinship units as well as *collegia* grounded in fictive rather than actual kinship relationships. Incorporating a class analysis with a reading of some of the social constructs in the gospel from the point of view of the women of the community causes a different picture to emerge.

First, the public/private division is not nearly as rigidly depicted as Love's analysis suggests.[86] Key women characters encounter Jesus in the public arena (9:20-22; 15:21-28; 20:20-22; 27:55-56; and 28:9-10) and women as well as men are clearly members of the crowds that follow Jesus, much of the ministry occurring, in fact, in the open space. Women emerge out of the crowd—the woman with the hemorrhage and the mother of the sons of Zebedee.[87] They are among those not counted at the multiplica-tion of the loaves, their mention, however, recognizing their presence (14:21; 15:38). They follow Jesus on the journey up to Jerusalem and watch faithfully with him during his execution (27:55-56, 61). Class may be significant here also as the lives of poor women were lived much more in the public arena, a factor not taken account of by Love when he points to a woman's wage earning bringing public dishonor to her husband and women being sequestered in special rooms.[88] Poor women often worked to supplement the low wages earned by their husbands, and their small houses and often cramped conditions meant that many activities, even the preparation of meals, took place in public courtyards or food was pur-chased on the streets when cooking facilities were not available. In these public contexts, preparing family and household food, working in fields or marketplaces, women's informal networks were established, networks of power and agency, and here stories were told. Groups of women who had come to believe in Jesus no doubt shared the stories that they had learned and even told new ones.[89] My earlier study suggested that in women's storytelling, female characters and women's concerns received significant attention and only in the telling of the male storyteller was their participa-tion lessened and men dominated the supposedly privileged spaces. We have failed to recognize that the latter perspective was a male one rather than necessarily that of the entire community.

Similarly, women or young girls function as significant characters, and it is their stories that are told in a number of the household contexts. Mary is present with her child in the first house reference (2:11); Peter's mother-in-law is healed in his house, the story being told not just as a healing but also as a call story parallel to that of the call of Matthew (8:14-15; 9:9); the ruler's daughter is healed in his house; and a woman anoints Jesus in the house of Simon the Leper. Only the house of the centurion (8:5-13), the unnamed house in which Jesus teaches and explains the parables (9:10; 13:36), and the house in which Jesus celebrates a final meal with the disciples are characterized as locations of male-centered stories. Reading such data from the reconstructed experience of first-century women, the house is a place where they too exercised significant influence or authority and where power structures were more egalitarian.[90]

Such an analysis from the point of view of women's participation both in the foundational context of the early Christian community, namely the household, and their active engagement in early Christian storytelling is in keeping with the model of power proposed by Foucault rather than the more traditional "revolutionary" model that Love seems to employ—if women's participation did not "burst the societal boundaries of the household of advanced agrarian societies"[91] then it must have been merely an incongruity. Jana Sawicki, however, outlines a three-point analysis of Foucault's theory of power that is in harmony with what has emerged above:

1. Power is exercised rather than possessed.
2. Power is not primarily repressive, but productive.
3. Power is analyzed as coming from the bottom up.[92]

Women's power as depicted in the gospel story consists in giving birth, following Jesus, hearing his teaching, being fed with the crowds, claiming healing, entering into debate in a way that changed Jesus' perspective on his ministry, exercising *diakonia*, remaining faithful at the site of Jesus' death, faithfully visiting his place of burial, encountering the risen Jesus, and going off to proclaim that Jesus had indeed been raised from the dead. While this story line, this voice, this expression of women's agency and power may not be the most audible in the written gospel, its continued presence and the signs of struggle around a story like that of the Canaanite woman suggest that there was resistance in some house-churches to the storytelling that may have been becoming more dominant in the whole community and may have been finding its voice in the official scribe(s).[93] In the telling of this story of the Canaanite woman it seems that there is a coalition of ethnic and gender voices; in others, class and ethnic and perhaps class and gender voices will combine. As Sawicki notes, "There are no privileged or fundamental coalitions in history, but rather a series of unstable and shifting ones."[94]

In listening to the multiple voices in the different contexts of interpretation, different coalitions of voices will be heard speaking of Jesus and the reign of God movement as characterized in the Matthean gospel. From these multiple reading contexts, genre, characterization, and metaphor will be read by undertaking a number of "soundings" in different parts of the Matthean narrative. In this way the new map or reading model of chapter 2 will be tested; more important, a reading/writing of the Matthean Jesus from a feminist perspective will be enacted. We shall indeed look for Another.

*Part III*

# Attending to the Soundings

# 4

# Of Rachel's Lineage—
# Endangered Child/Liberated Liberator

## *Matthew 1-2*

The opening words of the Matthean gospel—the book of the origin or birth or genealogy of Jesus Christ—focus the reader's attention immediately on Jesus *Christos*, the key character in the story to follow but presented in a context evocative of Israel's story of origin. In fact, the opening phrase, "book of the origin," invites or suggests a reading or rather a rereading of the Jewish scriptures.

The reader constructed by the opening verse is Jewish.[1] Intertextually, Jewish readers would hear resonances in the first half of the verse of two texts from the first "book" of their scriptures—Genesis 2:4 and 5:1—"this is the book of the origin/*genesis* of the heavens and the earth" and "this is the book of the origin/*genesis* of humankind." Genesis 5:1 not only parallels Genesis 2:4, but 5:1b-2a echoes Genesis 1:27—the "human one" in the image of God male and female. The female in the narrative genealogy of Genesis 5 is, however, virtually erased except for the passing references to daughters in each generation (Gn 5:4, 7, 10, 13, 16, 19, 22, 26, 30).

The intertextual possibilities in the opening of the Matthean gospel prepare readers to encounter a new book, a book of origins like the first book of their scriptures, a beginning of a new story. This new story holds promise of a new creation like the first creation and a new humanity reconstituted in the image of divinity, male and female.[2] The rupture in the echoed texts holds these two aspects of re-creation in tension. The ideology of Genesis 5 undermines the vision, but as Peter Miscall suggests, this new text (Mt 1:1a) displaces or decenters the earlier texts,[3] with the textual displacement functioning rhetorically to construct its readers as a community seeking a new self-definition by "undoing" its dominant narrative and "retelling it in such a way as to invite new interpretation and conclusions."[4]

The first mention of Jesus is linked rhetorically to this new vision, so rich in imagery and yet containing within its intertextual resonances the possibility of transgressions or erasure. As the reader plumbs the richness of the imagery, the new story or new reading is focused in Jesus/*Jeshua*, introduced and identified by this common name, which is linked to *Christos* or "anointed one," used also as name,[5] and qualified by the designations "Son of David," "Son of Abraham." The new story—and Jesus, in whom it is embodied—is inserted radically into Israelite culture and religion.

The term *Christos,* which is the first feature to characterize Jesus, would have carried rich resonances for both Jewish and gentile readers. Longing for a liberator was not peculiar to Judaism but characterized a number of religious groups in the Greco-Roman world who believed that history was in the hands of the deity or divine powers, named according to their religious beliefs. Jesus is named and characterized as just such a liberator.

Richard Horsley and John Hanson offer a significant threefold warning to contemporary interpreters of this characterization—first, that our understanding of the term *Christos* is "heavily influenced by western christological doctrine"; second, that a loose use of the term *messiah* has left us with confused understandings of popular Jewish messianic and prophetic movements; and third, that there was no unified expectation for "the Messiah" in first-century Judaism.[6] First-century hearers of the gospel story would have brought heteroglossal understandings of this term to the story, ranging from the hope of those supporting a royal ideology, generally among the elite class, to that of the more popular nonliterate or peasant community, which linked *Christos* with David but in a way that evoked other ancient traditions, especially those of popular kingship.[7] Such movements characterized the period at the end of the reign of Herod, the period in which Jesus was born, as well as the time of the Roman War, a time when the gospel traditions were being formed and received.

Both the royal and popular kingship ideologies and the movements they spawned were concerned with the liberation of the Jewish people from oppressive rulers, but the latter, the popular ideology, arose from among the people and received their acclaim. For this group within the Matthean community the designating of Jesus as *Christos* and Son of David, the one born of the woman Mary and adopted by her husband Joseph, may well have functioned to legitimate Jesus as the liberator in their midst, the one who required their acclaim and their allegiance to carry out his task. Whether the popular traditions through which the peasant and lower classes heard the Jesus story enabled them to counteract the class ideology inherent in the subsequent genealogy is impossible to ascertain. Levine's recognition of the gospel's own distinction between "elites and marginals" as depicted in the infancy narrative gives weight to the possibility of such a rhetorical effect of the opening of the gospel.[8] It is only as the Matthean story unfolds that this designation of Jesus takes on the meanings unique to this story. At the outset, however, Jesus as anointed one is linked by way of symbolic sonship to Abraham, the father, the progenitor of the nation Israel, and to David, who crafted its statehood and kingship. It would seem, therefore, to be a metaphoric designation with both socio-political and religious connotations.

### OF WHOSE LINEAGE?

The genealogy or patrilineage that follows the opening verse (1:2-17) is a particular and highly constructed reading of Israel's story.[9] It is read as a patrilineage (male was the father of male) encoding the text of the dominant kinship structure,[10] and it draws its reader into an ordered, coherent, and patterned structure bespeaking completion and fulfillment, a single unitary reading that is both cultural and religious. Lucretia Yaghjian says of the genealogy:

> What a birth certificate or passport is to ours, a genealogical record was to Matthew's world: it certified the bearer as an official member of his culture in good standing, and conferred upon him the cultural credentials of role and status apposite to his ancestral heritage. . . . To claim, then as Matthew does, that David (Israel's prototypical shepherd-king) and Abraham (through whom all the nations become heirs of Israel's blessings) are both primogenitors of Jesus is to invoke the book of the culture no less strategically than the book of the covenant.[11]

As well as honoring Jesus by inserting him into Israel's history, which is its history with its God,[12] the genealogy also, by its three-part structure—culminating in David, the exile and return, and Jesus—creates expectations that in Jesus a new "anointed agent" of liberation was due.[13] This story as encountered by its hearers is not simply a story about the person Jesus.[14] It is a story about what God is doing in human history in this person.[15] For those who believed that this history continued in their communities, it is a rereading of an old story, creating a new story about God's continuing participation in the lives of a people whose identity is being shaped by the memory, the story of Jesus creating and keeping alive his ongoing presence in their lives. The opening of the gospel story shapes community identity among it readers and constructs new kinships, a new household that gives identity.

There is, however, rupture and erasure in the opening of the story also. Male genealogy informs the initial interpretation of Jesus *Christos* and hence limits the intertextual possibilities of the new book of origins.[16] On the one hand, one might speculate whether within women's meaning-making in relation to Jesus and/or within some house churches, the influence might have flowed in the opposite direction. Might not the possibilities of a new beginning involving male and female in the image of God evoked by the opening phrase "book of the origin" have functioned to subvert the maleness of the metaphors initially predicated of Jesus—*Christos*, Son of David, and Son of Abraham?[17] Such a reading, reconfiguring the original vision distorted by the limitations of male genealogy, could have constituted reading subjects both female and male who envisioned their community as a new kinship structure.

The power of the patrilineage, on the other hand, undoubtedly would have functioned for many readers shaped by the unity and coherence of the text to construct the male as vehicle of divine action and the female as invisible vehicle of reproduction. The rhetorical effect of such a reading was to establish Jesus within a social fabric or kinship group defined by its male members. As such, it legitimated and secured the gendered division of the patriarchal world in which it was produced and received. It interpolated these readers/hearers into the gendered subjectivity that renders women invisible. The text's gaps, its erasure and exclusion, cry out, Is there neither mother nor daughter in Israel?[18]

The five patterned ruptures in the narrative (1:3, 5a, 5b, 6, 16) echo such a cry. A number of texts intersect here giving rise to tensive readings. From within the patriarchal register, these ruptures can be and have been read theologically.[19] These anomalous women, whose insertion into the patriarchal familial system is "irregular," are, nevertheless, the instruments through which the divine order, imaged as absolutely male-centered, reaches its completion or fulfillment.[20] From within the register of resistant readers, those in the reading community who identify with these powerless ones on the margins of society—the five women (Tamar, Rahab, Ruth, Bathsheba, and Mary) whose stories threatened the structure of the patriarchal family—open a small fissure in the symbolic universe that the patrilineage constructs.[21] Into this fissure can be drawn the names of the mothers and daughters who were likewise the ancestors of Jesus. Jesus, the anointed one, is therefore not only born of and into a family symbolically constructed as male-centered but also is born of and into a family in which the stories of women who symbolized an alternative to the dominant male ideology intersect with that dominant ideology.

Jesus is son or child of Mary, Tamar, Rahab, Ruth, and Bathsheba as well as of David and Abraham. A hint of alternative kinship structures and alternative memories, alternative readings of the biblical story, coincide with the dominant reading and at least momentarily decenter it. Verse 16 climaxes such a decentering, as the pattern is broken definitively with Joseph being identified as the husband of Mary and Mary designated the one from whom Jesus is born. In this verse, "Jesus who is called the Christ" is linked as closely with Mary, from whom he was born, as he was linked to David and Abraham in v. 1. At the end of the opening of the gospel Jesus is the one born of the woman Mary.[22] Such a gap is quickly covered over, however, with the recapitulation of the single unified reading of Israel's history in 1:17 and with the story of Joseph's agency in the birth of Jesus within the context of a divinely authorized Davidic family in 1:18-25.[23]

The reading strategies or competencies available to first-century readers/hearers of the Matthean patrilineage have pointed to first-century reception and characterization of the Matthean Jesus as not only single and unitary but plural and shattered. This leaves open the possibilities of the new story inherent in the gospel's opening phrase, at least for some reading communities.

Genre choices within different sectors of the community shaped by encounter with the text would also have been determinative of the rhetorical effects of these opening verses of the Matthean gospel story. The genealogy provided a prestigious family background for Jesus and would have functioned within the scribal or literate house-churches within the Matthean group to suggest the genre of biography. Within a Jewish matrix this genre may have been understood in terms of Israelite-Jewish biographies of heroic figures whose life accounts reiterated the link between Israel's history and its God.[24] From within a gentile matrix there may have been recognition of the story of Jesus as "bios," similar to biographies of Hellenistic and Roman heroes, political or wisdom figures.[25] Such choices may also not have been so clearly ethnically distinguished. One of the tendencies within such a genre choice, realized more fully in later theological tradition(s), was to separate Jesus as heroic one from the community of the reign of God, Jesus becoming exemplar or divinized one rather than one whose story was intimately engaged with the community's life. Socioreligiously, among the elite classes of the Matthean community, therefore, the patrilineage may well have functioned to insert Jesus into a royal ideology and theology popular in their circles and supportive of their world view.[26] It legitimated not only the gendered but also the class division within patriarchy. Even the Matthean popular audience's tendency to read a hero narrative within either its Jewish or gentile matrix[27] may have held the seeds of separation and idealization of Jesus. On the other hand, those house-churches that read the beginning of a story of identity, grounded in Jewish tradition and yet interpreted in new ways (cf. 13:52), would not have isolated Jesus from but would have embedded him within God's engagement with them as a people in their unfolding history.[28]

Looking to the possible rhetorical effects of an alternative reading of the patrilineage of the Matthean gospel from a contemporary feminist perspective, it is clear that women can take up subject positions in relation to Jesus and can do so with all the complexities, anomalies, or differences that those subject positions entail. Jesus *Christos* embedded within a movement of popular resistance provides the possibility of a variety of oppositional subject positions that may be influenced by class, race, or any number of other marginalizing factors. Although only a hint at this point in the narrative, it has been shown that the opening words of this gospel story, "book of origins," link the Jesus story with the creation of the heavens and the earth (Gn 2:4) and with the establishing of a new kinship (Gn 5:1). The story, therefore, can evoke for contemporary readers the profound link between the Jesus story, as we seek to interpret it today toward justice and integrity of life, with the new story of the universe. As such, it challenges integrity of relationships not only between ourselves and the divine or transcendent whom we name in various ways, but among ourselves as human community and also with the entire universe of which we are a living part.[29] The weaving of this thread in the tapestry being created is another significant aspect of a responsible feminist ethical theology in today's society and church.

As the story continues to unfold, characterization of Jesus is predominantly through others: the divine messenger, Joseph, the Magi, and Herod. The action centers around the birth of the child, Jesus, but he is a child in an adult world, powerless in contrast to the political and socio-religious power of Herod and the Magi even though he is by implication designated "King of the Judeans" (2:2) and a threat to Herod's hegemony.[30] He is hunted by the powerful Herod. There is instability in the story surrounding Jesus and tension at the discourse and rhetorical levels, and it is these points of instability and tension that allow for alternative reading strategies and interpretations.[31] Interestingly, in this regard, the child is never alone but is always with his mother, Mary (1:25; 2:11, 13, 20, 21). He is, throughout, "Miriam's child."

## ENDANGERED CHILD

The narrative of the birth of Jesus (1:18-25) seeks to cover the transgression that reference to Mary in v. 16 created. It does this by negating female agency and female sexuality. Mary, who conceives and gives birth to the child, neither speaks nor acts, is not addressed, nor are her thoughts, feelings, or characteristics recorded. Even the details of her situation are shrouded in silence and innuendo. Jesus' birth is legitimized through the righteous man, whom the law protects and whose obedience to divine command establishes him as the legal father of the child, thus giving closure to the patrilineage.[32] Throughout the narrative, however, until the point of Joseph's acceptance of the child and mother into his home and family kinship, the endangered child is linked to Mary, his mother; he is in a dangerous and anomalous situation in relation to patriarchal family and kinship and thereby a threat to this structure. The voices of both the narrator and the divine messenger explain this anomaly theologically—the child has been conceived in the womb of Mary "by a spirit that is holy" (1: 18, 20)—thus guiding reading. One wonders, however, whether some readers were still able to discern possible memories and traditioning of women regarding the anomalous birth of Jesus within the fissures of this narrative. These were, seemingly, quickly closed over by the dominant reading of virginal conception by the end of the first century and subsequently. The endangered child had become the one born of "a spirit that is holy." I agree, however, with the growing number of scholars who claim that this would not have been understood within the first century as attributing divine sonship to Jesus at this point.[33]

Meaning-making for readers is stretched when the endangered child is named Jesus, a name that carries with it a task or mission, as the voice of the divine messenger indicates (1:21). This child will *save* or liberate the *people* with whom he is identified by way of genealogy. This is both a prophetic and a royal task. The designation resonates with the vocation given to Saul and David to save/liberate Israel from the hands of the Philistines (1 Sm 9:16; 10:1; 2 Sm 3:18). In the post-exilic literature it was the role of God to liberate the remnant people of Israel (Is 63:8; Ez 13:21; 37:23; Hb 3:13; Zec 8:7; 9:16). There is no resonance in the Jewish scriptures, however, of the phrase *saving from sin*. In Israel's historical and prophetic tradition, political calamities were interpreted in terms of infidelity to God's ways and hence the results or manifestations of sin in Israel (Dn 9:15, 16, 20, 24; Jer 14:10; 16:10). It is from these that the king or God liberates. The divine voice in this narrative, therefore, situates the task given to this child within a context of political suffering or sin, a context that will become even more explicit in the following chapter. The notion of "anointed one" is further explicated in that the child's task will be like that of Saul and David, a royal task. This task, however, had to be undertaken by other anointed ones of God when the kingship disappeared. The child is, therefore, anointed for the task that is ultimately God's—to save God's people from all the manifestations of the breakdown of the divine-human relationship that were called sins.[34]

The narrator adds another perspective by indicating that the birth of this child is also in fulfillment of what Israel's God had spoken through its prophets, in particular Isaiah 7:14. The reader is shaped by the narrative to see clear parallels between narration and citation. The woman found to be with child of the Holy Spirit (v. 18) is the one named *parthenos*, virgin or young woman of child-bearing age who shall be found to be with child,[35] bearing a son as the angel predicted (v. 21). The second part of the Isaian verse parallels the one to be named Jesus Emmanuel, God with us. Not only is God on the side of this child but God is with God's people to bring about prophetic renewal in the birth and prophetic mission of this child. This entire narrative, however, raises significant questions for a feminist reader. Was the spirit that is holy, the God who is with the "us" of the narrative, understood by first-century readers as the God and spirit of the patriarchs, imaged as male and supportive of the negation of the female? On the other hand, would the memories, the erasures, the gaps in the narrative in which alternative traditions could be glimpsed have meant that some house-churches would have perceived in this a different understanding of God and the divine spirit, one who was with the marginal and the oppressed or endangered? The scandal of the endangered one prophesied as being liberator may have been the reading most operative in those households of alternative vision.

Rhetorically, these verses may have evoked two aspects of prophecy or prophetic activity that characterized first-century Judaism.[36] The first was that of the popular prophetic movement whose adherents believed they were participating in another of God's great acts of liberation and deliverance, as had the followers of the great prophets of old like Moses and Joshua.[37] The angel's explanation of the name of Jesus may have evoked these memories or shaped such beliefs, especially among those of the community who shared an oral culture as well as a belief in their continued participation in such a movement by the way they shaped their lives as a community in response to the Jesus story and by their ongoing *poiesis*. The second tradition is more closely linked to the literate or scribal classes, and it involves the interpretation of present events in light of the prophetic tradition, the tradition used in Matthew 1:22-23, as a way of proffering an explicit and unified meaning.[38]

Jesus who is called *Christos* is not only embedded in a family and a people characterized by continuity but by radical rifts in that continuity. Jesus is the "anointed one," the endangered child of the endangered woman, Mary; it is this child—whose credentials are surrounded with suspicion within the perspective of the reigning theology and ideology—who is designated liberator of the people. As this "anointed one" undertakes the prophetic task, God is with God's people, not just with Jesus, as the liberating task is foreshadowed. Read in this way from many different reading sites in our contemporary world, especially those where liberation from dominant and oppressive theologies and ideologies is a key concern, this narrative opens up new possibilities. God is with God's people as the frame of the Matthean gospel indicates (1:23 and 28:20) in radical discontinuity, in persons and movements whose presence and activity threaten the status quo. While this child, Jesus, has been depicted as male, Jewish, artisan class, and many other particularities, the child of radical discontinuity, the prophet of liberation, may be female or male, poor, middle class, or rich, Jewish or Muslim, colored or white. Where liberation from sins—from all that mars God's dreaming with humanity that humanity and the universe may live in right order and hence fullness of life—continues, there God continues to be with God's people. Jesus is with us to the close of the age.

## LIBERATED LIBERATOR

It is the Exodus and especially the Mosaic tradition in its biblical and popular Jewish expositions that is reread to interpret Jesus in Matthew 2.[39] The Matthean reading was one among many such readings in different Jewish communities within the first century of the Common Era (Josephus,

*Ant.* 2.212, Tg. Ps.-J on Exodus and *The Biblical Antiquities* of Pseudo-Philo, to name but a few).[40] Links to the prophetic tradition and liberation motif begun in the previous story are further developed in that each of these rereadings has a prophecy about the coming liberator conveyed by way of a dream. We have already noted that in Pseudo-Philo's *Biblical Antiquities*, however, it is upon Miriam that the "spirit of God" comes in a dream.

This and the repeated references to the presence of the mother, Mary, with the child (2:11, 14, 20, 21) may have shaped some readers to read the significant omissions in the Matthean rereading of the early Exodus narrative, namely, that of the Hebrew and Egyptian women who in that narrative were the instigators of Israel's liberation—Shiprah and Puah, Miriam, Jocabed,[41] and the daughter of Pharaoh (Ex 1:8–2:10).[42] While Exum draws the attention of contemporary readers to the ideology inherent in the Exodus texts, which portray these active and subversive women as "mothers" of the male liberator in a way that obscures their collaborative subversion of oppressive authority,[43] such omissions are further amplified in the Matthean rereading of Exodus with only a slight trace of their memory in the shadowy figure of Miriam/Mary, the mother of the child. Rather, the Matthean rereading situates the birth of the liberator, Jesus, completely in the context of male power struggles, focused particularly in Herod, who is designated king, as was Pharaoh (Mt 2:1; Ex 1:8). There is a significant reversal in this reading, however, with Joseph being commanded to take the child and his mother and flee into Egypt in order to escape Herod's plot against the life of the child (2:13). Oppressive hegemony is shifted from Egypt to Israel with Egypt becoming the place of sanctuary. This reading is itself quickly decentered by the introduction into the text of Hosea 11:1b as a fulfillment of what was spoken through the prophet (Mt 2:15)—"out of Egypt I have called my son." Political and oppressive hegemony is plural and not limited to any one particular location.[44]

The story of the visit of the Magi is also the site for alternative readings and characterization of Jesus. These strange visitors from the East may signify a wisdom tradition, attention to which led these sages to search for the new liberator, whose birth was heralded by a star and whom they designated by the title "king of the Judeans."[45] Their wisdom was portrayed in contrast to or perhaps in addition to Herod's appeal to the biblical historical/prophetic traditions as the source of knowledge of the liberator and the location in which this liberator could be found. A new motif has been introduced into the narrative of Jesus' birth, that of wisdom, a tradition or a "reflective mythology" familiar to those who knew the later writings of the Jewish scriptures, the so-called Wisdom Literature, or were participants in the transmission of traditional wisdom sayings.[46]

For those hearing Matthew's gospel, the wise ones from the East were more likely to represent the wisdom of the elite, the courts, and the scribal schools rather than of the homes and the villages. For the literate in the community, the story of the Magi, with the interpolation of the prophetic fulfillment text of Matthew 2:6, may have drawn together the wisdom and prophetic traditions into the interpretation of the story of the birth of Jesus. This juxtaposition and this interweaving will be traced through the unfolding of the story. For the present, however, it raises a retrojective question in relation to the first century as well as to contemporary audiences. This evocation of the wisdom tradition at this early point in the story may have raised echoes in relation to the understanding and interpretation of the Emmanuel reference in 1:23 for some readers. As well as its clear relation to the prophetic tradition of Isaiah, the narrator's translation of the name *Emmanuel* as "God with us" could have recalled for listeners and/or readers those wisdom songs in which Sophia sang of her delight to be with the human community (Prv 8:22-31, especially v. 31), her setting up of her dwelling place in Jacob, being established in Zion (Sir 24:8-12), her appearance on earth and dwelling with humankind (Bar 3:37). Such readings also may have opened up an alternative understanding of the God who is "with us" in Jesus, the Sophia God of some women's traditioning.[47] And even were such readings not made by any members of the first-century Matthean community, which is highly unlikely given the significance of the wisdom tradition in the early *poiesis* of Jesus, it still remains possible for twenty-first-century readers to read such heteroglossal potentialities.[48]

The Magi may also have suggested a political subtext. They could have signified alternative liberation or resistance traditions, those which originated among the aristocracy in the East in contrast to the popular resistance movements of first-century Palestine. The star that accompanied them would have pointed to the divine significance of the child, as it had for other political figures in Greco-Roman literature.[49] Both the child and the Magi, therefore, pose a threat to Herod and imperial power and these forces interlock within the Matthean story.[50] Horsley notes the reversal or the irony being played out in the narrative when he says: "Far from the restoration of the great Persian kingship in all its splendor for which they had long propagandized, the Magi now take the initiative in revealing that the hoped-for liberation from foreign domination has begun in this birth in a little town in the tiny principality of Judea."[51]

A child is called the *Christos*, the one who is claimed as fulfillment of the prophetic hope for a new Davidic figure who would liberate Israel from foreign domination. The powerless child is called "king" and "ruler" but is contrasted to the might of the Herodian machinery. As the scene closes, the Magi enter the house, see the child with Mary, do obeisance to this awaited deliverer, and offer gifts. Once again, a contrast. The scene is not in the palaces or fortresses of Jerusalem or the many other cities secured by Herod or the palaces of the East. The origin of this liberation movement is in a "house," the location that Crosby notes is the key metaphor in the Matthean gospel.[52] It is here that relationships are realigned when aristocrats acknowledge a child and resources are shared when the rich give to an ordinary Judean family, one which probably represented the majority of Jewish families impoverished by Herodian, Roman, and temple taxation. It was indeed the house in which this new resistance movement spread among the variety of social classes who gathered in houses across the Greco-Roman world to remember and to proclaim the birth, the life, the death, and the resurrection of this Jesus whose birth story is here told. The other most extraordinary inclusion in v. 11, which seems to carry through the subversive element noted above, is the presence of Mary in the house for this paradigmatic scene. What might this suggest for women's participation in the resistance movement that is the Jesus movement? If one of the aspects of this movement was a realignment of relationships between women and men, then her presence and this scene as a whole may have constructed gender, status, and ethnicity in new ways among those in the Matthean households who did not take offense at such a challenge.

The two scenes that follow this extraordinary story, like so much of the infancy narrative, invite a rereading of Israel's sacred story toward a *poiesis* of Jesus. In this instance the reading is of two great paradigmatic events in Israel's story—the Exodus and the Exile—as indicated by the prophetic verses cited in Matthew 2:15 and 18. Even though these two events had been incorporated into Israel's sacred story and given significant theological meaning, they were both highly political events. The stories that developed around them became resistance stories, continuing therefore the political subtext of the Magi story in the Matthean text. Jesus, like Israel in slavery and Israel in exile, was in need of being liberated from the political hegemony of Herod. This final aspect of the infancy narrative would have shaped a particular understanding of Jesus for readers/hearers. Jesus the liberator is not a hegemonic political leader whose liberation emerges from external power that dominates and subjugates. Rather, Jesus is identified with and characterized among those in Israel's past and present who were in need of liberation. It is from this experience that characterizes his infancy that he is able to become the type of liberator characterized in the unfolding narrative and that the reign of God movement can continue as one of liberation.

Like Israel, Jesus goes down into Egypt and is rescued from there by God; he is like Israel, who was called "son" by the divine parent of Hosea 11:1, the text cited in Matthew 2:15. The readings of this characterization of Jesus would have been heteroglossal among first-century households in the Matthean community, and some of these will emerge as the story progresses. At this point, however, it would be clear to Jewish readers that Jesus represents Israel as son. Within a patri/kyriarchal context, the God evoked by the Hosean text would be symbolized as father.

Such a reading, if dominant, would have functioned either in tension with or to silence potential readings within those households where wisdom traditions and alternative imaging of divinity played within the religious consciousness. From within such a context the Hosean imagery may have been heard in maternal terms, especially since the imagery predicated of divinity in the Hosean poem (Hos 11:1-7) is predominantly that of the mother. The tasks of teaching children to walk, lifting them up and healing them, holding them to one's cheek, and bending down to feed them (Hos 11:3-4) would have been heard as maternal by most first-century listeners.[53] Through this lens divinity imaged as male and female calls forth a new exodus, a new liberation, so that God being with God's people constitutes a new humanity and not just a male savior.

Overman notes the scribal activity that sought to give unity and coherence to the *poiesis* of Jesus within the community by way of fulfillment quotations, which abound in the infancy narrative.[54] The poetic nature of the texts cited and the richness of the reading communities' intertextual competencies meant, however, that meaning could not be contained. The danger the infant Jesus, identified as potential king of the Judeans, faced at the hands of Herod was metaphorically linked to that encountered by the children of Israel who were led north out of the city on their way to exile. Rachel, the ancient mother of Israel whose tomb was located in the region around Bethlehem—but whom the poem associates geographically with the northern route out of Jerusalem—is imaged in the Jeremian poem as weeping for her children who suffered such grievous political degradation: "A voice was heard in Ramah [the northern outskirts of Jerusalem] wailing and loud lamentation, Rachel weeping for her children; she refused to be consoled because they were no more" (Mt 2:18, Jer 31:15).

There is an extraordinary contrast set in place here between the two representations of Bethlehem at the beginning and end of the action set in motion by the arrival of the wise ones from the East. In 2:5-6 the chief priests and scribes, bureaucrats of the Jerusalem political system, cite the prophet Micah, who longed for a ruler like David who would come forth from David's city, Bethlehem, to shepherd or to rule Israel, an attempt at a coherent interpretation of Jesus. As the story draws to a close the narrator evokes the prophet Jeremiah to link Bethlehem not with the political David but with the weeping woman, Rachel. Difference and intertextuality combine to suggest alternative readings that would have shattered the order that fulfillment sought to establish.

The voice of Rachel weeping uncovers a silence in the text—the mothers of Bethlehem weeping for their children, refusing to be consoled because they are no more (not just taken into exile as were Rachel's metaphorical children, but slaughtered at the hands of a tyrant king). Their voices cry out to and against the intervening God of the infancy narrative. Their story, or rather their absence from the story, is surrounded by four dream appearances (2:12, 13, 19, 22) serving the rescue of Jesus, the favored child. Does this God only intervene on behalf of favored male children like Isaac and Jesus and not on behalf of innocent women and children (cf. Jgs 19, Mt 2:16)? The silence in the text cries out for an answer.

It is the raised voice of Rachel that pierces the male world of power, of slaughter, and of divine favor. She stands in the place of the erased women, but she also stands in the place of divine compassion, likewise erased. Just as the Hosean citation three verses earlier drew into the Matthean narrative images from the poem that it heads, so too the citation in Matthew 2:18 of Jeremiah 31:15 reads the slaughter of the children of Bethlehem in light of the entire poem of Jeremiah 31:15-22. The divine voice that responds to Rachel is a voice that promises return from exile, a voice more difficult to hear in the Matthean narrative in the face of the finality of death. For participants in the reign of God movement, however, resurrection was becoming an interpretive lens that was beginning to shape their reading of tragic death. The divine voice of the Jeremian poem—they shall return from the enemy's land—may well have been read through this lens (Jer 31:16).

The weeping and loud lamentation of Rachel creates a further fissure in the well-ordered Matthean narrative. She stands in the place of divine compassion imaged as female in continuity with the maternal imagery of Matthew 2:15. Phyllis Trible translates verse 20b of Jeremiah's poem in these words: "Therefore, my womb trembles for him; I will truly show motherly-compassion upon him."[55]

The extraordinary poem of Jeremiah does not end there. Its final verse (22b), drawn into the Matthean narrative by way of the image of Rachel, forms an inclusion with the Matthean narrative's opening verse (1:1a). Jeremiah's poem ends with God creating a "new thing" on the earth, female/woman surrounding/encompassing male/man.[56] The image of female in the final verse of the poem evokes Genesis 1:27, considered above. In contrast, however, the terminology used for male is not that of Genesis 1:27 but *geber*, which is more generally associated with the virile male or male warrior than the generic.[57] The resistant tears of the female, Rachel, which virtually conclude the Matthean infancy narrative, can also encompass or surround it, decentering male hegemony in whatever form it appears—sexual, military, political, religious.

For the communities of readers resistant to the male-centeredness of the opening verses of the narrative, Rachel's resistant tears point back to the beginning of the narrative, to its hope and possibilities. They also break open the closures that the narrative seeks to impose upon its readers. This new advent of God with God's people is focused in Jesus, who is to be read in metaphorical terms that are plural and shattered, not single and unitary. Jesus is not only in the lineage of David and Abraham but also in the lineage of Mary and Rachel.

This brief study of the interplay of genre, characterization, and metaphor in the heteroglossal making of Jesus and of first-century reading

communities in and of the Matthean infancy narrative has revealed a richness of meaning-making potentialities for contemporary feminist readers.
Individual male power, whether of patriarchal generativity or hegemony,
is decentered. The infant Jesus is located throughout in the presence of
the woman Mary, designated in the text as "his mother" but evocative of
those women whose anomalous stories challenge patriarchal family structures. He is attended by wise ones, resistance figures whose presence
challenges political hegemony. Metaphorically, he is linked to Israel as
community, imaged as "son" and as community of gender reversal in which
female "surrounds" male. Indeed, it could be suggested that we have here
the birth story not only of an individual but of a movement, the reign of
God movement. Characteristics of that movement have shaped dialogically the Matthean characterization of Jesus in the narrative, and the story
of Jesus could have been read as the story of the movement also. It is a
movement, at this point in the narrative, in which God is present with
God's people to bring about liberation/salvation. Jesus, characterized in
the lineage of Rachel, endangered child and liberated liberator, shaped
readers to enter the narrative open to the creative possibilities that the
initial verse evoked. Such characterization also allows a variety of subject
positions for contemporary feminist readers as they continue reading the
narrative.

# 5

# Wisdom Is Justified—
# Doing Her Deeds and Bearing Her Yoke

## *Matthew 11:1-30*

*Now when Jesus had finished instructing his twelve disciples, he went on from there to teach and proclaim his message in their cities.*
—Matthew 11:1

This opening verse of Matthew 11 acts as transition for the attentive reader/listener. Together with the verses that follow it draws together many of the narrative threads of the gospel that have begun to unravel meaning-making in relation to both Jesus and the reign of God movement to this point in the gospel story. For the reader already familiar with the gospel performance, the beginning of 11:1—"now when Jesus had finished . . . "—is a formula text designed to indicate the conclusion of one of the five discourses in the gospel (see 7:28; 13:53; 19:1, and 26:1) and a move into the subsequent narrative. In this instance it draws to a close Jesus' instructions to the disciples regarding their participation in the spread of the reign of God movement. They are to preach as Jesus preached that the reign of God was at hand (10:7) and to perform the works that characterized the movement—healing the sick, raising the dead, cleansing lepers, and casting out demons (10:8).

The verse recalls or recapitulates the discourse of the previous chapter and rhetorically reiterates the intimate link being constructed for the Matthean communities between the mission/ministry of Jesus and their own. The narrative weaves the threads of Jesus' ministry with the mission given to disciples in order to authorize the Matthean communities by providing them with a foundational story in which prophet and prophetic community are intimately connected.[1] This may have been the reading constructed by the different households and different groups within those households.

Some Matthean readers or reading communities, however, may have experienced a transgression in the narrative at this point. For some, the disciples, whom they have interpreted as representative of themselves and their communities,[2] are limited to "the Twelve," since the naming of them in the previous discourse has alerted readers to the exclusive maleness that characterizes the group. These readers would have been shaped by the historicizing tendency in the narrative in relation to the Twelve that had shifted understanding from the "eschatological-symbolical" of earlier layers of traditioning (see 19:28) to the "historical-masculine."[3] Fred Burnett suggests that the origin of the tradition of the Twelve and its preservation within the gospel narrative may have been to legitimate distinctions within the communities.[4] Within the Matthean context it may have functioned, at least in some of their communities, to authorize growing claims to exclusive male leadership (see 16:13-20 and the discussion in the next chapter of this book), claims that replicated the kyriarchal structures of imperial institutions that characterized their society. Even if this were not so, the tradition has certainly functioned in that way in subsequent centuries. Stories of female discipleship, however, uncover an underside to the narrative—subjugated knowledge or traditions of resistance within some communities of reception. As one would expect, over the centuries this knowledge has become even more silenced than it was in the Matthean narrative and communities.

The second half of v. 1 returns the focus to Jesus and his ministry, continuing the narrative thread of 4:23-25 and 9:35, Jesus teaching and preaching in the cities. There is a gap in the narrative for the attentive reader. Have the disciples departed on their mission while Jesus continues his, thus developing the foundational narrative of the prophetic community intimately connected with Jesus? Or did those house-churches in which the authority of Jesus was believed to be invested in an exclusive group of male leaders continue to read an encomium or biographical work of praise focused on Jesus in which disciples were considered secondary to the Jesus narrative?[5] The continuation of the narrative may offer further clues in response to these questions.


### DOER OF DEEDS

Verses 2–6 form the first narrative segment in the chapter, which in its turn introduces an integrated unit to v.19. In this entire section Jesus is characterized in relation to John. The reference to John at the beginning of v. 2 recalls 3:1-17, while the location of John in prison points toward 14:1-12, which provides the reader with the reason for John's imprisonment and narrates his death at the hands of Herod. For the first-time reader, the reference to John's imprisonment and the memory of his eschatological preaching (3:7-12) might have evoked intertextually the fate of the eschatological prophets of old (Jer 37:11-16); therefore, the narrative link between John and Jesus would have been read beyond v. 19 into the eschatological preaching of Jesus (vv. 20-24).

The narrator speaks of John's having heard of the "deeds of the *Christos*," a phrase for which the reader may have been a little unprepared since *Christos* has not been used since the infancy narrative (1:1, 16, 17, 18; 2:4).[6] It would carry here for the different readers the diversity of intertextualities already discussed in the previous chapter, but its meaning-making potential for readers would be extended in this segment of the narrative by way of its interconnectedness with other titles, metaphors, and the very narrative itself. The most immediate link is with "the coming one" in the question of John—are you "the coming one" or shall we look for another? Earlier, John indicated that there was one coming after him (3:11), so that the use of the phrase "the coming one" in 11:3 would not have been completely surprising to readers/listeners. As a possible designation for Jesus and its immediate link with *Christos*, it would have recalled for the reader expectations of a new prophet like Moses (Dt 18:15-18); an eschatological prophet like Elijah (Mal 3:1-4); an anointed one, either Davidic or priestly.[7] Overman also points to the political implications that John's question may have had for those households that were experiencing significant imperial oppression and who had continued to interpret the traditions of Jesus according to a political trajectory of meaning-making.[8] The question would have been asked whether Jesus was the deliverer/liberator from Roman oppression.

These verses, together with the response of Jesus (vv. 4-5), hold in tension two aspects of characterization that subsequent theology has separated, namely, the identity or naming of Jesus and the deeds of Jesus. In the opening verse of this section it was the hearing of the deeds of the *Christos* (the *erga tou Christou*) that prompted John to ask whether Jesus was "the coming one." The reply of Jesus turned attention not to titles but back to what had been seen and heard, the deeds or *erga*—the blind receive their sight and the lame walk, lepers are cleansed and the deaf hear, the dead are raised up, and the poor have good news preached to them (Mt 11:5). Jesus is a doer of deeds rather than a bearer of titles. What is seen and heard, in its turn, gives meaning to the title *Christos* and the metaphor "the coming one."

Many commentators have pointed out that the list of deeds pointed to fulfillment of prophetic expectation (Is 29:18-19; 35:5-6; 61:1-2).[9] Sharon Ringe goes on to suggest overtones of the Jubilee,[10] and Michael Crosby adds further that the "deeds" or "works" evoke the original work of creation, a Matthean intertextuality already elicited in the opening verse of the gospel. Crosby writes, "Matthew sees Jesus Christ continuing the work of reordering creation through a reordered religious and economic base, namely the household."[11] Such a reordering, a doing of prophetic deeds, is indeed political, a politics of democracy rather than a politics of identity.[12] One is led to question whether even within Christian communities like Matthew's at the end of the first century, there was tension and struggle between households. Some may have sought a unified center or titular identity in their *poiesis* of Jesus, while others were more engaged in the doing and telling of the deeds, the continuing of the reign of God.

Although the narrator does not specifically link the "deeds of the *Christos*" or the list of Jesus' works seen and heard by the disciples of John to the reign of God in this section of the narrative, such a link may well have been made by those participating in the performance of the gospel. Jesus' entire preaching is characterized by the reign of God being at hand (4:17). The first summary verse (4:23) links the preaching of the gospel of the *basileia* with healing. The poor in spirit and those persecuted for righteousness are promised that the kingdom of heaven is theirs (5:3, 10), and conditions for entry into the *basileia* are laid out in 5:20 and 7:21. The preaching of the reign of God (5–7) is accompanied by the works of Jesus (8–9) and it is to this same mission that the Twelve are sent (10:7). God's dreaming with and within humanity is being realized in the deeds of Jesus and shall continue to be realized in those communities of believers who shaped their lives according to the foundational story proclaimed among them. For those house-churches it was, therefore, not titles, names, symbols, or metaphors that finally answered John's question, but it was what was seen and heard, the deeds. And this reign of God with which Jesus is so intimately connected was not exclusive. It had drawn in both women and men, boys and girls, ethnic "outsiders" and "insiders," clean and unclean (8–9). It was imaged as a *basileia* quite unlike that of Rome, which was grounded in the patriarchal and hierarchical family or *oikos*[13] and structured according to status.[14] Status, ethnicity, and gender were beginning to be constructed or read differently in these communities.

For the households characterized as more scribal or literate, for whom the gospel narrative was read as a life of Jesus, the holy one, the signs or deeds of greatness narrated in Matthew 8–9 and summarized in 11:4-5 gave further foundation to their genre choice. Such households, as we have already seen, may have had significant influence on the shaping of the gospel narrative as well as its reception, and it may have been that for them the narrating of the deeds of the *Christos* characterized him as not just a "holy one" generally but as sage or even divine sage. Patricia Cox has assessed the paradigm of divine sage and the biographies of such sages, pointing out that for the biographers there was a complex set of characteristics that might signify divinity.[15] She makes it clear, however, that in the Roman imperial era "the idea that men could be divine did not include absolute identification with the supreme god."[16] Such a recognition is important for contemporary Christian interpreters who wish to reconstruct first-century communities of reading and interpretation, so that they don't impute to those communities theological categories developed at a later date.

Cox's analysis demonstrates that the divine sage is characterized as "son of god" by two distinguishing features: divine parentage, which some Matthean readers may have read in Matthew 1, and miraculous and prophetic powers "far beyond human capacity,"[17] predicated also of Jesus by the signs of 11:4-5. It is thus possible to construct one possible reading of Jesus in the opening verses of Matthew 11 as divine sage, bearer of wisdom, and doer of deeds. From a gender perspective such a reading, because of its participation in the metaphorical designation of the sage as "son of god," may have functioned to underscore the maleness of Jesus by way of his likeness to other divine men and to legitimate the centrality of maleness to the imperial sex/gender system as it functioned within certain Matthean households.

Mary Gerhart, on the other hand, reminds the contemporary reader of the transgressive nature of narrative, pointing out that "gender and genre are made most evident when their conventional forms are transgressed either by the reader or by the text."[18] This can be considered with Cox's claim that "what is most characteristic of the philosopher who is considered to be a son of god is that he is *sui generis*, in a class by himself. . . . He occupies this special, sacred territory, which is inaccessible to others."[19] There is, therefore, a transgression in the Matthean narrative from the ideal type of the divine sage; readers would have known from the previous gospel segment (10:1-42) that Jesus had shared his own miraculous and prophetic powers with his disciples. These disciples were signified male in that section of the narrative, but that very categorization was transgressed in the narrative as a whole. Also from a gender perspective, the accounts of the miraculous deeds of Jesus and of his proclamation of the good news to the poor have been inclusive of both female and male recipients. The characterization of Jesus in the opening verses of chapter 11 is not, therefore, single and unitary but plural or polyvalent within the unfolding of the narrative and its heteroglossal reception.

For those who read Jesus and the reign of God in terms of and constructive of the status quo or the imperial kyriarchal world or even in terms of certain expectations characterized of John,[20] then the deeds of Jesus could have been a "scandal," an "offense," or a "stumbling-block" (11:6). Jesus was mere man, Israelite, even marginal Jew,[21] associating with those on the margins of respectable society, and yet he is characterized as *Christos* and "the coming one," "divine sage" and "Son of God" doing those deeds that characterize God's desire for humanity, God's reign. The narration of his preaching and actions and those of his disciples in the ongoing reign of God movement lack closure, however, in their narrative context, and hence they challenge worlds and expectations that are fixed and stable.[22] The reader/hearer constructed in 11:6 as "blessed" for not taking offense at this Jesus, can and even must always look for another in the multiple voices that read Jesus in the Matthean narrative. Such readers/hearers construct a counter-story for their communities of resistance within first-century Judaism and Imperial Rome, reconfiguring through a variety of intertextualities new readings of God's being with humanity and humanity's participation in divinity.[23] And such readings open new possibilities for contemporary feminist women moving within the openness of the *ekklesia* of women.

## SAGE, TEACHER, PROPHET, AND WISDOM JUSTIFIED

The didactic nature of Matthew 11:7-15 and the parable and parabolic saying of 11:16-19 represent Jesus as teacher and sage. The narrative content amplifies the relationship between Jesus and John, v. 7 opening with Jesus beginning to speak to the crowd about John and vv. 18-19 closing the section with a linking of what Wendy Cotter calls "the two ways to wisdom" represented by the life paths of John and Jesus.[24] Darr suggests that in the Lukan narrative the characterization of John and Jesus is developed by way of *sygkrisis*, that ancient rhetorical pattern of comparison and contrast.[25] We have already seen the use of this technique in the Matthean infancy narrative, but not as in Luke in relation to John and Jesus. In the developments in Matthew 3, however, it would seem to be an important rhetorical strategy, as it is in Matthew 11.

The words of Jesus, the parabolic teacher, turn attention to John and tease the minds of both crowds and readers through a series of rhetorical questions regarding John. Even the conclusion to vv. 7-9 is open-ended, claiming John's prophetic role in the line of the prophets of old but also claiming that John's presence and work in the Judean desert rather than in the houses of kings opens out beyond what the Jewish nation already expected in its prophets (11:9, 11). John is exceedingly honored by Jesus. The scribal community's meaning-making in relation to Jesus reflects this honor back onto Jesus by its appropriation of the combined texts of Exodus 23:20 and Malachi 3:1. This was an act of *poiesis*, giving meaning to Jesus by weaving together biblical texts so that they are now appropriated to Jesus by way of their metaphorical function. The "coming" of God that will be prepared for by God's messenger, according to Malachi, is interpreted as realized in John and Jesus. As John is constructed open-endedly, more than messenger and prophet, so too readers are challenged by way of the rhetoric to understand Jesus open-endedly.[26] The play between least and greatest, between John the Baptist and the reign of God in v. 11, invites such an interpretation. Both John, the greatest of those born of woman (11:11a), and Jesus, "the coming one," are to be understood in relation to the reign of God (11:11b). Matthew 11, to this point, rhetorically constructs the manifestation of God's reign in Jesus as a sign of God's being with humanity. It is to that that attention must be directed rather than to the identity of either John or Jesus. In an agonistic society, however, and in the Matthean context in which some households considered themselves as deviant within their Jewish matrix, v.11, with its lesser and greater comparisons, could also have been read as making prominent the believers in Jesus over against the wider Jewish community represented by John, their prophet.[27] It is also this danger, which has characterized later Christian tradition, that must be avoided in contemporary feminist readings of Jesus.

As in the preceding section, vv. 12-13 give meaning to Jesus only indirectly, the focus being on the *basileia*. These two verses certainly challenge contemporary interpreters by their seeming paradox, and it might be imagined that such was the case for first-century readers also. Gerd Theissen's recent study suggests that a stigma developed against the reign of God movement within its Jewish matrix—Jesus and his followers as revolutionaries against the "will of God"—is turned to advantage so that it becomes charism rather than stigma.[28] Those households shaped by traditions of greater political engagement may well have understood the language politically, recognizing that "the kingdom of heaven has been challenging forcefully . . . [and that] those who are fully determined, forceful men are the ones who will lay hold and take possession of the kingdom."[29] It is the courageous determination that one sees in John, imprisoned for preaching the reign of God[30]; in Jesus, who is beginning to draw opposition for the same; and in the Canaanite woman, who is forcefully determined to claim the works of the *basileia* for herself and her daughter (15:21-28). It may have been the case, however, that those households that had suffered persecution because of their beliefs recognized their own experience in these words—the reign of God movement had suffered violence and the violent had confronted it to take hold of it and destroy it.[31] The closing words of vv. 7-15 called on those listening to hear the open-ended challenge toward a new future that is of God and God's *basileia* in the unfolding narrative, the narrative representation of John, Jesus, and all the courageous prophetic participants in the reign of God movement rhetorically constructing such a challenge for the readers/listeners.

Jesus as parabler, teacher, and sage who teaches by way of parables continues the challenge to openness and newness by way of a short, antithetically parallel, parabolic saying and its interpretation in vv. 16-19. Indeed, this parable and its content may have recapitulated for the reader as well as prepared for the more extensive characterization of Jesus as parabler in subsequent chapters (13, 18, 20–22, 25). The rhetorical effect of this aspect of the Matthean narrative is perhaps captured by John Meier in his explanation of parable:

> Though usually drawn from vivid, realistic events in ordinary life, the parable often functions as a type of riddle, intended to startle or tease the mind of the audience, forcing it to ponder both the parable

and their own lives as challenged by the parable. Far from being just another pretty story, the parable can embody a fierce polemic thrust. Full of surprises, paradoxes, and sudden reversals, it can be an "attack" on the very way the audience views God, religion, the world, and themselves. The parable is thus often a challenge to change one's vision and one's action; in short, it is one of Jesus' favorite ways of calling people to repentance, a basic change of heart, mind, and life.[32]

By way of this parable both John and Jesus are interpreted in terms of response to their preaching and lifestyle. Wendy Cotter has pointed out convincingly the irony in the parabolic context conveyed by way of its language. The image of one seated in the marketplace addressing the crowd does not belong to the world of children but of judicial courts, an aspect that would be immediately recognized by a Mediterranean audience.[33] To place a child in such a context is subversive of the adult world and opens the way for the interpretation of the parable that follows. Both John's ascetic lifestyle and Jesus' boundary-breaking table-companionship, representative of two different lifestyles or wisdom paths, subverted expectations of those who encountered them. This parable and its interpretation solidifies for readers who have ears to hear the challenge to be open to the unexpected, almost the unthinkable, in relation to both John and Jesus, whose lives interpret one another as well as the reign of God. While the link between an ascetic lifestyle and a ministry of eschatological prophecy may have been subversive of the world view of only certain segments of the Matthean community,[34] the characterization of a divine sage as "friend of tax-collectors and sinners" is completely deviant[35]; yet both the parable and the concluding statement of 11:19b challenge acceptance of such deviance. It is here that those households that had taken up such a challenge would have found another genre pointer to the gospel as a foundational narrative for the reign of God movement within the matrix of their broader Jewish context, in which they were considered deviant.

The seemingly unobtrusive substitution of the metaphoric title, or perhaps even simply designation, "the human one" (traditionally translated "Son of Man") for Jesus in 11:19 may have evoked a variety of reader responses.[36] Intratextually, it has already designated Jesus in his itinerant ministry in 8:20 and his sharing in the divine prerogative of forgiveness of sins (9:6); in 10:23 it functioned to alert the reader to the coming of a future "promised one." As it appears in the context of 11:19a, and given the extensive comparison between the life and ministry of John and Jesus begun in 11:2, we can imagine that for many of the Matthean audience, especially the broader popular audience, this phrase may well have been simply a circumlocution for "I" or "this man."[37] Meier suggests that it may have functioned, for those attentive to the narrative context of Jesus the parabler, by teasing the audience into meaning-making as an aspect of that mind-teasing.[38] What did it mean for Jesus the parabler to designate himself "human one"?

Intertextually, within the variety of first-century Judaism the metaphor carried a number of connotations. For those shaped by the prophetic tradition, the phrase may have evoked the self-designation of the prophet (Ez 2:1, 3, 8; 3:1, 4; 37:3, 11, 16) or the vision of Daniel of a "human one" who would come on the clouds of heaven for judgment (Dn 7:13-14). For those whose genre choices moved them to interpret Jesus as divine sage, and perhaps for others among whom the apocalyptic tradition was strong, the "human one" of 11:19 may have been evocative of 1 Enoch, in which traditions of the figures of divine wisdom and the "human one" merge. Just as Sophia/Wisdom, who dwelt in the heavens, went out to find a dwelling place among humanity (Enoch 42:1-2), so too "the Son of Man was concealed from the beginning, and the Most High One preserved him in the presence of his power; then he revealed him to the holy and the elect ones" (Enoch 62:7). Such a group's participation in the shaping of the Matthean text may be visible in Matthew 11:19b—Wisdom is justified or made righteous, language reminiscent of both the wisdom tradition as well as the Enoch apocalyptic. Within a community performance of the Matthean text different meanings evoked by the metaphor of the "human one" may have played among and between the audience. Contextually and intertextually, it not only characterized Jesus but also was a response to Jesus.[39]

Since in its original context of meaning it is unlikely that Jesus' self-designation as the "human one," with all its heteroglossal implications, functioned to universalize or even specifically signify the maleness of Jesus, contemporary insistence on the androcentric interpretation of the titular nature of the phrase and its translation as Son of Man must be challenged. Within the symbolic universe of contemporary christology, which privileges the titles Son of God and Lord discursively, and within liturgical contexts in which these same titles dominate and their metaphoric qualities are silenced, Son of Man functions to symbolize Jesus in absolute male terminology. The intertextual possibilities of an alternative translation of the phrase makes possible a subversion of this dominant ideological perspective and opens up alternative contemporary *poiesis* as new interpretations/translations such as "the human one" or "the promised one" are explored.

Within the reception of Matthew 11:1-19 first-century readers gave meaning to Jesus by an intertextual weaving of prophetic and wisdom traditions. Such an interweaving would also have rhetorically shaped meaning for readers in the ongoing performance of the gospel. As with the *sygkrisis* characteristic of this section of the narrative, the Matthean combination of wisdom and prophetic traditions means that they function together to interpret one another and, in their turn, interpret or give meaning to Jesus and his embeddedness in the reign of God movement. This complex finds a particularly explicit expression in the conclusion to this section of the Matthean narrative, 11:19b.

The forensic imagery of 11:16 is continued in the language of 11:19b—yet Wisdom/Sophia has been justified/recognized as just from her deeds.[40] It is as though response to John and Jesus is judged as response to Sophia/Wisdom, the female gestalt of divine wisdom of the sapiential tradition.[41] In light of the previous parable readers may well be reminded intertextually of Wisdom who "cries out in the street and in the squares . . . raises her voice" (Prv 1:20). She says of herself, "I have called and you refused, have stretched out my hand and no one heeded" (Prv 1:24). More remote, it would seem, are the references to Wisdom's works in Wisdom 14:5 and Sirach 1:9. Sirach 18:1-4, however, may have enhanced the early Christian meaning-making in relation to Jesus. In these verses, the Living One is proclaimed as having created the universe and is the one who alone will be justified (future passive of the verb used in the aorist passive in Matthew 11:19b). Sirach 18:4 further amplifies the distinctiveness of the Creative One by acknowledging that no one has been given power to proclaim this one's works/deeds, nor can anyone plumb their depths. Wisdom 9:9, on the other hand, identifies Wisdom as the one who knows these works, being present at the creation of the universe. Solomon prays that she be sent forth; 1 Enoch 42:2 imagines her going forth to dwell with "the children of the people"; and in Sirach 24:8-12 the Creator chooses a place for her tent among "an honored people." Intertextual voices play in this meaning-making both toward its writing and toward its rewriting as it is heard, read, and performed.

Sophia/Wisdom is rendered justified in the deeds of John and Jesus. Such a meaning would have been even stronger for those who had retained echoes of the Q tradition—Wisdom is justified by her children. The path of wisdom chosen by the ascetic eschatological prophet and that chosen by the prophet of inclusive table-companionship, both of whom are Wisdom's representatives or prophets, are ways by which Wisdom's righteousness is rendered visible. The contemporary reader catches a glimpse here of possible subjugated knowledge, the recognition of both John and Jesus as prophets of Sophia, pointing to the significance of the sapiential or wisdom traditions among early Christians in making meaning of Jesus' life and death.[42] Such traditions have certainly become subjugated in later Christianity both in their own right as well as in relation to Jesus and contemporary Christian *poiesis*.

Matthean readers, however, also would have found their understanding of Jesus shaped by the *inclusio* of vv. 2 and 19—the deeds of the *Christos* paralleling the deeds of Sophia. Sophia and *Christos* are both linked metaphorically with Jesus. New meanings are given to Jesus as readers identify him with the rich intertextual layers of the words *Christos* and *Sophia* in both their socio-cultural context and in this narrative context.

The Sophia imagery, however, is also transgressive. On the one hand, it identifies the male Jesus with Sophia, genderized female, with such identification carrying all the transgressive aspects that the sapiential traditions and their representation of Sophia/Divine Wisdom as female evoke.[43] Jesus is Jesus Sophia and, like Sophia, unites the human and the divine by way of theological evocation that breaks open gender distinctions.[44] On the other hand, the metaphor represses the cross-genderization and its possible rhetorical effect by way of its identification with the male Jesus in a symbolic narrative whose world is significantly androcentric. For those Matthean households whose storytelling shaped a community identity that was inclusive of genders, ethnicities, and classes, the image of Jesus Sophia may have functioned as boundary-breaking and been linked intimately with the boundary-breaking aspects of the works of the *basileia*. The links would have tended to be with the more popular community or folk wisdom tradition, which was more inclusive of women and men, than the scribal or school tradition, which speaks strongly in the wisdom literature of the Jewish scriptures. For those households, especially those influenced by that scribal or school context that was male exclusive, such an interpretation would have been an "offense" or "stumbling block," and its subversive aspect could very readily be suppressed to "Son of Man" imagery and to the "father" and "son" imagery that will characterize the subsequent narrative.

Contemporary meaning-making that seeks to subvert the ideological sex/gender system as it has functioned not only to make meaning of Jesus but also of the lives of Christians might identify and emphasize the rhetorical effect of such cross-genderization in subverting the centrality of the maleness of Jesus within Christian theological discourse. This might then open up the possibilities of contemporary *poiesis* that can draw on additional female symbols and metaphors in constructing christologies that will, in their turn, contribute to developing female and feminist subjectivities. This is the work of the *ekklesia* of women for which the Matthean storytelling provides a prototype.

The deeds of the *Christos*, the deeds characteristic of the reign of God movement, are the deeds of Wisdom. But Wisdom's deeds, as well as being salvific or liberating deeds (see Wis 10–19) are also creative; she is present at the very shaping of the universe (Prv 8:22-31; Sir 24: 1-22; Wis 9:9). The intertextuality evoked in the opening verse of the gospel continues here. In Jesus, and even more especially in the deeds of Jesus *Christos*/Jesus Sophia, the works of the *basileia*, the creative works of the Living One, continue. A new creation is being wrought in the works of righteousness, the reordering of resources and relationships, whereby Wisdom is rendered right or just in the sight of humanity. She is called on to respond to her prophets, whether they come in the guise of an ascetic preacher living on the edge of civilization inviting people to come to hear or an itinerant preacher speaking in the midst of the people in their cities and villages, on their mountain tops, and by their lakesides. For contemporary feminist interpreters this points toward new possibilities of meaning-making and storytelling that will shape a consciousness adequate to the response necessary for the reordering of life for the sake of the planet and all its species—a creative and a liberating praxis.[45]

Why the image of Jesus Sophia was suppressed invites consideration, but few firmly founded conclusions are possible. Luise Schottroff suggests that Israel's sapiential traditions belonged predominantly to Israel's elite males, scribes, and teachers, and that the *Armenevangelium*, the good news to the poor, finds its home among women and other dispossessed.[46] The first tradition, therefore, would seem to have excluded the second and became the dominant one. The multiple voices from earlier and later layers of traditioning heard in the Matthean narrative suggest, on the other hand, that the prophetic tradition with its liberation and justice aspects and the sapiential, which in its later stages combined the liberating deeds of Sophia God with reflection on her giving of wisdom to all, were combined and functioned within Matthean traditioning to read those ancient traditions in a new way as well as to give meaning to Jesus.[47]

Silvia Schroer points out that Israel's wisdom traditions were vitally concerned with questions of righteousness or right ordering of the resources and relationships within a universe in which divinity would be at home, and she marks out the relationship between the prophetic and sapiential traditions in early Judaism. She sees the prophetic being engaged in social protest and critique, while the wisdom tradition appeals to the well-to-do not to exploit the poor.[48] She also demonstrates that in first-century Palestine there was a tradition of folk wisdom on which the Christian traditioning drew, using Matthew 13:54 (// Mk 6:1-2) by way of example. It has likewise been shown above that the Jesus traditioning that linked the prophetic and sapiential metaphors and images was open-ended and nonhierarchical, constructing such identities in deviant or resistant communities. It would seem, however, that control of Jesus' identity and hence of community identities led some communities to choose a more agonistic understanding of Jesus as greater than John, a more male-centered imaging that privileged metaphors of "Son of God" and "Son of Man." This may have occurred as more hierarchical structuring and more male-dominated power and control began to characterize the community toward the end of the first century, leading to a silencing but not a complete erasure of the open-ended storytelling and wisdom traditioning. It may have been the female imagery that linked humanity and divinity within that tradition that was its greatest challenge and hence cause for its subjugation. It is this very gap or fissure, however, that makes new readings possible.

Rhetorical hints have already prepared the reader to link the images of Jesus that play within this section of the narrative with that of eschatological prophet, one who challenges and who faces rejection. That rejection is narrated graphically in Matthew 11:20-24, rather than being hinted at parabolically as in 11:16-19. The grounds for eschatological condemnation of the cities in which Jesus had preached is a failure to recognize the *dunameis*, the mighty deeds Jesus performed there. Intratextually, the attentive reader would recall immediately the *erga* or deeds of *Christos/ Sophia* of the previous section, vv. 2-19. While this section speaks to the reader of failures to respond to Jesus' message, no doubt it resonated in the Matthean Galilean-Syrian arc of cities in which internal strife was dividing Judaism, expressing the disappointment, the hostility, and the pain that a Judaism in crisis created for its people.[49] The narrative then moves on quickly, however, drawing readers into an intricate weave of the threads of this section of the narrative and the weaving of new strands that will move the narrative and its imaging of Jesus and the reign of God movement forward.

## BEARING HER YOKE

The tone and style of the narrative changes quite dramatically in the concluding verses of chapter 11, which can be divided into two segments— vv. 25-27 and vv. 28-30—both of which function significantly in the characterization of Jesus. The first segment is in the form of a prayer or divine address on the lips of Jesus. It is the prayer of the holy one, the divine sage, and it draws together sapiential, prophetic, and apocalyptic threads into these few short verses that have been given extensive scholarly attention.[50]

Language of "father," "son," and "to reveal" permeate vv. 25-27. The opening of the prayer—I bless you, Father, Lord of heaven and earth— brings together titles that are not combined in this form elsewhere in the Christian Testament nor in exactly the same way in other extant Jewish literature, although elements of the combination are familiar. The most immediate recognition and meaning-making would seem to come from the sage's prayer in Sirach, especially Sirach 51:1, which begins in the same way but uses the address "O Lord and King." In Sirach 23:1,4, however, the sage begins a prayer, "O Lord, Father." Mary Rose D'Angelo and Eileen Schuller have offered much more extensive intertextual resonances from intertestamental literature and early Judaism, especially Qumran, Tobit, and 3 Maccabees.[51] For the reader shaped intertextually by some of these possibilities, the divine address is that of the holy one at prayer in time of need, of refuge, or of forgiveness, as well as an acknowledgment of divine power and providence.[52] The prayer renders Jesus as holy one or divine sage, while the Matthean language of "Lord of heaven and earth" invites readers into the symbolic universe that the Matthean narrative constructs, a universe linking earth and heaven (5:18; 6:10; see later 24:35; 28:18). The language of Jesus, the holy one, at prayer points to a recognition of the divine engagement with and among humanity, using terms familiar from Jewish prayer to evoke this.

The titles "Father" and "Lord" also contain meaning from another context in which the Matthean households were grounded, namely, the Empire. Both terms encode linguistic referents to the male head of the household, *kyrios* or *paterfamilias,* as well as the male ruler of the Empire.[53] Use of these titles may have had a twofold rhetorical effect. On the lips of Jesus, the radical preacher of the reign of God as alternative to the imperial vision, they shape readers' consciousness and imagination toward a new or alternative family or fictive kinship within a new world vision or empire, that of God, and toward legitimate resistance to the empire of Rome. That such a vision challenged patriarchal family structures and began to construct gender alternatively has been demonstrated in my previous work.[54] The stumbling block created by such a vision in some households would have been great, and it is likely that the intimate connection made between these imperial titles and the Empire in subsequent centuries may have stretched back to Christian leadership within the Matthean community that was, even then, desirous of imitating leadership of the Empire. Matthew's injunction against titles in 23:10-11 may point to such a trend, however slight. The titles themselves have become an offense to many contemporary feminist Christians, because they have been used to close off the gospel meaning rather than open it up to new articulations consonant with twenty-first-century rather than first-century experience.

As at the beginning of the chapter, the Jesus who here addresses God as "Father" and "Lord" was characterized by the deeds of the reign of God. In the context of the entire segment of the narrative, it would seem that the *tauta* ("these things") of v. 25 are a reference back to the *dunameis* done in the cities (11:20), the deeds of the *Christos*/Sophia (11:2, 19). In the wisdom language evoked by these verses the work of the sage is a work of revelation and, as Deutsch points out, it is "a source of wisdom for the community."[55] Jesus, the sage, is never separated from the community or from the works of God for, with, and among the community. The "babes" or "infants" who receive the revelation (11:25) would be recognized by many listeners as themselves, the ones receiving the story of Jesus and the reign of God and thereby participating in its ongoing open-endedness.[56] The interplay of concealment and revelation with its apocalyptic overtones suggests the incompleteness of any storytelling, any imaging of Jesus as representative of God among us. The incomprehensibility of the intimate relationship between divinity and humanity imaged in incarnation will always stretch out in front of each community of believers and point to the limitation of any attempts to articulate it definitively.

In the language world of the Matthean community, especially its households of alternative vision, the exclusive father/son language of 11:27 creates tension. For many listeners the language continues sapiential with faint apocalyptic echoes. For those familiar with Wisdom 2, the righteous one who suffers at the hands of the ungodly (Wis 1:16) is the one who calls God "Father" and is tested to see whether such a claim is true (Wis 2:16-17). Wisdom is the one to whom it has been given to know, to recognize the ways of God, and who likewise passes on what she has learned. The "son" here takes the place of Sophia, a substitution not surprising to the reader who has encountered a similar meaning-making device in 11:19, and that son passes on the revelation in a chain of tradition that will become familiar later in the Tannaitic literature.[57] What *is* surprising, however, is the exclusive note introduced into v. 27b. Inclusive revelation not only for the wise and the powerful but for the little ones of the *basileia* functions in tension with the claim to exclusivity in a male line of authority. Schüssler Fiorenza says that "the introduction of father-son language into early Christian sophialogy is intrinsically bound up with a theological exclusivity that reserves revelation for the elect few and draws the boundaries of communal identity between insiders and outsiders."[58] Such imagery creates a tension in a symbolic universe characterized by open-endedness and the expansive participation of Sophia God and Sophia's prophet, Jesus, among humanity. At this point it is a minor fissure in the narrative structure, but, given the wider narrative context, it can be read to repress the female imagery for God and Jesus that has characterized at least this section of the narrative; it thus opens the way for the more dominant male imagery in order to create cohesion, a tendency that will characterize subsequent readings of the Matthean gospel down through its history of reception.

Another source of intertextuality, available more readily perhaps to the scribal households, is that of the Moses typology.[59] Allison finds three crucial texts functioning intertextually. They narrate the reciprocal knowledge between Moses and God which functions as a type for the reciprocal knowledge 11:27 proposed between the "father" and the "son" (Ex 33:11-23; Nm 12:1-8; Dt 34:9-12). Just as Sophia's unique knowledge of the ways of God was claimed for Jesus, so too the claim that no prophet has arisen in Israel like Moses, who knows God face to face, is now predicated of Jesus. While the language of the text seeks exclusivity, its intertextual links—which give it meaning—subvert such exclusivity. Just as Moses and Sophia were types for Jesus, so too Jesus is a type for all those who enter into a special knowledge relationship with the God of Jesus. Such readings would have created identity for those households constructing a story of origin for themselves. They too knew and were recognized by God and passed on the tradition in an ongoing chain.

The last three verses are an invitation to readers in both sapiential and prophetic language. One or the other of these traditions may have shaped particular households' reception or reading of these verses depending on the more prevalent tradition in their house-church, but perhaps the interplay of language also challenged them toward an interpretation that combined the two worlds of meaning.

The sage of Sirach 6:18-37 and Wisdom herself (Sir 51:23-30) invite disciples to come to Sophia and to learn from her without labor and toil. The language of both of these invitations resonates in the invitation of Jesus, characterized as both sage or teacher of wisdom, and Wisdom herself. The promise of rest is a promise made by Wisdom (Sir 6:28), but it is also a promise of God made through the prophets. In sapiential language, the prophet Jeremiah calls those faithful to the covenant to stand at the crossroads and ask for the good way, because the walking of it will give rest for the soul (Jer 6:16). God also gives rest to Moses (Ex 33:14), a theme familiar to first-century Judaism, as indicated by Josephus's *Antiquities* 3.61. Jesus, the sage or prophet, speaks the assurance of Sophia and the Covenant God. Intertextually and intratextually, the hint of rest also evokes the new creation and its culmination in a Sabbath of renewal of creative energies (Gn 2:2-3), developing the thread that began to unravel in the opening verse of the gospel and whose meaning was amplified earlier in this section in relation to Sophia's creative deeds.

In Jesus' second invitation to take up "my yoke," the voice of the sage disappears, and it is the divine voice that speaks.[60] Wisdom's yoke is not difficult to bear (Sir 51:26-28; 6:29-31), a claim that is meant as encouragement to take up wisdom, which Sirach equates with Torah. It is in this regard that the language of "yoke" may have had meaning for the Matthean households familiar with Jesus as a prophetic and wise interpreter of Torah. Indeed, the sapiential language of v. 29 may have evoked a link for some between Jesus and Torah. For households seeking an identity in the following of Jesus according to a new interpretation of Torah, this invitation to take up the yoke of Jesus, the meek and gentle one, would have encouraged discipleship.[61]

Overman notes that the dramatic contrast in this language of discipleship compared to that of the woes of the Galilean cities might indicate the ambivalence experienced by many house-churches in relation to the reign of God movement.[62] This ambivalence may have been internal also, as for some the notion of "yoke" meant sovereignty, and the taking on of a yoke could mean domination, or it may also evoke the struggle involved in the yoke of justice familiar within the prophetic tradition.[63] The prophetic evocation of the meekness and humility of heart of Jesus (Zec 9:9; Zep 3:9-13) assures the Matthean households, especially if they are threatened by intra-Jewish strife and/or suffering under the Roman yoke of oppression, that the way preached and lived by Jesus and the prophets of the reign of God movement is easy and light and provides strength in the struggle. The Jesus who speaks in the language of the gospel continues to speak in the prophetic and wise preachers and teachers of the Matthean community, those who follow the way of Jesus and truly learn discipleship. These continue the interpretation of Torah, continue the wisdom teaching begun in Jesus.

This chapter of the Matthean gospel offers the contemporary feminist interpreter a prototype for interpreting Jesus. The narrative tension between identity and works, between concealment and revelation, acceptance and rejection, closed categories of comparison and open-ended processes of understanding provide the reader with those fissures in the text that invite creative ongoing interpretation rather than closed cohesive meaning that is established once and for all. The contemporary feminist reader is invited into the reading process, bringing rich layers of intertextuality from present reading sites as well as the history of reception of this narrative critically evaluated. The reader has been alerted to some aspects of the text that have been universalized and used to legitimate domination of women and to prevent gender, race, and class alternatives during the history of reception. However, the possibilities of ongoing open-ended interpretation have been uncovered. The *ekklesia* of women and its *poiesis* of Jesus is one possible site in which such possibilities can be realized.

# 6

## As She Desired and He Confessed—
## Boundary-Walker and Deconstructive Builder

### Matthew 15:21-28; 16:13-20

*Matthew 15:21-28 is from beginning to end the story of the Canaanite woman. She initiates the movement of the story with her first petition, refuses to be silenced or ignored, and in the end goes away victorious, having been answered and heard by Jesus. She is insistent, demanding, and unafraid to state her claims. She is the lifeblood of this story. Any attempt to classify this text by placing Jesus at its center will ultimately be inadequate.*

—Gail R. O'Day[1]

These words of Gail O'Day seem to render strange the choice of at least the first of the two pericopes for consideration in this chapter. I readily agree with O'Day that the Canaanite woman, Justa,[2] is the protagonist of the story in Matthew 15:21-28; and a number of studies in recent years have highlighted Justa's significance.[3] As well as its gender implications, though, her story demonstrates, as did Matthew 11:1-19, that character interaction is one of the key rhetorical devices in the development of characterization. It will be from this perspective, therefore, that this chapter will explore how the story of Justa and her interaction with Jesus was shaped by and also shaped different meaning-making in relation to Jesus within the variety of Matthean households.[4]

Matthew 16:13-20, or the Petrine confession, as it is so often designated, appears much more readily to contribute to the gospel's characterization of Jesus, especially given its repetition with variation of the "who do you say I am?" question. It has certainly received extensive scholarly attention in relation to Matthean christology.[5] One aspect, however, that has been entirely overlooked by scholars, as far as I can determine, and that has captured my own attention in recent years, is the parallel between the two stories. Given that contemporary scholarship has considered 16:13-20 central to a reading of the Matthean Jesus, this study provides a more than suitable site for exploring my intuitions regarding the narrative relationships between the faith claims of both Justa and Peter and their contribution to a reading of the Matthean Jesus.

Contextually, these two pericopes function within the long narrative section between the parable and the community discourses of Matthew 13 and 18 (13:53–17:27).[6] Elsewhere, I have demonstrated that the story of Justa, together with the preceding discussion on the tradition of the elders (15:1-20), belongs at the midpoint of a chiastic structure framed by the feeding of the five thousand and four thousand (14:13-21; 15:32-39); reference to the "little faith" of disciple/s (14:28-33; 16:5-12); and the healing of many (14:34-36; 15:29-31).[7] One could argue that this chiastic structure is itself framed by two parallel stories—the rejection of Jesus at Nazareth, in which the identity of Jesus is a central concern (13:53-58) that parallels the questioning of Jesus' identity at Caesarea Philippi (16:13-20); and the death of John the Baptist (14:1-12), which symbolically parallels the death of Jesus predicted in 16:21-23.

A number of interlocking narrative threads and thematics play within this section, and these in turn would have evoked different emphases from within the variety of reading communities. The identity of Jesus and response to what one understands of that identity certainly constitute a significant thread running between the story of the residents of Nazareth who seek to make meaning of the wisdom and *dunameis* or mighty deeds of the one whom they have known as Miriam's son (13:54-55) and the very short account of Peter's inability to accept that the prophetic, messianic one in their midst will suffer as a result of the path chosen as the righteous one of God (16:21-23). The *dunameis* of Jesus, which the Nazareans grappled to understand, continue to be manifest in multiplication of loaves (14:13-21; 15:32-39), walking on water (14:22-33), and numerous healings (14:34-36; 15:29-31), that of Justa's daughter being given narrative development and focus (15:21-28). Bread is a prominent thematic (14:17, 19; 15:2, 26, 33, 34, 36; 16:5, 7, 8, 9, 10, 11, 12) and metaphors and titles in relation to Jesus are reiterative and interactive, as the subsequent study will indicate.

Since this chapter focuses on two pericopes, it will assist the subsequent analysis to highlight here at the outset some of the parallels or relationships between the two. The first similarity is that both stories are structured as dialogues or debates with a significant repetition at the beginning of most verses of either the verb "to say" (15:22b, 25, 27; 16:13b, 14, 15) or the participle of the verb "to answer" together with a form of "to say" (15:24, 26, 28; 16:16, 17). The dialogue format is more fully developed in 15:21-28, so that the story could be said to resemble a rabbinic debate, but in both pericopes the verbal interaction with Jesus structures the story.

Both dialogues are framed by very brief narrative settings and conclusions (15:21-22a, 28b and 16:13, 20), with Jesus narrated as approaching the region of Tyre and Sidon in 15:21 and of Caesarea Philippi in parallel phraseology in 16:13. From within either Jewish or Greco-Roman contexts, the narrative structures may have initially shaped a characterization of Jesus as teacher, either rabbinic or philosophic.

Socio-culturally, both stories may have been read through the lens of the honor/shame system. Justa's encounter with Jesus contains classic elements of the challenge/riposte of an agonistic society. Her request for help challenges Jesus, whose initial response is a scornful or disdainful rejection. Justa does not accept the rejection and makes a further request, which is met with a counter-challenge that she, in turn, counter-challenges.[8] Had Justa been male, this would have been read by many first-century readers and contemporary critics as an excellent example of Jesus being bested in the public arena of challenge to male honor and his recognition of that in the granting of the request, contrary to his original intention. The extraordinary transgression in this story from a cultural point of view is that Justa is female, alien to the male world of honor and contravening the code of female shame by engaging Jesus in the public arena. It is difficult to imagine that this was accidental and would have gone unnoticed within the first-century contexts of reading. Rather, it needs to be considered with other transgressions in this story in relation to the characterization of Jesus. Within the Caesarea Philippi incident, it is Jesus' question about how he is identified by others that would have evoked the honor system of the first-century society. In this story there is little transgression, with most readers likely to characterize the "disciples" to whom the question is addressed as male (even though discipleship could be construed within the unfolding narrative as male and female).

A final parallel relationship between the two pericopes is that both are concerned not only with the identity of Jesus but seem to be sites of contention around the identity of the community and its emerging structures of participation. This is particularly explicit in the Caesarea Philippi incident, in which Jesus names the community *ekklesia*. While not so explicit in Justa's story, the question of the boundaries of Jesus' own commission would have raised questions about community boundaries of inclusion and exclusion. At the point of the Matthean reception of the text within its communities of reading, such questions, as well as dealing with the community's outer boundaries, may also have been symbolic of other boundaries within the community in relation to liturgical leadership and participation.[9]

## OF BREAD AND DOGS AND JUSTA'S DESIRE

The narrative introduction to Matthew 15:21-28 is characterized by ambiguity, if recent scholarly interpretations are any guide. Certainly for contemporary interpreters it seems impossible to determine with certainty whether Jesus has entered or simply approached the region of Tyre and Sidon and whether Justa left this territory for Jewish soil where she encounters Jesus.[10] The same ambiguity may have prevailed among first-century readers. Indeed, the very ambivalence or ambiguity in the text may have influenced readers to read both characters introduced in the opening narrative, Jesus and Justa, as boundary-breakers or, as McCracken calls them, "characters in the boundary."[11] Both appear in this narrative on the threshold, and it is only in the dialogic relation between the characters in this encounter that each is constructed.

Justa, according to this narrative, is out of place, a *skandalon*, a boundary-walker.[12] It is from this site that is neither her own nor that of Jesus, the liminal or threshold point that allows a "crossing over" to occur, that Justa cries out her plea.[13] O'Day characterized Justa's stance before Jesus and the structuring of the narrative around her pleas (vv. 22, 25) as a "narrative embodiment of a lament psalm."[14] Elsewhere I have also demonstrated that at least some of those within the matrix of the Jewish religion would have recognized the language of the psalms in Justa's cries for mercy and assistance.[15] Perhaps in this liminal narrative they may have interpreted this marginal woman to be an embodiment of the petitioner who cries out in great need to the One who can offer relief. Her cries may have also prefigured for those familiar with the unfolding story the final cry of Jesus (27:50) on the cross. There may have been for the attentive reader the slightest hint of a crossing over of characterization between the woman and Jesus, prepared for by the threshold space created in the opening narrative sector. Like Justa, Jesus too is or will be, as the narrative unfolds, the embodiment of lament. The story may have functioned in this way in particular for those alternative communities of resistance who shared the liminal space of the margins and for whom the Jesus story was constituting gender and ethnicity in ways that differed from the dominant Jewish-Christian and Greco-Roman cultural matrices.

It is from this same liminal space that Justa counter-challenges the final obstacle that Jesus places before her. In reply to her cry for help, Jesus counters that "it is not fair to take the children's bread and throw it to the dogs" (15:26). Jesus' reply transgresses the liminal space created by the narrative introduction, locating Jesus and Justa not together on the boundaries but one as insider to the household imaged by reference to children and one outside with the dogs to whom bread is thrown. This reply completes the transgression of the pericope's narrative space already begun with Jesus' ignoring of Justa's first request and his reiteration of his commission only to the lost sheep of the house of Israel (15:23a, 24; cf. 10:5-6). His position is fixed and closed. Justa, however, moves the reader back to the place of possibilities beyond the boundaries Jesus has established. She does not accept the dichotomies of insider and outsider within which Jesus functions but creates a new space that is inside the house and that allows both the children and dogs to be fed within that household, both from the same table.

Justa's role in this story is prophetic and transgressive. She is counter-cultural in that she accepts the challenge to her honor and responds accordingly, just as the reader has expected of Jesus as a result of a number of challenges (8:5-13; 12:9-14, 22-30, by way of example). It is also her counter-challenge (v. 27), out of fidelity to her desire for healing for her daughter, which is recognized by Jesus as being in keeping with God's desire for humanity (let it be done as you desire).[16] Justa is prophetic teacher who brings Jesus to a new understanding of his mission.[17] She stands in the place that the reader would have come to expect of Jesus in keeping with a number of threads in the unfolding narrative. In the liminal space on the boundaries, there is the possibility of cross-characterization. As the christic one, Justa challenges Jesus to a new and more broadly prophetic understanding of the reign of God movement intertextually in line with the vision of Isaiah (Mt 12: 15-21; cf. Is 42:1-4, 9; 60:1-16).

Justa is also the wise one who turns Jesus' vision back to the inclusive sapiential perspective that readers have already encountered earlier in the narrative. We saw in the previous chapter that Jesus Sophia called *all* who were in any way burdened to come to her for rest (11:28). And yet the Jesus presented in 15:21-28 seems to contravene this invitation. Intra-textually, it is Justa who now stands in the place that Jesus stood earlier, constructed according to the imagery of Wisdom. Justa is like Mother Wisdom, who desires to feed her child with bread (Sir 15:2-3), but Justa transgresses the imagery because it is not her son but her daughter for whom she desires bread. By way of her challenge to the exclusive house-hold imagery of Jesus, she envisages another house (v. 27), one in which Sophia's invitation to "come and eat of my bread" (Prv 9:1-5) can be extended to all. As we have seen earlier, the prophetic and sapiential tradi-tions intersect in the Matthean narrative to interpret Jesus, but in this story the sapiential, like the prophetic *poiesis,* functioned through cross-characterization, a very significant rhetorical device, to shape reading. It could be suggested that this *poiesis* may have been predominantly women's.

Within those households who read the Matthean gospel as the story of origin of the reign of God movement in which they were participants—a movement that had begun the task of constructing gender and ethnicity in ways that differed, however slightly, from that of the dominant cultural matrix—Jesus and the Jesus vision could be read in this story as inextrica-bly linked to the prophetic/sapiential spirit embodied in the community and its members.[18] In their narrative it was the doubly or triply marginated woman who embodied a scandalously new vision and new wisdom and whose story functioned not only to construct Jesus but also to construct gender and ethnicity in ways undreamed of and only possible from the place on the boundary, the threshold. In situations encountered in the ongoing life of the Matthean households, this story could have challenged the community to recognize others also whose stories and whose interaction with the community would construct Jesus in the new ways that would enable the house-churches to face new situations, especially issues of inclusion. As McCracken indicates, "It is not just characters in the text who are brought to the threshold; the gospels themselves act as occasions for offense to their readers."[19]

As Justa and Jesus negotiate their encounter within the liminal space in which the narrative places them, a new vision of the reign of God movement and of Jesus within that movement is being constructed around the image of household introduced into this story by way of Jesus' reference to the "house of Israel." It is a tensive image for readers from within both Jewish and gentile households. While the use of the image in this context suggests limitation and boundaries, its link with the mission of seeking out the lost sheep would recall intratextually for some readers the earlier reference to Jesus as having compassion on the crowd, who were "harassed and helpless, like sheep without a shepherd" (9:36). In this first instance different readers would have understood the extent of that compassion differently depending on the link they made between the summary statement of 4:23 and 9:35. Matthew 4:24-25 located the response to Jesus' preaching, teaching, and healing (4:23) "throughout all Syria . . . from Galilee and the Decapolis and Jerusalem and Judea and from beyond the Jordan," while the parallel reference to Jesus' preaching, teaching, and healing in 9:35 is followed by the image of the crowd as sheep without a shepherd. The sheep could certainly have been understood as located beyond the boundaries of Israel. The temporal axis of limitation of mission boundaries was, however, introduced into 15:24, as it was also in 10:5-6, the commissioning of the disciples.[20]

The parabolic statement of 15:26 continues the household imagery, constructing an inside and outside through the related imagery of "children's bread" and what is thrown to the dogs. The children belong in the house and the dogs outside.[21] It is this which the reply of Justa subverts, bringing the dogs into the house to eat crumbs from the same table as the children (v. 27). She acknowledges difference but not dichotomy and locates these differences within the same household, at the same table. When Jesus confirms Justa's desire and her daughter is healed, the subversion is complete. The boundaries of the reign of God movement have been constructed not from within according to the vision of Jesus, but from the margins. Jesus has encountered an "outsider" who brings him, through response to that encounter, to the new vision that is in accord with God's desiring of right relationships. For those of the Matthean community who now sought to live in the new vision, this story may have been legitimating of the communities they had established. Justa's multiple marginality—gender, ethnicity, and religious affiliation, to name the obvious—would have continued to challenge such households to ongoing openness to the invitations and encounters that came from those on the boundaries, those whom the community encountered in liminal spaces, the place of new vision.[22] The reading of Jesus would have shaped the visioning of the community's responses in new situations.

One of the most extraordinary transgressions of the boundaries, imaged by the geographic and ethnic identifications of Justa and Jesus, occurs in Justa's addressing of Jesus in the titles or metaphors whose meaning context is the Jewish religious tradition (vv. 22, 25). Both titles—Lord and Son of David—belong within and contribute to the household imagery central to the pericope and yet they are on the lips of the woman on the boundary. *Kyrios* (Lord) could be seen simply as a title of social respect, but its most common referent was to the male head of the household in the Greco-Roman society, the one who had both power and authority over the people and resources that pertained to that household. As a title of address in the unfolding Matthean gospel, it has been heard on the lips of supplicants—a leper (8:2); a Roman centurion (8:6); the disciples and Peter under threat by the waves (8:25; 14:28, 30); and the two blind men (9:28). It is a recognition of power and constructs the reign of God as a new fictive kinship. To this point in the narrative, the participants in the new kinship have been explicitly or implicitly male. Justa invites readers to an expansion of the boundaries of this new kinship to include women— and not just as supplicants but as participants in the shaping of the vision of the reign of God. The new imaging of the household may have functioned to subvert some of the familiar connotations in the title. It must be remembered, however, that metaphorically Jesus as *Kyrios* suppresses the world of mothers and daughters. But, in the tensive nature of metaphor, it also carries the traces of what it has so suppressed.[23]

The title "Son of David" is not only a household metaphor in keeping with the later reference to the "house of Israel," but it also carries hierarchical and monarchical overtones that for both Jew and Gentile could have evoked the political and subversive subtext of the narrative already noted in earlier chapters, especially given its metaphorical and fictive use in Matthew. Dennis Duling has provided a detailed study of the plurisignificance or multivalence of the title.[24] On the lips of Justa in Matthew 15:22, it could have recalled for readers the locating of Jesus within an ancestral kinship or household (1:1-25) as well as the therapeutic understanding of the title encountered in the cry of the blind men, which parallels Justa's (9:27). As such, it could signify either a closed household as constructed by Jesus within this pericope or an openness toward a mission of compassion (see later 21:14-15), depending on how this heteroglossal image was read by Matthean households.

Justa's words set the "house of David" already characterized according to its male lineage (1:1-17), over against another household, that of a mother and daughter. The latter is a household not characterized by power and honor but by need; it is a place symbolized in the narrative as demon-possessed. For many readers it would have been seen as foreign, as other, and the stance of Jesus in relation to Justa, who represented this house-hold, would have confirmed such a reading. Through the interaction between Justa and Jesus, however, a third household is evoked (v. 27). It is one in which the foreign mother and daughter share from the same table as the children of the *kyrioi*, one that the explorations of the previous chapter indicate could be envisaged intertextually as Wisdom's house. It is not yet the household of radical equality. Difference and hierarchy persist in the imagery of the narrative, but for many readers the story may have functioned as subversive, as legitimating or challenging the community toward the ongoing process of subversion of those boundaries that even Jesus had to learn to cross.

The possibility of first-century Matthean households reading this story as a "threshold dialogue" is supported by Bakhtin's recognition of this genre as "widespread in Hellenistic and Roman literature, propagated chiefly through the Socratic dialogues and Menippean satires, the latter of which . . . had a great influence on ancient Christian literature."[25] In Justa's story, however, the threshold dialogue is itself transgressed as Justa is the stumbling block, the one in whom Jesus encounters another who leads him to new faith.[26]

The history of reception of this story and the theological world view that it continues to structure and legitimate today suggest that not all the Matthean households characterized Jesus according to the reading indicated above. There were those communities, whether Jewish or gentile, in which a patriarchal world view persisted, and whose genre choice for this story of Jesus was the hero narrative, the biography of a man endowed with divine power. They would have read Jesus as chief protagonist. As a result of such a genre choice, Justa's addressing Jesus as *Kyrios* and Son of David would have been seen as rightfully honoring Jesus as the one who shared the power of the divine *Kyrios*, strange perhaps on the lips of this woman from the boundaries, but even this could have given an even stronger indication of the universality of his power.

The household imagery constructed from within such a reading site would have legitimated rather than critiqued the kyriarchal household and imperial structure in which the community participated. Their *kyrios* is Jesus, the symbolic authority in the household authorized as the avenue for God's salvific action in Israel, the house of David. Jesus is indeed privileged son and heir within this household, receiving his power from the divine *Kyrios* (11:27). He has the power, therefore, to grant or refuse Justa's request, to test her faith[27] by ignoring her request and by his disdainful designation of her and her daughter as "dogs." From this perspective it is not Jesus who has changed; he remains universally in control. It is Justa who has been tried and proved faithful and who can then pick up the crumbs.

The symbolic universe of this household is androcentric and power is highly genderized. Gender and ethnicity are constructed according to the center, which is male and power-dominant, and Jesus is located at that center. The reading of Jesus from this site legitimates hierarchy as well as gender and ethnic dichotomies. The "great faith" of Justa is not that of defiant resistance to the limitations that placed her on the margin and outside the community of reception of the fruits of the *basileia*.[28] Rather, it is recognition of and submission to kyriarchal power that provides her with the crumbs that fall from the masters' tables.

The power attributed to Jesus within such a reading is universal and dominant. Associated with divine power, as it is in the Matthean text generally, it veils the violence that can be inherent in such power, a violence that emerges close to the surface in the story of Jesus' encounter with Justa. It is the only story in which Jesus so forcefully ignores a supplicant, places the obstacle of ethnicity across the path of a plea for help, and then reiterates the obstacle in language that is offensive. The actions and the words of Jesus speak a violence against women and other outsiders that is always present within patriarchy but that becomes more visible when the hold over dominant power is threatened. It suggests, therefore, that this story was a site of struggle around the identity of Jesus and the construction of the Jesus community—whether to comply with the social constructions of the society in which the Matthean communities were embedded or to face the difficult and sometimes overwhelming task of structuring an alternative.

Within this segment I have suggested two very different readings of Jesus and of the reign of God movement within Matthean households. In that context, more heteroglossal possibilities would have emerged than it has been possible to demonstrate here. For contemporary readers aware that such heteroglossal *poiesis* exists in today's contexts of reading, the second reading sounds a warning in its starkness. Embeddedness within patri/kyriarchal world views has shaped in the past and will continue to shape a reading of Jesus that is oppressive of women and others designated as outsiders. Such a reading supports a power structure within the community, supposedly authenticated by Jesus, which is contrary to God's dreaming with and for the human community. The alternative reading, on the other hand, demonstrates that the kyriarchal power predicated of Jesus and the androcentric metaphors that proclaimed such power may well have been—and hence can continue to be—deconstructed. From within contemporary communities of resistance such readings will invite cross-characterization of Jesus as these communities are challenged by encounters emerging from their life situations. Jesus as read today will not be universal and dominant within the community authenticating other forms of universal and dominant power. Rather, Jesus and the community of believers' self-understanding will be read and written from the boundaries, from the threshold space that is not owned or controlled but that is the liminal space from which new understandings and new possibilities of encounter with Another are able to emerge.

## OF ROCKS AND KEYS AND REVELATION OF JESUS

Matthew 16:13-21 begins in a parallel manner to 15:21-28. There is no reference to Jesus' withdrawing, as in 15:21, but, just as he entered the region of Tyre and Sidon, so too he comes into the region of Caesarea Philippi. In this second instance there is no sense of ambiguity as to boundaries. Jesus has clearly entered into the region. Overman and Davies and Allison note that the named city is gentile, while the region is under the control of the Herodian, Philip. Its population, no doubt, is ethnically diverse.[29] The exact import of the geographic location on character interaction and interpretation is difficult to determine. Within the narrative it is not a site for Jesus' ministry; rather, a dialogue with the disciples takes place there. It is the most northern point of Jesus' journeying, furthermost from Jerusalem, the center of Jewish life and religion. In accordance with Levine's analysis, it is on the periphery, a point that deconstructs all notions of fixity and centrality.[30] The mention of Caesarea Philippi would have also carried connotations of political and socio-economic power and may have stood as representative of the circle of Galilean cities to the south—Tyre, Ptolemais (Acco), Scythopolis (Beth Shean), Tiberias, and Sepphoris.[31]

What takes place in this context is a dialogue similar to that of 15:21-28; again, discourse rather than action constitutes the scene. The two stories differ significantly, though, as the debate element is missing from the Caesarea Philippi incident and Jesus is not challenged to enter into the encounter but rather initiates the dialogue. He asks the disciples how people identify or situate the "human one." The gender and ethnic tensions at the heart of Justa's story are absent from the Caesarea Philippi encounter. It would be reasonable to assume that most Matthean readers would have imagined this scene in male and Jewish contours and, as it develops, the androcentricity of its symbolic universe will become more obvious.[32]

Malina and Rohrbaugh point out that Jesus' question as to his identity would not have been heard by a Matthean audience in terms of contemporary understandings of individuality and identity.[33] Rather, it is a question regarding one's placement in relation to others and the honor that derives from being so identified. One wonders about the impact for the Matthean audiences of the designation "human one" in the opening question of Jesus (v. 13b).[34] Given the close parallel with the similar question asked in 16:15—"Who do you say I am?"—in which "you" clearly parallels "the people" of v. 13, it is possible to assume that "human one" parallels "me/I" in the second question. Read in this way, it is simply a circumlocution for "I."[35] The appearance of the term and its metaphoric function earlier in the narrative would have suggested to many readers a more multivalent reception. Its use in Jesus' question could have raised the possibility of the revelation of the hidden "human one" of Enoch (1 Enoch 48.7; 62.7;

69.27). It could also have recalled Jesus' itinerant ministry (8:20) and his sharing in divine power, namely, that of forgiveness of sins (9:6). It may even have functioned evocatively as indicator of Jesus' entire ministry up to this point in the narrative in a way that the simple use of "I" certainly would not have accomplished.[36]

The reply given by the disciples is presented as the popular view of Jesus—that Jesus was a prophetic figure. If Verseput is correct in recognizing the rhetorical effect of 13:52–16:20 as eliciting from the reader confidence in Jesus' mighty power,[37] then the acclamation of Jesus as prophet in the line of such oracular and eschatological prophets as John the Baptist, Elijah, or Jeremiah[38] would, for many readers, have characterized Jesus within the popular prophetic movements of first-century Judaism. Such an interpretation would be a more-than-appropriate response to Jesus' question, as it locates Jesus within a movement, and within the first century it was such a social location that provided identity.

Horsley and Hanson have noted that it was predominantly among the poorer classes that such popular prophetic movements arose and that it was the peasantry who recognized the prophet as their spokesperson against the ruling classes, which were more hostile to such prophecy and movements.[39] Those readers who remembered Jesus' response to John's question about the identity of Jesus (11:3)—Go, tell what you see and hear: blind see, lame walk, lepers are cleansed, deaf hear, dead are raised and the poor have the good news preached to them—would recognize in the disciples' reply a valid interpretation of the ministry of Jesus. In Jesus, the powerful deeds of divine liberation were manifest as they had been in the prophets remembered intertextually in the biblical tradition and intratextually in the tradition of John the Baptist (3:1-12; 11:7-19 and 14:1-2). Jesus' response to his rejection in his own hometown likewise links prophecy to *dunameis* or mighty deeds (13:54, 57-58). For the Matthean reader, therefore, the popular interpretation of Jesus was aligned with Jesus' own interpretation of his identity. It would have functioned as an authoritative interpretation among the poor of the Matthean reign of God movement in the arc of cities and neighboring regions of the gospel's reception.

Within such an interpretation, Caesarea Philippi could have represented symbolically the Matthean cities that were likewise centers of Herodian and/or imperial rule and exploitation of the masses. The poor are not distinguished by gender and are therefore male and female; hence, Jesus is designated prophet by women and men who see themselves as participating with Jesus within the prophetic reign of God movement. The identification of Jesus with John, Elijah, and Jeremiah could have functioned metaphorically, however, to suppress the prophetic role of women, a role that Justa actualized in her claim on Jesus' healing powers in the parallel story of 15:21-28.

The reiterated question of Jesus (v. 15) suggests that the prophetic identification of Jesus is not closed or complete. The disciples are asked directly whom they understand Jesus to be in a way that subverts any single or unitive interpretation of Jesus. It renders the identity question open and tensive allowing for new *poiesis*. Simon Peter answers on behalf of the disciples, "You are the *Christos*, the Son of the Living God." The use of the name Simon Peter makes links with two earlier references to Peter by way of the phrasing, "Simon who is called Peter." It is Simon Peter who is first called and then who is named first among the commissioned apostles (4:18; 10:2). The name Peter stands alone in the story of the dramatic walk by the disciple across the water toward Jesus (14:28). We see in the narrative movement of disciples speaking on behalf of the people and Simon Peter on behalf of the disciples a dangerous development, especially in relation to the gospel's characterization of Jesus. It is the silencing of the voices of the many by the use of a representative voice. In this instance that representation is genderized so that the male and female participants in the reign of God movement are represented by the disciples, who are characterized as male, and then the disciples are represented by the lone male, Simon Peter. It also places the more elite scribal interpretation rather than the popular one on the lips of the representative voice. Such a development has the potential to shape reading and community consciousness toward a valuing of the representative voice, which is single and unitive. It silences the plural and shattered voices identifying Jesus. It is this very development and its exclusive genderization in the history of the reception of the gospel and Christian tradition that have led to the limited and oppressive interpretation of Jesus outlined in the initial chapter. This development has silenced the interpretive voices of women, of ethnic minorities, indeed of almost all who are not Western, male, and in some traditions, clerical.

Although the identifying statement of Simon Peter in 16:16 is hailed by some interpreters as central to the gospel's proclamation of Jesus,[40] the above warning should give us pause before such a claim. Indeed, the response of Peter would have come as no surprise to gospel recipients. We have seen that the narrator has already designated Jesus as the *Christos* in the infancy narrative (1:1, 16, 17, 18) and has focused some of the heteroglossal possibilities of the metaphor in 11:1-19, discussed in\ the previous chapter. In this context and given the link back to the identification of Jesus as prophet, the title *Christos* recognizes Jesus' place within the popular understandings of royal or messianic movements characterized by saving or liberating deeds.[41] It carries significant political overtones. Its link forward to the metaphoric title Son of God, opens up other possibilities.

It could be argued that the Petrine confession has acknowledged the characterization of Jesus popular among the poorer strata of the Matthean communities with the use of *Christos*. The Petrine confession then moved to a scribal interpretation, one that would have resonated more readily with the *poiesis* of the scribal and literate sectors of the community. The metaphor "Son of God" creates meaning intertextually and intratextually. The "beloved Son" imagery of Matthew 3:17 evokes both Isaac and Israel typology (Gn 22:2; Is 42:1). Jesus is tempted as "Son of God" in Matthew 4:1-11, a text rich in intertextual imagery for the Jewish scribal readers as differing interpretive or poietic voices drawing imagery from both Psalms and Deuteronomy clash.[42] Like Israel personified in prophets such as Moses, Elijah, and Jeremiah, Jesus correctly interprets God's word because he is the beloved Son of the one named as "Father"; as 11:27 makes abundantly clear, he has received both the power of prophetic deeds and also prophetic words from that Father. The disciples' statement of recognition of Jesus' sonship in 14:33 is a further identification of Jesus' sharing in divine power. The *Christos*/"Son of God" metaphoric relationship in Matthew 16:16 carries, therefore, heteroglossal meaning-making potential within the predominantly literate strata of the reading communities, whether shaped by Jewish biblical intertextuality or the Greco-Roman matrix in which "Son of God" designated likewise a sharing in divine power manifest in human authority and saving deeds.[43]

Read interactively with the open-ended *basileia* vision associated with the *Christos* imagery of Matthew 11:1-19, Jesus as "Son of the living God" could connote life for all in the new household or fictive kinship that the familial imagery constructs.[44] For those weighed down by the Herodian and imperial rule symbolized by the Caesarea Philippi context, this is a *poiesis* that gives hope in the struggle and locates that hope in Jesus and the ongoing reign of God movement. This is where the living God can be found and where one can participate in the life of divinity shared with humanity. Such a reading made on the margins or the periphery of Jewish religious life—away from the centers of power in Jerusalem—may have functioned to shape the image of religious meaning-making differently within the reign of God movement. It is not under the control of those at the center where it becomes fixed, rigid, and closed. Rather, it emerges on the margins, from those who have participated with Jesus in the reign of God movement regardless of class, status, or gender.

From within a reading regime in which power and struggles over questions of leadership were operative, the metaphorical potentialities of Peter's identification of Jesus could have been significantly restricted. Subsequent verses that locate leadership in a designated individual and their tensive relationship with a more communal vision (18:15-20) and Jesus' critique of titles and places of honor (23:2-12) would suggest that such struggles were familiar to the Matthean reading communities. Peter as representative leader could be read to signify kyriarchal power as representative; the recognition of Jesus as "Son of the living God" images divine power and its human manifestation as male within an androcentric and kyriarchal fictive kinship or household. Women and other minorities and social sub-groups are excluded from power, and the female is repressed in the symbolic universe in which power is so genderized. From within such a frame of reading it is impossible to speak power and leadership in female terms or in other inclusive perspectives. Read in this way, the Caesarea Philippi location and all that it symbolizes are merely reproduced in the religious and political life of some Matthean communities or households, as they would be in later receptions of this tradition. Meaning-making is thus closed and controlled.

Such a reading is not alien to contemporary women, for whom Jesus imaged as Christ and Son of God has been used to exclude them from leadership within ecclesial communities and more particularly from mean-ing-making or creative *poiesis* in relation to divinity and its incarnation within humanity. The sonship metaphor has been locked into rigid trinitarian formulations that have stifled meaning-making both in relation to Jesus and to divinity itself.[45] The familial imagery of father and son has functioned to exclude and suppress the female in the imaging of divinity. Alternative reading sites beyond kyriarchal power and control and new modes of reading will enable the Matthean metaphors to open out into the potentialities toward which the Matthean text points, some of which would have been beyond the imagining of many of the households of reception because of the limitations of their location and world view.

In conclusion, brief attention will be directed to Jesus' words to Peter (16:17-19) and to their contribution to the characterization of Jesus and the reign of God movement from which his identity cannot be sepa-rated. Just as Peter identified Jesus within a socio-cultural and religious matrix—"You are the Christ"—so too Jesus identifies Simon—"You are Peter"—locating him within a related socio-cultural and religious matrix that Jesus names as his *ekklesia* (16:16, 18). Malina and Rohrbaugh note the political implications of Jesus' words, claiming that "names were given at significant junctures in a group's life to persons who figured promi-nently in the life of the group."[46] Also, the beatitude pronounced over Peter as recipient of revelation links him inextricably with Jesus (11:25-27) and with those who humbly and with open eyes and ears receive the message of the *basileia* from both the revealing father and the parabler of the *basileia* (11:25; 13:10-17, 34-35). Peter is honored within the reign of God movement, and hence his earlier identification of Jesus (16:16) is rendered more authoritative.

The household imagery of v. 16 is made more explicit in the words of Jesus to Peter—"You are *petros*/Peter and on this *petra*/rock, I will build my *ekklesia*/church." Jesus builds or constructs metaphorically; he names the new community with whom he is identified. It is not the Temple located in Jerusalem, the center of socio-political and religious power that is corrupt and corruptive (Mt 24: 1-2; 26:61). It is an *ekklesia* imaged intertextually through both the lens of the assembly of Israel as God's people and the Greco-Roman socio-political structure. In Deuteronomy (4:10; 9:10; 18:16; 31:30), Israel is the people formed by God's liberat-ing action in the Exodus and by their receiving of God's word as they assemble in community. By the first century of the Common Era members of this assembly met together in a synagogue or *ekklesia*. Jesus' *ekklesia*, constructed from the periphery and in tension with other socio-political structures within its context, is the assembly formed by Jesus' liberating action in the unfolding gospel story and focused in 13:53–16:20, for which these words of Jesus provide a conclusion. Jesus' imagery would also have had profound political implications for both Jewish and gentile recipients embedded within the Roman imperial system in which the *ekklesia* of freeborn elite men was the governing structure for the city. The *ekklesia* of Jesus built on Peter would provide an alternative to the *ekklesia* of Caesarea Philippi.[47]

This study's focus on difference brings to light the realization that the *ekklesia* metaphor could have functioned within different reading sites either to subvert dominant theologies and ideologies or to support them. Even within Deuteronomy, in which the metaphor predominates, Israel's assembly or *ekklesia* is constituted by its sons and not its daughters (see Dt 4:10, 45; 6:2, 21; and passim). The story of this people is that of its heroic males. At the beginning of the Common Era its religious center, the Temple, as well as its meaning-making by way of liturgy and officially recognized tradition-making, were the domain of men, generally a select and stratified group of literate men. This is the intertextual lens through which many readers heard the story of the Matthean Jesus and gave it meaning. Likewise the Greco-Roman *ekklesia*, constructed according to a theory of democracy and participation, was in fact constituted on the exclusion of women, children, and other men who were considered unfit to rule. It was a highly stratified and genderized system that shaped the world view of all those participating in it.[48] If the *ekklesia* of Jesus was read according to this model, then Jesus' maleness and the honor accorded to him by way of his family and his relationship with divinity would have constructed him as a powerful figure who ruled by domination. The images and metaphors proclaiming Jesus would have been read through such ideo-theological lenses within some Matthean households.

In these short verses two other metaphors characterize the commission Jesus gives to Peter and reflect back on Jesus' own characterization. In contrast to the table bread that symbolized the new community vision to which Justa's encounter with Jesus gave rise is the rock on which the *ekklesia* is built. Bread continually needs to be produced, as does the open-ended community shaped by new encounters. The rock, on the other hand, connotes fixity, permanence, constancy. It is a multivalent image in the gospel, however, and was so within early Christian traditioning. In Jesus' parable of 7:24-25 the wise builder constructs a house upon rock so that it will endure. Alternatively, in the parable of the sower the rocky ground prevents the seed from taking root (13:20-21). For readers who may have been familiar with Pauline traditions, intertextual readings of Isaiah 28:16 and 8:14 had already transferred the twofold imagery of the foundational rock and the rock of stumbling that caused offense from God to Jesus (1 Cor 10:4; Eph 2:19-21; Rom 9:33; cf. 1 Pt 2:8).[49] Matthean readers would already be familiar with Jesus as *skandalon* or stumbling block (11:6)[50] and would have imagined him as the rock on which his *ekklesia* would be built. There is here, as in 15:21-28, a cross-characterization that shapes reading; in this case it moves, as more normally expected, from Jesus to Peter. One wonders in the reading/writing of early Christian tradition, especially as communities grappled with the absence of Jesus, whether traditions that earlier characterized Jesus were transferred to roles and role-bearers in the community to give them cohesion. As earlier memories were erased, readers were shaped by the coherent and unifying reading.

The second image is that of the keys, which is here linked to binding and loosing and with which, Bernard Robinson suggests, the image "has little in common."[51] The key-bearer image is not typical intertextually, with Isaiah 22:15-25 being one of the rare texts that it may have evoked from the Jewish scriptures. The image is contextualized within the household and its authority structure, where the keys would normally be given to the son or to the faithful and designated master of the household (Is 22:15). I do not want here to explore in detail the multivalent possibilities of binding and loosing[52] but simply to acknowledge that it is clearly an authorization to set limits and boundaries, probably within the Matthean context in relation to membership as well as the teaching and instruction developing within the community's ongoing traditioning process. At least some segments of the community, and perhaps it was those who were assuming power and leadership of a more kyriarchal kind, would have welcomed and perhaps even developed this tradition. The danger inherent in such authority, however, is warned against in the woe of Matthew 23:13, which may have legitimized alternative leadership and power structures in some households as would the tradition of Matthew 18:18.

It is clear that these images which connote fixture, permanence, reliability, certainty, and authority, mixed as they are within Matthew 16:17-19, have within them the element of self-deconstruction inherent in all figurative language.[53] First-century readers may not have been deconstructive readers according to the mode of contemporary critics, but shaped as they were by different socio-cultural, economic, and gendered locations, it can be argued that they read and in their reading wrote the multivalent narrative differently. In this way they may well have created in their act of reading/writing the "tears in the fabric," the "inconsistencies in its pattern" that contemporary critics uncover.[54] These same tears and inconsistencies would, on the other hand, have opened up heteroglossal reading potential within the communities of subsequent reception.

A number of studies have demonstrated the way in which the Matthean narrative and its overall characterization of Peter transgresses the imagery of 16:17-19—giving authority to the entire community (18:18) or leadership group (28:16-20); warning against the type of authority established in 16:17-19 (23:2-12, 13); and presenting Peter as one of little faith or failing in understanding (14:31; 15:16; 16:23; 26:33-35, 40, 69-75). Augustine Stock questions whether it is "ironic"[55]; Arlo Nau reads the Petrine tradition in Matthew as an encomium or biography of "dispraise"[56]; and Bubar concludes that the author "is constantly chiselling away at the very rock that serves as the foundation of the church."[57]

Many first-century readers would not have seen these tears because of their reading for coherence and for the rock-solidity they desired to authenticate leadership positions within certain households and even the very security of the Matthean group generally. For other households threatened by fixed positions and structures developing in their midst, the inconsistencies made possible a transgressing of a tradition that may have been becoming dominant. They were able to undertake a resistant reading that authorized alternative constructions of power, leadership, status, and gender. For them, Jesus as deconstructive builder could continue to challenge roles and structures that became fixed and dominant, inviting the community to continue the process Jesus began of building upon rock but ensuring that each building project had within it the seeds of its own deconstruction.

"Son of God" and Petrine leadership may have proved adequate titles, metaphors, and models for an emerging patri/kyriarchal church determined to maintain its androcentric power base, but they were clearly inadequate for more inclusive communities. In the ongoing tradition the voices of the latter have been subjugated. Within contemporary communities of resistance seeking "Another" adequate to developing feminist and alternative subjectivities, attention to the multivalent reading possibilities within the Matthean text and its first-century reading context provide surprising avenues of exploration. The stories of Justa and Peter encountering Jesus have suggested that the character of Jesus is not fixed or closed, not rock-like. Rather, the table of shared bread could symbolize the Matthean narrative. Different characters eat this bread from their different locations, thus constructing Jesus and themselves multivalently. This is the process available to those engaged in contemporary *poiesis* in relation to Jesus and the community of the reign of God praxis.

# 7

# The Liberator Liberated,
# the Crucified One Raised

## *Matthew 27:32-28:20*

*We must read these early Christian attempts of theological meaning-making as critical arguments that begin with the very real experience of Jesus' dehumanization and crucifixion as a political criminal. . . . They begin with the historical "fact" of unjust oppression, the experience of struggle for a different world, and an encounter with the victimization and death of the dehumanized person.*

*Faith in resurrection and hope in the overcoming of brutal suffering and execution celebrates "the Living Ones." It does so with ever new names and images that reconstitute the human dignity, agency, and memory of those killed . . . enabl[ing] us to understand the meaning of resurrection as a political, "real" vindication of struggle for a world free from hunger, abuse, and injustice.*

—Elisabeth Schüssler Fiorenza[1]

The accounts of the death and resurrection of Jesus have a long history of traditioning, some of which took place within the Matthean communities.[2] They are the result of long-term Christian *poiesis*, shaped by the traditioning and meaning-making of women and men who struggled to make sense of the death of their companion and friend, Jesus. While Brown and Senior have not given attention to women's participation in this traditioning process, more recent works by Sawicki,[3] Corley,[4] Schüssler Fiorenza,[5] and my own earlier work[6] have recognized the significant contribution of women's *poiesis*, especially to the traditions of the cross and empty tomb with which they are intimately connected. In this chapter attention is directed to those stages in the traditioning process beyond textualization, namely, the reading or reception of the Matthean text within the variety of contexts and from the different contextual perspectives with which we have become familiar in this study.

The textual focus of the chapter will be the death of Jesus on the cross and the account of the empty tomb together with Jesus' final gospel commissioning (27:32–28:20). This forms the climactic conclusion to the Matthean narrative and its rhetorical effects in the making and characterization of Jesus. I am aware, however, of the limitations of choosing only a small segment of the passion narrative (26–27) for consideration, but what is begun here can be extended to the entire narrative by others.[7]

## THE LIBERATOR LIBERATED

The narrative of the death and burial of Jesus (27:32-66) is stark in terms of plot and action, especially in relation to Jesus, who is the victim of a cruel political execution not graphically detailed.[8] It is given texture and meaning by way of a rich intratextuality, drawing together diverse narrative threads; by way of character response to Jesus' death, what a diverse range of characters say and do in response to that death; and by way of what Crossan calls "intensive intertextuality," the heteroglossal literary and socio-cultural texts that intersect in this early Christian meaning-making.[9] It is these three aspects of the text's characterization of Jesus that are encountered by readers and that are directed by them into new meaning-making; at the same time this characterization shaped and constructed those readers religiously, ethnically, and as gendered readers.

The genre choices that have dominated the reading of the Matthean gospel narrative to this point no doubt continued to function as readers encountered what Crossan calls a "narrative passion" that historicized the "prophetic passion," the rich intertextual readings of the death of Jesus, and that also historicized the passion and resurrection.[10] Readers would have come to expect such a historicized narrative, witness to the scribal hand. We have already noted, however, that different communities of reception read this historicized narrative as encomium or biography of praise for a great hero or divine sage, as popular hero narrative, as continuation of their sacred story of God's dealings with Israel, or as foundational myth for an alternative community, a counter-story. The genre competencies developed in engagement with this story, attention given to the narrative unfolding of the character of Jesus, and recognition of some of the diverse intertextuality that gave it shape would have guided the reading of Jesus from within the different communities of reception through these last sections of the narrative.

For many Matthean readers familiar with and subject to the highly charged political situation under Roman occupation, the beginning of this section of the narrative—the procession outside the city to the place of execution or crucifixion (27:32-33)—would have evoked the political connotations of Jesus' death, read in connection with the Roman trial (27:1-2, 11-26).[11] No doubt for the poorer members of the community—slaves and the lower class, who were more readily subjected to crucifixion—as well as those for whom the Jesus story gave foundation to their political engagement, the political aspects of the death of Jesus were central to their reading. *Intratextually*, readers were prepared for other layers of meaning, predominantly religious. The parable of the vineyard (21:33-41) characterized the broker/son cast out of the vineyard and killed by its tenants, contributing, no doubt, to the interpretation of Jesus' death as rejection by the Jewish leaders at that time. Given the intra-Jewish polemic of the Matthean context, such an interpretation would have functioned together with other aspects of the gospel to shape an emerging "Christian-Jewish" identity over against Rabbinic or Formative Judaism and subsequently to construct Christian anti-Judaism.[12] Such a reading must be situated within its first-century religio-political context and not be given universal meaning within contemporary feminist interpretations of Jesus or any contemporary Christian meaning-making.[13]

Many aspects of the subsequent narrative (27:34-50) have been informed not only by the spirit but also by the texts of Israel's psalms of lament (especially Pss 22 and 69). This will be considered in more detail below, as will the responses to Jesus. It is sufficient to note here, in terms of intratextuality, that as Justa was characterized as embodied lament in Matthew 15:21-28, Jesus is now likewise portrayed. He embodies the prayer of the righteous or just one who suffers unjustly.[14] While this is the work of the scribal community, lament and especially these psalms of lament would not have been far from the heart and lips of the poor of the community, who experienced rejection and abandonment daily. From their reading location, and indeed from a variety of Matthean reading locations, Jesus would have been understood as the innocent one who suffered unjustly at the hands of both political and religious powers.

The brief reference to Jesus' crucifixion (27:35) would have recalled the earlier predictions of Jesus (20:19; 26:2) as well as his recognition of the fate of God's prophets, wise ones, and scribes (23:34). It placed Jesus, the crucified one, among those prophetic, sapiential, and scribal interpreters who read the politico-religious context in which they were located in light of God's dealing with humanity articulated in their sacred texts. The reader could recognize that Jesus had rightly interpreted his own future, and hence there would have been expectation even in the face of this appalling death that the hope of being raised articulated in 20:19 and linked to that same predicted hope in 16:21 and 17:23 would, in fact, be realized. Such an interpretation and its narrative threads intimately link the death of Jesus with resurrection, an aspect that is key to avoiding some of the christological minefields detailed in chapter 1.

The political and religious titles of kingship used to mock Jesus (27:37, 42) as well as the challenge to Jesus to save or liberate himself take on a depth of meaning when considered intratextually. The charge "King of the Judeans" was highly political and, as well as being placed over the head of Jesus on the cross, it was also the grounds for Pilate's questioning of Jesus (27:11) and the soldiers' mocking of him after the trial (27:29). It was an ironic metaphor to associate with Jesus. The reader would have recalled its association with the powerless and politically vulnerable infant of 2:2, but at that point in the narrative there would have been heteroglossal expectations in relation to the title. As the narrative unfolded, however, Jesus never held political power, never constituted an army, never established himself in a royal household clothed with soft raiment (11:8). The metaphor was, therefore, finally deconstructed as Jesus hung naked upon the cross. One wonders whether the deconstruction of the title put to death all imperial and hierarchical titles within those communities for whom the Jesus story shaped an alternative consciousness regarding many socio-political and religious structures.[15]

For the scribal community, on the other hand, both writing and reading for coherence and fulfillment and also less desirous of challenging the status quo, the political aspects of the kingship titles would have been subverted to the religious and linked with "Son of David" and "*Christos*" or anointed one of God. Such an interpretation obscured the powerlessness of both the infant Jesus and the crucified one in the face of the imperial system and interpreted Jesus' death within that kyriarchal system of meaning, even if ironically or symbolically.[16] This would have also been enhanced by certain textual links between the kingship metaphor and that of "saving" or "liberating."

The charge over the head of Jesus named him first before identifying him with the kingly title (27:37). The name *Jesus* would have taken on meaning for the readers throughout the entire narrative, but it is most explicitly linked to the designation "he will save his people from their sins" (1:21). Burnett says of this phrase that it "inscribes Jesus in some sense into the narrative as the savior."[17] It has already been demonstrated that this would have been understood intertextually as a prophetic as well as royal task, sharing in the divine undertaking of liberating humanity from all that marred the divine-human relationship as well as from political and religious oppressions.[18] Throughout the narrative Jesus has liberated others from harm, from danger, even from threats to their lives (8:25; 9:21, 22; 14:30). He is challenged by both the passers-by as well as the leaders to save himself (27:40, 42). Understood in light of Jesus' own exhortation to lose one's life in order to save it (16:25), and the prayer of Jesus, "not what I want but what you want" (26:39), there may have developed among some Matthean readers seeking to make sense of Jesus' death an interpretation of that death as being willed by God and loss of a life as being salvific in and of itself. Within a kyriarchal system such interpretations sowed dangerous seeds that have ripened into some of the theologies critiqued earlier. The victimization of the innocent either at the hands of the divine or human kyriarch can all too readily be religiously authorized and can construct the poor ones who suffer unjustly as legitimized victims. This fissure is there in the Matthean narrative, and it has opened up such meaning for many interpreters. Schüssler Fiorenza sounds a similar warning:

> Early Christian interpretations of Jesus' execution must be understood as sharing in the kyriarchal framework and androcentric language of their time. Hence, they ought to be critically assessed and rhetorically reconfigured in a different frame of meaning. . . . A theology that is silent about the sociopolitical causes of Jesus' execution and stylizes him as the paradigmatic sacrificial victim whose death was willed by God or was necessary to propitiate God continues the kyriarchal cycle of violence and victimization instead of empowering believers to resist and transform it.[19]

There is, however, another possible convergence of the kingship titles and the liberating thematic that needs to be explored.

The political aspects of those titles within the narrative of the death of Jesus, may have evoked for many readers the cost of participation in the reign of God movement as they strove to bring about the *basileia* of God as both preached and practiced by Jesus. In the gospel story Jesus preached the *basileia* as future hope and present reality as well as made it present in his inclusive table-companionship and ministry of healing and liberating. This central metaphor and praxis of Jesus was both religious and political and it was this would have been evoked for many Matthean readers by the kingship titles given to Jesus in the trial and on the cross. The vision and praxis of Jesus, God's covenanted presence with humanity symbolized as *basileia*, were being put to the test on the cross by alternative powers and kingdoms.[20] And at this point in the narrative there was no projected outcome save hope generated by the story as it had unfolded. The one characterized as liberator and his vision of liberation were now in need of that liberation.[21]

Intratextualities abound in the Matthean narrative of the death of Jesus that cannot be given further detailed attention in this study, but before turning to a consideration of the responses to Jesus' death, two related instances will be noted. Simon of Cyrene, an unknown character in the narrative to this point, carried the cross of Jesus (27:32), pointing to the absence of the disciples of Jesus who had been commissioned with such a task (16:25). This absence was likewise apparent to the attentive reader in Jesus being flanked on the right and left by two bandits or wrongdoers while being charged as "king" (27:37, 44). Misunderstanding the nature of God's *basileia* as proclaimed by Jesus, the mother of the sons of Zebedee requested that James and John be given places on the right and left of Jesus in his *basileia* (20:21). Ironically, when he was being charged as "king," these two disciples had fled with the rest of the male disciples (26:56). In death as in life, Jesus was situated among the outcasts of society (Mt 9:11; 11:19). The narration of the death of Jesus not only constructed Jesus but also the followers of Jesus by way of absence as well as presence. Even alone on the cross, Jesus was not characterized as separate from his followers or from the reign of God movement, an aspect of the narration that would have been read and understood by those households reading the gospel as founding myth for communities of *basileia* praxis.

The *responses to Jesus,* both negative and positive, in the account of his death on the cross contributed to his final characterization in the narrative. We have already noted that the imperial soldiers, the passers-by, and the chief priests, scribes, and elders all mock the dying Jesus using titles, metaphors, and claims that have characterized his life and *basileia* ministry. He is called "King" (27:29, 42), challenged to save himself by coming down from the cross (27:40, 42), and tested to see if he is "Son of God" as he claimed (27:40, 43). Later, certain bystanders interpret Jesus' cry from the cross as his calling on Elijah (27:47), and others raise the challenge whether Elijah will come to save him (27:49). As in the trial scene and the temptation narratives of 4:1-11 with which they are linked intratextually, the charges are densely interwoven. The only one to stand alone is the "false" accusation from the trial that Jesus would destroy the Temple and rebuild it in three days (27:40; cf. 26:60-61).

One way to understand these charges and to reconstruct how they may have been read and understood by Matthean readers is through the labeling and prominence models and processes within the honor-shame system explained in detail by Malina and Neyrey.[22] Jesus on the cross is "out of place" or deviant, an offense and a *skandalon* according to the well-developed maps of peoples and places constructed by the "moral entrepreneurs" or map-makers of Greco-Roman and Jewish first-century society.[23] Previously in the narrative Jesus has been a boundary-walker, but in the account of his death the boundaries have been breached radically.

The voices that we have already noted making charges against Jesus that render him deviant may contain traces of historical memories. They may have been read as representative of the opponents to the gospel and its households within Matthean Judaism or of those questioning the meaning of Jesus' criminal death in the face of a growing belief in him as founder of a new prophetic movement within Judaism. These voices cluster around the claim that Jesus will destroy the Temple and in three days rebuild it. Within the Jewish belief system, this was one of the most radical challenges of deviance because the Temple expressed the presence of God to Israel as the Holy One in their midst.[24] The naming of Jesus as Emmanuel, God with us, and the promise of Jesus to be present where two or three gathered in his name (18:20), together with Jesus' own prophetic breaching of the Temple (21:12-16), at least gave meaning to the charge.

The shaping of the gospel and the reading of the unfolding narrative while containing the deviant-producing voices also enacted a process of acclaiming Jesus as prominent. Malina and Neyrey call this christology "from the side."[25] In the light of the different contexts of reading within the Matthean group of households, this process would have functioned differently within these differing locations. We have already seen this in relation to the kingship titles, with different readings of this metaphor being brought into tension within the Matthean group. The deconstruction that such narrative tension makes possible means that contemporary meaning-makers must choose how they read the Matthean Jesus in the passion narrative. The reading of Jesus that deconstructs hierarchal titles and affirms the preacher and practitioner of the reign of God as religious and political present reality and future vision best informs contemporary feminist *poiesis* of Jesus.

The attentive first-century reader may have questioned the charge that Jesus claimed to be "Son of God." In the unfolding narrative and its acclaiming of Jesus metaphorically by way of this title, twice a heavenly voice acknowledged him so (3:17; 17:5). He was challenged twice by Satan, testing to see whether he was the divine son; and the Gadarene demoniacs questioned him under the same nomenclature. The disciples (14:33) and Simon Peter (16:16) acknowledged him as "Son of God" and "Son of the Living God" respectively. The only two instances that might be construed as a claim to that title would be 11:27 in the proverbial saying about son and father and the apocalyptic contention about the final day and hour being known only to the Father (24:36).

Readers would have incorporated the metaphor into their reading of Jesus as prominent, because it combined both divine recognition and acknowledgment by disciples that could counter the challenges to Jesus' authority by demonic forces and the charges of deviance (26:64; 27:40, 43). The metaphor may have functioned as heteroglossal within Matthean households. In some, it may have been a legitimation and further honoring of male familial relationships, extending their actual and symbolic power to the detriment of women and others within the households. It may also have privileged male images of the divine, rendering God as Father central to the religious symbolic universe of the community and hence marginalizing other metaphors like Jesus as prophet of Sophia/God. Those communities reading a foundation myth for their resistance to the legitimized status quo may have imaginatively construed the metaphor in terms of intimacy, love, and fidelity within the familial world of imagery. This is, however, to read the metaphor resistantly, but it opens up possibilities for further subversive readings today.

The charge that Jesus was unable to save himself was placed likewise within the gospel process of deviance/prominence. Readers would have been shaped by participation in the narrative to understand that all liberating power was God's and that even the one designated savior or liberator may need liberating in the face of unjust political power. This was to shatter any understanding of Jesus that was fixed, closed, and divinized. The gospel story directed those readers who had ears to hear beyond the deviant labeling to the *skandalon* of the cross, which challenged them to a participation in meaning-making that was open to boundary-breaking rather than boundary-making. The need to liberate the liberator could have challenged all readers who were able to read beyond coherence and familiarity.

This process of labeling would have been a familiar one within the circles of the scribal and literate class as well as the power-brokers in the community. It was a process that constructed or named the crucified one/the suffering just one by way of male metaphors. Those engaged in the deviance and prominence processes, who struggled for authority over the body of Jesus and the textualization of that body, were likewise predominantly male. Female suffering and female meaning-making were silenced and hidden.

It is only within the final verses of the account of Jesus' death (27:55-56) that a small group of women emerge within those groups who render the final responses to the death of Jesus. They are surrounded, however, by the centurion, who keeps watch with other soldiers; Joseph of Arimathea; and the chief priests and Pharisees. The centurion and those keeping watch with him (cf. 27:36) see the earthquake and other cosmic phenomena accompanying the death of Jesus and they exclaim: "Truly this man was God's Son" (27:54). There are a number of possible readings of this response. For gentile readers and/or households, Jesus' death could here be given meaning within their symbolic universe. The cosmic phenomena and the death of Jesus within these happenings would have pointed to his divine favor or divine sonship.[26] This was the death of a great hero, acknowledged as were other heroes as "a child of the gods."[27] Others may have located the centurion in a trajectory that linked the Capernaum centurion (8:5-13) and Justa, the Canaanite woman (15:21-28), with this centurion and the others keeping guard. They could have been read as representative of those gentiles who recognized the authority and power of Jesus and acclaimed it, thus symbolically prefiguring in the narrative the discipling of all nations (28:19). As such, they may have been seen to authorize the participation of gentile believers and householders within the Matthean reign of God movement, especially in light of the climactic moment of the cross. Jesus on the cross was portrayed as physically present within the group of respondents gathered around his body and struggling for authority over his name, just as he had promised to be present within the ongoing reign of God movement that would likewise gather (18:20).

Joseph, the rich man from Arimathea, one who was being discipled to Jesus, requests permission to take the body of Jesus from the cross and to bury it. Control over the body of Jesus was finally in the hands of a disciple. Read generically as a historical narrative, Joseph's story does not leave Jesus abandoned in spite of the flight of his named male disciples

(26:56). He does what a disciple should do; he "came and took the body and buried it," as did the disciples of John (14:12). Such action authored the body of Jesus in a new way. It deconstructed some of the shame of crucifixion, after which the bodies of the crucified were either left on the cross for carrion or thrown into a mass grave.[28] Read symbolically within communities of meaning-making, the rock/*petra* in which the body of Jesus was placed (27:60) evoked polyvalent possibilities. As symbol of fixity and solidity, it could have closed off the story of Jesus, his body finally sealed within rock. It could be read also as a sign of contradiction causing offense, a *skandalon,* raising questions as to whether this was indeed the end. We have already noted that the narrative deconstructs the *ekklesia* built on rock. For many readers the question must have arisen, Could this rock likewise be deconstructed, especially given the hint of such in 27:51 with the tearing apart of the rocks at the death of Jesus? Perhaps for these readers the request of the chief priests and Pharisees (27:63-64) represented the fear of the scribes and power-brokers of the Matthean communities of just such a deconstruction, that this body could not be contained even in rock. It could not be contained in life and perhaps not in death. The actions of Joseph may have raised new questions and new expectations in relation to Jesus.

But what of the women at the cross and at the sepulchre? Corley, in a very detailed study of women's association with death and lamentation in Greek, Roman, and Jewish literature, suggests that the portrayal of the women at the cross does not necessarily fit the stereotypical gender role given to women in such situations.[29] They are not said to mourn and lament as would have been expected but assume the silent role of male mourners. She demonstrates, however, that the women's presence pointed to their discipleship, and even though their ritual laments were cast in male terms silencing their mourning, they indeed honor Jesus, the suffering righteous one, by being present at his death.[30] Her conclusion that "the tradition of the women at the cross and the tomb persists in spite of the obvious attempts by every gospel writer to contain it"[31] points to the presence of women's meaning-making and preservation of their traditions in that meaning-making, a sign of resistance to scribal power and a *poiesis* of Jesus that shaped inclusive communities.

Two recent characterizations of these women may provide further clues as to the way the presence of Mary Magdalene, Mary the mother of James and Joseph, and the mother of the sons of Zebedee (27:55-56) may have been either minimized or suppressed in some first-century readings shaped by the sex/gender system that was in place. Both Brown and Heil cast the women's response either as not reacting as well as did the centurion and Joseph of Arimathea[32] or as "passivity."[33] As support for his argument, Brown suggests that readers would not have been led to compare the presence of the women at the cross with the absence of male disciples mentioned "some sixty verses before," an argument that seems to ignore the characterization of these women in discipleship terminology—they have *followed* Jesus from Galilee and they have been *ministering* to him as his own life has been characterized by ministering (20:28). The transgression of socio-cultural gender expectations evoked by the presence of these female disciples in this place of public execution would surely have spoken loudly of the absence of the males who had been portrayed as constantly with Jesus during his ministry. On the other hand, Brown sees no problem in setting the "one male disciple," Joseph, over against "the most famous male *disciples* of Jesus (the Twelve) who had fled" despite the "sixty verses" that separate them![34]

Brown and Heil both denigrate the women's response by privileging male confession over female faithful presence. We have already seen that the centurion's "confession" may have been read polyvalently, not necessarily as representing a full confession of faith in Jesus but as a recognition of divine favor. Even read as recognition and confession, it is momentary and single, whereas the women's fidelity has been throughout the ministry of Jesus to the foot of the cross.[35] One wonders, however, whether Heil and Brown have not alerted us to possible struggles within Matthean contexts of meaning-making. The scribal and predominantly male mode of confession could have been read in tension with the faithful discipleship of Jesus that gave meaning to Jesus and the reign of God among women and other non-elites. The narrative, however, leaves the tension stand rather than privileging one response over the other as do the two contemporary interpretations. Just as female and non-elite resistant power and subjugated knowledge could deconstruct male voice and privilege where necessary, so too for today's feminist interpreters, faithful discipleship can continue to challenge and subvert confession located in the hands of male elites and hence deconstruct kyriarchal power as the source for the naming of Jesus.

One final consideration before leaving the narrative of the death of Jesus is the use of *intertextuality* to give meaning. This, like intratextuality, provided readers with rich potential for characterizing Jesus, and it is beyond the scope of this study to plumb these depths with any degree of comprehensibility. Attention will be given simply to those intertexts that construct Jesus as the suffering just one who embodies lament.[36]

Senior would seem to be correct in suggesting that not only some of the content and spirit but even the very structure of Psalm 22 may have had a significant influence on the Matthean account of the death of Jesus.[37] It is reasonable to assume that many of Matthew's Jewish readers would have given meaning to the Jesus of this section of the Matthean gospel intertextually with Psalm 22. Psalm 69 and Wisdom 2:12-20 and 5:4-5 could likewise have provided sources of intertextuality at this point in the narrative. Psalms 22 and 69 are psalms of lament and could be even more specifically categorized as psalms of the suffering just one. Wisdom 2:12 also begins with a threat against Sophia's righteous one, and it is this that characterizes the entire section. While we can assume scribal familiarity with these texts, it also seems reasonable to argue that the poor, the suffering, the non-elite who bore economic, political, and even religious burdens, would have known these cries of the heart that echoed their pain so well. The language of the texts constructs the sufferer as male, but in those house-churches in which women used the scriptures (as seen in Justa's story) either in worship or in meaning-making, the gender construction may have been transgressed. The intertextual reading could have opened up a small fissure in the text for such readers. Psalm 22:9-10 recalls God, who took the just one from her mother's womb and who kept her safe on her mother's breast. And yet, like the cry of Rachel that opened the fissure in the text of the infancy narrative, allowing readers to hear the cries of the silenced and absent mothers, so too this small intertextual fissure may well have opened the text to the cry of Matthean women, their lamenting with Jesus, their lamenting with and in their own communities. It may also have pointed, with the absence of Sophia from the account of the righteous one's suffering in Wisdom 2:12-20, to the absence of any of their female imaging of the divine from the entire passion narrative.

With the possibilities that these gaps opened for attentive readers before us, let us examine what a first-century reader may have heard echoing from the scriptures. The offering to Jesus of both gall (27:34) and vinegar (27:48) echoed the fate of the just one of Psalm 69:21 under persecution.[38] The suffering one of Psalm 22 cried out to God who seemed to have forsaken the sufferer as did Jesus (27:46, 50). The mocking of the enemies who wagged their heads in scorn is the fate of both (Ps 22:7; Mt 27:39), as is the dividing up of garments (Ps 22:18; Mt 27:35). Both are mocked and faced with the charge that reliance on God will bring rescue (Ps 22:8; Wis 2:18; Mt 27:43). In Ps 22:8, it is God who is challenged to save the righteous sufferer, in contrast to the challenge offered Jesus that he save himself (Mt 27:40, 42). Finally, the enemies of Sophia's righteous one tested the righteous one's claim to be "child" of God to determine whether the righteous one was authorized to name God father (Wis 2:13, 16-18; 5:4-5). Jesus too was so challenged (Mt 27:40, 43). Psalm 22:27, the vindication of the just one characterized by all the ends of the earth and all nations returning to God, may have even for some echoed through the response to Jesus of the gentile centurion and those keeping watch with him (Mt 27:54).

Clearly Jesus would have been interpreted by many as the suffering just one who remained faithful to God even in the face of unjust persecution and torment at the hands of enemies.[39] In so characterizing Jesus, God was also constructed for the reader intertextually in very significant ways in this section of the narrative.[40] God was the one who could be trusted (Ps 22:4, 5) to hear the cries of the sufferer (22:24), because it was God who had the power to save or to deliver, to liberate (Ps 22:5, 8, 20, 21; 69:1, 13, 14, 18).[41] Jesus' preaching of and fidelity to the righteousness of God's

*basileia* vision (Mt 3:15; 5:6, 10, 20; 6:1, 33) had indeed made him enemies among those who would seek to name and control true righteousness
(5:20; 21:32). It was fidelity to that vision which brought Jesus to the
cross. Intertextual voices would have assured the reader that God would
be faithful to and present with this suffering just one, Jesus. Even as the
favored one of God who could liberate others, Jesus did not/could not
liberate himself, but God could be relied on to liberate this faithful liberator of God's people (1:21). Matthew's gospel does not suggest that fidelity
to God's *basileia* and the liberation of God's people necessarily led to the
cross or that the cross was sought for itself; however, it promises that
should such fidelity lead there, God could be relied upon through the
suffering of the one who preaches and lives this *basileia* vision.[42]

Such a reading would have given hope to Matthean readers engaged in
political struggles, those ostracized because of their commitment to an
alternate vision that challenged the power of the status quo, and those
poor who bore the weight of taxation and other burdens. It should be
noted that readers did not find here the language of fulfillment of scripture familiar in the infancy narrative, which could have led to an
interpretation that would have given kyriarchal legitimation to their suffering, an interpretation that seems much more commonplace among
contemporary critics.[43] It is such contemporary readings that a feminist
rhetorical *poiesis* critiques because of the divine legitimation given to suffering. Rather, the reading proposed here points to the hope that is beyond
the cross, the trust that sustained the suffering just. It affirms, as does the
Matthean narrative, that crucifixion cannot be severed from resurrection.


## THE CRUCIFIED ONE RAISED

In the final segment of the Matthean gospel, especially 28:1-10 and
28:16-20, which will be the focus of this last section, readers encountered
the textualization of traditionings of the resurrection of the crucified one
developed within contexts of female and male meaning-making.[44] Both
Schüssler Fiorenza and Sawicki locate the shaping of resurrection faith and
tradition within contexts of "teaching and/or catechesis on the one hand
and baptismal and/or eucharistic liturgy on the other."[45] These have generally been viewed as male contexts, but a recognition of women's
participation in early Christian *poiesis* and the confluence of the traditions
within the Matthean storytelling suggest that in the catechetical and liturgical contexts in which the gospel continued to be told, both male and
female readers were shaped by and shaped the meaning of both stories as
a fitting climax to their story of Jesus. As I explore the meaning given to
Jesus through the interpretation of these two stories, attention will be
given to the way in which they functioned together to commission both
female and male Matthean readers beyond the Jesus story.

Both Matthean accounts of resurrection and appearance contain cosmic or apocalyptic thematics that intimately linked the raising of Jesus with God's judgment on his crucifixion (28:2-4; cf. 27:51-53). That divine power, the authority of heaven and earth, is given to Jesus (28:18) and will therefore remain by way of the promise of Jesus' presence till the close of the age (28:20). The seismic power that split open the rock/s, the *petra/i,* that entombed the holy ones (27:53) and Jesus (27:60; 28:2) is, as Raymond Brown suggests, a witness to the power of God's action more than to the identity of Jesus and would have been recognized and interpreted thus according to both Jewish and Greco-Roman matrices of meaning.[46] For many readers this may have placed the reign of God movement associated with the vision and praxis of both Jesus and the Matthean communities firmly within the context of participation with and in divine power. As the community projected itself beyond the Jesus story, it may well have been reminded of the opening of that story with its vision of a new heaven and new earth, new kinship possibilities (1:1). Just as this divine power was manifest in the final gospel stories to those women and men who encountered the risen one, so too it could continue to be manifest in kinship structures and households where power and authority were likewise shared.

The Jesus whom readers encountered in these final narratives was, in fact, simply Jesus. The angel recognized that the women had come to seek Jesus, the one who had been crucified (28:5), but pointed out that the crucified one was not to be found in the tomb—"He is not here"—but had been raised as he had said. The crucified and resurrected one cannot be separated; both designations are located in Jesus and in that name. The name Jesus would henceforth carry dual signification. When the Eleven go to the mountain in Galilee, it is Jesus, the crucified and risen one, whom they encounter, all other titles and images having been eclipsed.[47] As Schüssler Fiorenza says, while crucifixion is taken seriously, it does not have the last word.[48]

It is the risen one who dominates the two stories that conclude the gospel,[49] and it is the Jesus who has been raised who goes before disciples into Galilee. It is here, on the open road going toward Galilee with fear and great joy, that the women, Mary Magdalene and the other Mary, encounter Jesus. It is the potential of this aspect of the resurrection traditions that Schüssler Fiorenza develops, stressing the significance of the "open road" tradition for interpreting both crucifixion and resurrection, offering a space in which meaning can be made of both the suffering and victimization as well as the agency and potentiality for "becoming the Living Ones."[50] She offers a direction for considering the significance of location in Matthean readers' *poiesis* of the resurrection traditions they received.

We have already noted the importance of location within the Matthean story, especially in light of Levine's interpretation of its center/periphery indicators. Mary Magdalene and the other Mary receive the announcement that Jesus has been raised at the opened tomb, the transformed place of death, outside the city of Jerusalem, the center of power (28:5-6). They are told that the Jesus who has been raised is going ahead of them to Galilee (28:7). Going along this road they are met by Jesus, who reaffirms their mission (28:9-10). Such a tradition and its association with women would have been a very significant challenge to scribal readers seeking coherence and closure to the Jesus story and to those in the community who may have been establishing new centers of kyriarchal power. It would also have failed to provide a fitting conclusion to an encomium or hero narrative. It could have provided authentication, on the other hand, for those establishing alternative kinship structures, rituals, and catechesis within their households of faith. It would have been more than a fitting conclusion to their counter-story, their foundational myth. The Jesus who went before the Galilean women along the open road would be seen as the one who continued to go ahead of them as they sought to bring the reign of God more concretely into their present.

The Matthean story narrates a second location of encounter with the risen Jesus. It is on a mountain in Galilee (28:16). There is an interesting fissure in the narrative at this point. Both the angel and the risen Jesus point to Galilee as the designated place of encounter, the place where the male disciples, who forsook Jesus during his death, could be reconciled with him (28:7, 10). Galilee as a region, we have already noted, is on the periphery, away from the cities as centers of power, especially Jerusalem. But it is not to the region that the male disciples go but to a mountain, and this location is authenticated in the narrative, contrary to the prior directions, with the phrase "to which Jesus had directed them."

The mountain within the Matthean narrative is a place of authority. It is on a very high mountain that Satan offered Jesus power and authority over all the kingdoms of the cosmos (4:8). An unnamed mountain in Galilee was the scene for Jesus' authoritative teaching (5:1; 7:28-29) and healing (15:29), and it was also his place of transformative encounter with God (14:23; 17:1-9). According to the narrative, it is here that the male disciples encounter the risen Jesus. The connotations of the mountain seemed not to suffice, however, to convey authority in this scene. It was reinforced by the words of Jesus—"All authority in heaven and on earth has been given to me" (28:18). Such a location must have evoked heteroglossal possibilities of interpretation. Read from a scribal perspective or from a perspective of those holding or claiming religious and administrative power within the Matthean group, the Jesus on the mountain could have been claimed as authenticating these perspectives. The mountain is a place of stasis, and hence it could have evoked stability, reliance on the Jesus who was interpreted as giving authority over interpretation, and ritualization within the community to those who claimed a line of authority with the eleven male disciples.

There is a tension or gap in the narrative coherence, however, because the mountain is on the periphery, in Galilee, and the disciples who encounter Jesus there are sent away from the place of stasis into the whole world. For those who read this fissure together with the location of Jesus on the open road, the risen Jesus would have been understood as one who sent disciples *away* from any fixed location, any fixed center of power and authority. The Jesus who is with commissioned disciples to the end of the ages (28:20), the Jesus who was named Emmanuel at the opening of the story (1:23), is with those sent on mission. That presence was not guaranteed on a mountain in Galilee. One wonders, on the other hand, whether the reiteration of authority by way of the mountain location and the words of Jesus did not function rhetorically to countermand a more open interpretation and to direct readers to give more significance to the second account than the first.[51] Contemporary readers can almost visualize this struggle for meaning within the Matthean communities, and it is one with which feminist readers are familiar in today's churches. Unfortunately, too often the tradition of the mountain in Galilee, associated as it is with male leadership and authority, is used to silence what Matthew narrates as an equally valid tradition of the "open road."[52]

The risen Jesus of both Matthean accounts is one who commissions disciples, female and male, to "Go"—away from the tomb, away from physical/visual or historicized encounter with the risen Jesus, away from the mountain (28:7, 10, 19).[53] In the Matthean account there is no attention given to Jesus' changed appearance (Lk 24:16; Jn 20:14-16; 21:4), to his capacity to overcome physical obstacles (Lk 24:36; Jn 20:19, 26), his eating with disciples as risen one (Lk 24:30; Jn 21:9-13), and his demonstrating his wounded humanity (Lk 24:39; Jn 20:17, 20, 27). The identity of the risen one is not a concern. The entire focus of the narrative is on the commissioning of female and male disciples.

Both commissions are directed toward action, action intended to have an ongoing effect in terms of the story of the crucified preacher of God's *basileia* who had been raised. Although, as Schüssler Fiorenza contends, the early resurrection formulations were confessional,[54] the Matthean resurrection commissions were not confessional but oriented to action, to opening up access to the risen one on the "open road" that leads into the future. Confession had within it elements of stasis that sought to hold and solidify a fixed *poiesis* from the past. Commissions to "go" pointed to the opening up of new meaning-making potential into the future.

Crossan has highlighted for contemporary interpreters the political implications of early Christian appearance stories. He suggests that they were not primarily interested in "trance, ecstasy, apparition, or revelation, but in authority, power, leadership, and priority."[55] He also distinguishes three types of recipients—specific leaders, leadership groups like the Twelve or the apostles, and the general community.[56] If appearance in itself, but even more so appearance together with commissioning, conferred authority in early Christian communities, then it is reasonable to assume that the combined traditions associated with both female and male disciples as climax to the Matthean gospel would have been read, at least by some, as authorizing women's and men's leadership. For others, no doubt, such a reading would have functioned as an offense, another aspect of the gospel as *skandalon*, which challenged recipients to a response that would shatter the boundaries of the status quo, in this instance, its authority and power structures.

The commission given to the women by Jesus, first through the angel and then in person, was twofold—to proclaim the message of Jesus having been raised to disciples (28:7), and to direct disciples who had alienated themselves from the crucified one to reconciliation with the one who had been raised (28:10). The eleven male disciples are likewise given a twofold commission, ritual and catechetical, under the umbrella of making disciples of all nations—to baptize and to teach (28:19-20). As contemporary readers we know that historically the women's commission has been read as single, momentary, with no lasting validity, while that to the male disciples has been interpreted as ongoing and authorizing male leadership. We can be sure, also, that it would have been read in that way within certain Matthean households. Given the agency of at least some Matthean women within certain contexts, as has already been established in this study, one could ask whether in those households in which the gospel functioned as counter-story, the male and female commissions may have been read cyclically as authorizing both women and men, thus crossing gender boundaries according to the way these have been constructed transgressively in this section of the text.

Within such households, resistant to or deviant within certain developing interpretations of Jesus and the reign of God movement that shaped their identity, it may have been that the raising of the crucified one was seen as beginning an open-ended and ongoing commission to make disciples. Those first commissioned could have been understood to have been given the message of resurrection, sent out into the "open road" and authorized to reconcile into a renewed kinship any discipled ones who had become alienated. The textual designation of that kinship was in male generic terminology, "brothers," but those transgressive aspects of the gospel story in relation to kinship already noted could have deconstructed a limited gender interpretation of the new kinship (28:10), at least for some readers. For these readers it was reconciled disciples who extended discipled membership in the reign of God to others, all boundaries to such discipleship being transgressed by the universality of the commission to include "all nations."[57]

Praxis within the Matthean households indicated that such new disciples were first baptized into the ritual life of the house-church. They would have then heard first and foremost and continually the proclamation that Jesus has indeed been raised, the heart of what commissioned disciples taught. As they became more fully incorporated into Matthean households they would need, as the gospel indicates, to be reconciled across differences and even betrayals and alienations (18:15-20) in order to carry on the work of the house-churches of proclaiming Jesus' resurrection, teaching all that he had taught, and ritualizing new membership. Within such Matthean households of reading and creative *poiesis*, Jesus could have been understood as one who transgressed gender boundaries in a way that authorized the entire community's participation in the universal mission. Such an interpretation may have reflected as well as authorized Matthean inclusive communities of ritual and catechesis. They may not have been the dominant voice in the Matthean group, and we know that their *poiesis* was not permitted to influence later ecclesial traditioning. These voices can, however, be recovered not in silences but in textual possibilities and potentialities that intersected with communities of interpretation in which gender, socio-economic, and ethnic boundaries had been transgressed by the reign of God movement.

The conclusion to the Matthean gospel makes clear that it was in the going and doing that Jesus would be present with communities of disciples and that in their so going and doing their story would be heard dialogically in the story of Jesus.[58] There is, however, a dangerous potential in such a promise of presence—that it would be controlled by those claiming authorization and that it would be linked with stasis. We have already noted this mode of interpretation and its function within the Matthean context. The tradition of the open road endures within the narrative and its interpretation, however, to continually disrupt such control. We have noted too that the Matthean resurrection accounts gave no titles to Jesus, leaving open for future interpreters the possibility of new meaning-making. The only naming or title-giving within the close of the gospel is that into which new disciples would be baptized—the name of the Father and of the Son and of the Holy Spirit (28:19). While this cannot be interpreted as an early trinitarian formula, it could have indicated some of the alternative ways in which the gospel story of Jesus had shaped readers to understand how God's presence could be manifest.[59] We have already seen that other manifestations, other namings were available to Matthean gospel readers beyond the familial and gendered potential of this triadic formula. History has again demonstrated, however, that exclusive male traditioning has resulted from such naming.

The final commission to teach all that Jesus had commanded would have sent Matthean readers back into the gospel story and to its telling within their midst. It was there that what Jesus commanded would be found. Those teachings of Jesus were not concerned with his own identity but with the reign of God movement that he was preaching and facilitating by his healing ministry. They would have been interpreted variously, however, by gospel readers. Being authorized by Jesus, who had been given authority to both teach and heal (11:27; 28:18), they may have been read as coherent and final, Matthew 5:17-19 being adhered to strictly. If, however, the teachings of Jesus were understood as continually new as well as old (13:52), then even the scribal communities and leaders should have been constantly challenged in the ongoing work of teaching, which was where the risen Jesus was available to the Matthean households.[60] Readers could close off this presence or continue to evoke it as they brought new and old together in their communities' storytelling.

The conclusion to the Matthean narrative reclaims the resurrection tradition of women and men, not subverting one to the other. It also holds in tension the traditions of the "open road" and the authoritative mountaintop, aspects of the life of the Matthean group that may also have been in tension and so storied. The creative tension in first-century interpretation can function as a prototype for contemporary feminist exegesis. The seeking of the risen Jesus on the open road must continue to challenge liturgical ritual and catechesis that becomes fixed and rigid while authorized teaching and ritual must give ongoing shape and form to open-ended meaning-making. The close of the gospel likewise provides a location in which a feminist answer to the Baptist's question can be articulated. It commissions believers to continually look for "another," for the new ways in which divinity can be manifest and represented, for new ways of reading the story so that teaching can go on "to the close of the age," for new ways of telling stories of communities of resistance in conjunction with the Jesus story. The Matthean story indicates that it is in this process that the risen Jesus is to be found. For Matthean readers of the gospel story, however, that was promised only in their going away from tombs, even if they were empty; going away from mountains, even if they were centers of authority and authorization. New ways of reading this old story offer possible sites, therefore, where contemporary feminist women and men can name and proclaim Jesus beyond the current crisis of historical christological narratives.

# Conclusion

At the beginning of this work I drew attention to the dialogic interplay between the questions each interpreter brings to the biblical text and the questions the biblical text asks of the interpreter in each creative act of interpretation. My experience in addressing and being addressed by the textual question—"Shall we look for Another?"—within a context of feminist biblical *poiesis* and feminist Christian praxis has confirmed that initial insight.

Contemporary Christian women's agency within churches and within centers of theological meaning-making has brought to light critical issues for speaking and reading Jesus. It has changed the landscape of biblical interpretation, creating new communities of interpretation in which these issues and their related questions have given rise to new methods of reading. This study has provided one such new method, or new map, as I have called it. It drew on an insight awakened by contemporary experience; namely, that attention to the agency of women and others outside the centers of power and scribal activity leads to a recognition that communities of reception of the gospel were not monolithic, as so often constructed by scholars, but significantly diverse. Ethnicity, gender, and class were the three major categories chosen in the construction of this diversity in the Matthean context for the purposes of this study. Others may construct the diversity through the lens of different categories arising out of their social location and experience of those aspects of life that dominant theo-ideological discourses have silenced or marginalized in the past.

A feminist recognition of the limitation imposed by the necessity of choosing particular categories of analysis within the confines of a single work of interpretation has brought with it an awareness of the impossibility of activating the full potentialities of reading Jesus within the Matthean gospel. This study is one small contribution to that task. Insights developed in the interpretive work itself made it clear that there is no final word on the Jesus of the gospels. Attention to the particularities of socio-cultural context, reading competencies as a result of one's literary and cultural intertextuality, and a number of other factors meant that diversity of reading Jesus characterized the first century. Recognizing this process as prototype for contemporary Christian *poiesis* has opened up the richness of the heteroglossal possibilities of Christian meaning-making to others. Diverse voices of interpretation need to be heard so that the reading of

Jesus is not controlled or confined in the hands of a few, as it has been in the past, but is available to many and to the artfulness of the Christian imagination in communities of Christian faith and praxis.

The experience of bringing new questions to texts out of a different construction of its communities of first-century reception has confirmed the insight that the Jesus of the gospel cannot be spoken or read definitively. Texts that I had read carefully in the past with other questions in the foreground yielded up new meaning. I also became aware that there were avenues of exploration that I was not able to take. A more developed study of Greco-Roman political, socio-cultural, and literary intertexts, as well as the possibility of intertextual influences from other early Christian texts and traditions, are just two such areas.

The experience of engendering reading and the Matthean Jesus in light of the question—"Shall we look for Another?"—has yielded an affirmative response whose polyvalence points toward the open road that leads away from the empty tomb. Narrative, metaphor, and the imagery that have been used to construct Jesus have been and can be interpreted in ways that are oppressive and that constrict meaning simply to support the status quo. On the other hand, a feminist reading of that imagery within the creative meaning-making potential of narrative and attention to the agency of those previously silenced has yielded not only other ways of reading but also Another, the incarnation of divinity, which will not be confined and about whom feminist women and men can speak in new ways. This study closes, therefore, in the imaginative space of Christian feminist *poiesis* of Jesus, on the open road leading away from all empty tombs but open to the necessity of continuing to look for Another who will be seen and heard in Christian *basileia* praxis.

# Notes

## INTRODUCTION

[1] Rosi Braidotti, *Nomadic Subjects: Embodiment and Sexual Difference in Contemporary Feminist Theory*, not Gender and Culture (New York: Columbia University Press, 1994), 1. Braidotti's entire text has as one of its aims "to develop and evoke a vision of female feminist subjectivity in a nomadic mode."

[2] Mary Rose D'Angelo, "Re-membering Jesus: Women, Prophecy, and Resistance in the Memory of the Early Churches," *Horizons* 19 (1992): 202, explains the use of the hyphenated form of this word in relation to twentieth-century feminist approaches to Jesus in the gospels.

[3] Donna Haraway, "Ecce Homo, Ain't (Ar'n't) I a Woman, and Inappropriate/d Others: The Human in a Post-Humanist Landscape," in *Feminists Theorize the Political*, ed. Judith Butler and Joan W. Scott (New York: Routledge, 1992), 86.

[4] Diana Fuss, *Essentially Speaking: Feminism, Nature and Difference* (New York: Routledge, 1989).

[5] For an excellent overview of recent discussions in feminist theory, both European and North American, see Rosi Braidotti, *Patterns of Dissonance: A Study of Women in Contemporary Philosophy*, trans. Elizabeth Guild (Cambridge: Polity Press, 1991). For a location of these discussions within the context of postmodernism, see Linda J. Nicholson, ed., *Feminism/Postmodernism* (New York: Routledge, 1990).

[6] Within theological feminism, this approach has been theoretically articulated most comprehensively by Elisabeth Schüssler Fiorenza. See her "Transforming the Legacy of *The Woman's Bible*," in *Searching the Scriptures*, Volume 1: *A Feminist Introduction*, ed. Elisabeth Schüssler Fiorenza (New York: Crossroad, 1993), 1-24; idem, *But She Said: Feminist Practices of Biblical Interpretation* (Boston: Beacon Press, 1992); and idem, *Discipleship of Equals: A Critical Feminist Ekklesialogy of Liberation* (New York: Crossroad, 1993). In the realm of critical theory I find this position presented most convincingly by Braidotti, *Patterns of Dissonance*.

[7] Schüssler Fiorenza, *But She Said*, 8. See also the fourth chapter in this same book (pp. 102-32), for her more extensive analysis of systemic patriarchy.

[8] Such awareness has come as a result of the critique of the hegemony of white middle-class feminism by women of color from different parts of the globe. In Australia, such a challenge has come from migrant women (see Sennie Masian, "The Profile of Filipino Women—Not Read, Seen, or Heard," in *National Women's Conference 1990 Proceedings* [Canberra: Write People, 1990], 182-84); and from indigenous Australian women (see Anne Pattel-Gray, *Through Aboriginal Eyes:*

*The Cry from the Wilderness* [Geneva: WCC Publications, 1991]). It is personal and political in Audre Lorde's open letter to Mary Daly, in *Sister Outsider: Essays and Speeches* (New York: The Crossing Press, 1984), 66-71. See also Chandra Talpade Mohanty, "Feminist Encounters: Locating the Politics of Experience," in *Destabilizing Theory: Contemporary Feminist Debates*, ed. Michèle Barrett and Anne Phillips (Stanford: Stanford University Press, 1992), 74-92, for a theoretical articulation of the necessity to deal with the difference *within* feminist discourses. Judith Plaskow has for many years challenged Christian women regarding the anti-Judaism within their Christian feminist theologies. For a most recent articulation of her position, see "Anti-Judaism in Feminist Christian Interpretation," in Schüssler Fiorenza, *Searching the Scriptures*, 1:117-29.

[9] Teresa de Lauretis, *Technologies of Gender: Essays on Theory, Film and Fiction*, Theories of Representation and Difference (Bloomington: Indiana University Press, 1986), in particular pp. ix-x, 1-30.

[10] Braidotti, *Nomadic Subjects*, 158-67.

[11] Ibid., 172.

[12] Luce Irigaray makes the following plea in this regard: "Let us not forget, moreover, that we already have a history, that certain women, despite all the cultural obstacles, have made their mark upon history and all too often have been forgotten by us" (*Sexes and Genealogies*, trans. Gillian C. Gill [New York: Columbia University Press, 1993], 19). Feminist studies of biblical texts and the history of the ancient Near East as well as early Christianity and Rabbinic Judaism have done much to remedy the situation that Irigaray decries.

[13] See, however, Athalya Brenner and Fokkelien van Dijk-Hemmes, *On Gendering Texts: Female and Male Voices in the Hebrew Bible* (Leiden: Brill, 1993), for a perspective on female and male voices in the text.

[14] Elisabeth Schüssler Fiorenza, *In Memory of Her: A Feminist Theological Reconstruction of Christian Origins* (New York: Crossroad, 1983).

[15] Elisabeth Schüssler Fiorenza, "Zur Methodenproblematik einer feministischen Christologie des Neuen Testaments," in *Vom Verlangen nach Heilwerden: Christologie in feministisch-theologischer Sicht*, ed. Doris Strahm and Regula Strobel (Fribourg: Edition Exodus, 1991), 129-47; idem, *Jesus—Miriam's Child, Sophia's Prophet: Critical Issues in Feminist Christology* (New York: Continuum, 1994).

[16] Marianne Sawicki, *Seeing the Lord: Resurrection and Early Christian Practices* (Minneapolis: Fortress, 1994).

[17] I use the terminology "reign of God movement" in place of the more traditional "Jesus movement" in order to focus attention on the proclamation of the reign or kingdom of God, which is central to the Matthean gospel, rather than on Jesus as central to the movement. The more traditional focus often obscures the other participants in the movement and their contribution to the developing understanding of God's reign.

[18] Mary McClintock Fulkerson, *Changing the Subject: Women's Discourses and Feminist Theology* (Minneapolis: Fortress, 1994), 152, points out that "[a] reading writes a text anew, stimulates its flow of meaning in new directions." The same could be said of each oral performance, that it is "writing" the text anew. See Joseph A. Grassi, "Matthew's Gospel as Live Performance," *BibT* 27 (1989): 225-32, for a study of this aspect of the gospel.

# 1 "WHO DO *YOU* SAY THAT I AM"—
# LISTENING TO THE QUESTIONS

[1] See Jon Sobrino, *Christology at the Crossroads: A Latin American Approach* (Maryknoll, N.Y.: Orbis Books, 1978); D'Angelo, "Re-membering Jesus," 205; and Carter Heyward, *Speaking of Christ: A Lesbian Feminist Voice*, ed. Ellen C. Davis (New York: Pilgrim Press, 1989), 21.

[2] Sandra M. Schneiders, *The Revelatory Text: Interpreting the New Testament as Sacred Scripture* (San Francisco: Harper, 1991), 152.

[3] Fernando F. Segovia, "Cultural Studies and Contemporary Biblical Criticism: Ideological Criticism as Mode of Discourse," in *Reading from This Place*, Volume 1: *Social Location and Biblical Interpretation in the United States*, ed. Fernando F. Segovia and Mary Ann Tolbert (Minneapolis: Fortress, 1995), 1-17, details how the emergence of cultural studies and the recognition of differences among interpreters not only on the basis of gender but also socio-political and cultural, ethnic, racial, and religious differences have led to this awareness of the constructed nature of meaning.

[4] Jacquelyn Grant, *White Women's Christ and Black Women's Jesus: Feminist Christology and Womanist Response*, AARAS 64 (Atlanta: Scholars Press, 1989); Kwok Pui-lan, "Racism and Ethnocentrism in Feminist Biblical Interpretation" in *Searching the Scriptures*, 1:101-16; Virginia Fabella, "A Common Methodology for Diverse Christologies," in *With Passion and Compassion: Third World Women Doing Theology—Reflections from the Women's Commission of the Ecumenical Association of Third World Theologians*, ed. Virginia Fabella and Mercy Oduyoye (Maryknoll, N.Y.: Orbis Books, 1988), 108-17; Chung Hyun Kyung, *Struggle to Be the Sun Again: Introducing Asian Women's Theology* (Maryknoll, N.Y.: Orbis Books, 1990); and Anne Pattel-Gray, "Not Yet Tiddas: An Aboriginal Womanist Critique of Australian Church Feminism," in *Freedom and Entrapment: Women Thinking Theology*, ed. Maryanne Confoy, Dorothy Lee, and Joan Nowotny (North Blackburn, Vic.: Dove, 1995), 165-92.

[5] Elisabeth Schüssler Fiorenza continually emphasizes the necessity of this form of analysis. In relation to christology, see her article "Zur Methodenproblematik," 129-47, especially pp. 134-41. See also Grant, *White Women's Christ and Black Women's Jesus*, 195-230.

[6] Teresa Lynn Ebert, *Patriarchy, Ideology, Subjectivity: Towards a Theory of Feminist Critical Cultural Studies* (Ph.D. diss., University of Minnesota, 1988), 48-64, critiques what she calls an "essentialization of experience" that accepts women's experience as a "given" and fails to critique the way it is produced by "the ideological, political and economic practices of the culture." See also Joan W. Scott, "Experience," in Butler and Scott, *Feminists Theorize*, 22-40.

[7] The challenge of Audre Lorde, bell hooks, Gayatri Chakravorty Spivak, María Lugones and many others is significant here. See Lorde, *Sister Outsider*; bell hooks, *Yearning: Race, Gender, and Cultural Politics* (Boston: South End Press, 1990) and *Ain't I a Woman: Black Women and Feminism* (Boston: South End Press, 1981); and Rey Chow, "Violence in the Other Country," and other essays in *Third World Women and the Politics of Feminism*, ed. Chandra Talpade Mohanty, Anne Russo, and Lourdes Torres (Bloomington, Ind.: Indiana Univer-

sity Press, 1991), 81-100, to name but a few who offer a challenge to the universalizing tendencies of white middle-class feminism.

[8] There are now numerous feminist critiques of traditional christology and reclamations of the Christ figure from a feminist perspective. It is beyond the scope of this brief analysis to provide a comprehensive outline of either the critiques or the new possibilities emerging.

[9] For a very clear discussion of the distinctions among the actual Jesus, the historical Jesus and the proclaimed Jesus, see Schneiders, *The Revelatory Text*, 100-102. These categories will be discussed more fully in the following chapter.

[10] Elizabeth A. Johnson, *She Who Is: The Mystery of God in Feminist Theological Discourse* (New York: Crossroad, 1992), 152.

[11] Elisabeth Schüssler Fiorenza, *Jesus*, 34-43, analyzes the sex/gender system as a "discursive frame of meaning" in relation to christology.

[12] *Asian Women Doing Theology: Report from the Singapore Conference, November 20-29, 1987*, ed. Dulcie Abraham, et al. (Kowloon: Asian Women's Resource Centre for Culture and Theology, 1989), 165.

[13] Choi Man Ja, "Feminist Christology," in Abraham, et al., *Asian Women Doing Theology*, 175.

[14] Monica Melanchthon, "Christology and Women," in Abraham, et al., *Asian Women Doing Theology*, 183. Carr, "Feminist Views," 132, also states that "if Jesus was truly human, then his particular sex, like his ethnic heritage and historical provenance, was purely contingent." Such a recognition is essential to the recognition of ongoing divine incarnation in the multiple contingencies of the lives of those who participate in the reign of God movement. Incarnation did not cease with the earthly Jesus.

[15] Judith Butler, "Variations on Sex and Gender: Beauvoir, Wittig and Foucault," in *Feminism as Critique*, ed. Seyla Benhabib and Drucilla Cornell (Minneapolis: University of Minnesota Press, 1987), 128-42; and "Gender Trouble, Feminist Theory, and Psychoanalytic Discourse," in Nicholson, *Feminism/Postmodernism*, 324-40. See also Braidotti, *Patterns of Dissonance*, especially 128-31.

[16] Haraway, "Ecce Homo," 90.

[17] The literature on this question is vast. By way of example, see de Lauretis, *Technologies*; Jane Flax, "Postmodernism and Gender-Relations in Feminist Theory," *Signs* 12.4 (1987): 621-43; Joan W. Scott, "Gender: A Useful Category of Historical Analysis," in *Coming to Terms: Feminism, Theory, Politics*, ed. Elizabeth Weed (New York: Routledge, 1989), 81-100; and Nancy K. Miller, ed., *The Poetics of Gender* (New York: Columbia University Press, 1986). In relation to theology, see *Reflections on Theology and Gender*, ed. Fokkelien van Dijk-Hemmes and Athalya Brenner (Kampen: Kok Pharos, 1994).

[18] De Lauretis, *Technologies*, 1. Linda Nicholson problematizes gender in her introduction to the collection edited by her, *Feminism/Postmodernism*, 16, noting that "the very categories we use to liberate us may also have their controlling moment." Rita Felski, *Beyond Feminist Aesthetics: Feminist Literary and Social Change* (Cambridge: Harvard University Press, 1989), 58-59, argues for a dialectical interrelation between the subject and society as a way out of the either/or dichotomies that characterize patriarchy.

[19] Johnson, *She Who Is*, 154-56. For a more extensive development of a new anthropology, see Mary Aquin O'Neill, "The Mystery of Being Human Together—

Anthropology," in *Freeing Theology: The Essentials of Theology in Feminist Perspective*, ed. Catherine Mowry LaCugna (San Francisco: Harper, 1993), 139-60; and the excellent collection of articles in *In the Embrace of God: Feminist Approaches to Theological Anthropology*, ed. Ann O'Hara Graff (Maryknoll, N.Y.: Orbis Books, 1995).

[20] Johnson, *She Who Is*, 82.

[21] Ibid., 156. Johnson's position is similar to the "proliferation of difference and . . . the constitution of identity via the recognition and letting be of true difference." See Seyla Benhabib and Drucilla Cornell, "Introduction," in Benhabib and Cornell, *Feminism as Critique*, 15, wherein they describe the work of Butler, "Variations on Sex and Gender," in the same volume. See also Haraway's notion of "nongeneric humanity" in "Ecce Homo," 86.

[22] See Rosemary Radford Ruether, *Sexism and God Talk: Toward a Feminist Theology* (Boston: Beacon Press, 1983), 137; Ada María Isasi-Díaz, "The Bible and Mujerista Theology," in *Lift Every Voice: Constructing Christian Theologies from the Underside*, ed. Susan B. Thistlethwaite and P. Engel (San Francisco: Harper & Row, 1990), 264. Sandra M. Schneiders, *Woman and the Word: The Gender of God in the New Testament and the Spirituality of Women*, 1986 Madeleva Lecture in Spirituality (New York: Paulist, 1986), 58, argues in response to the critique of the maleness of Jesus that Jesus had to be male, given the nature of first-century society, in order to reveal the true nature of God and humanity. While she may or may not be correct in this, the problem lies in the universalizing of this first-century claim to God's manifestation in Jesus. Mary Daly, *Beyond God the Father: Toward a Philosophy of Women's Liberation* (Boston: Beacon Press, 1973), 69-71, provides a radical critique of the maleness of Jesus as masculine symbol of ideal incarnation. Schüssler Fiorenza, "Zur Methodenproblematik," 129, points out that generally the starting points of the discussion of feminist christology invariably are the maleness of Jesus and the meaning of Jesus' death on the cross as redemptive.

[23] Schüssler Fiorenza, *Jesus*, 119, says of such titles that they "are not definitions of the true being or nature of Jesus. Rather they are best understood as language models and metaphors that seek to 'make sense' . . . of Jesus." It is in this way that they shall be considered in this study.

[24] Johnson, *She Who Is*, 151, points out in her discussion of the "imperial Christ" that this aspect of christology is also radically critiqued by Latin American liberation theologians.

[25] Rita Nakashima Brock, "And a Little Child Will Lead Us: Christology and Child Abuse," in *Christianity, Patriarchy, and Abuse: A Feminist Critique*, ed. Joanne Carlson Brown and Carole R. Bohn (New York: Pilgrim Press, 1989), 43. Her critique, however, is not limited to the image of Lord or Suffering Servant (which we will consider below) but is directed to the Christian understanding of redemption needing to be wrought by the death of Jesus. This is developed in her *Journeys by Heart: A Christology of Erotic Power* (New York: Crossroad, 1988), 1-9.

[26] Choi Man Ja, "Feminist Christology," 176. Chung, *Struggle to Be the Sun Again*, 58-59, also demonstrates how some Asian women have reclaimed this image. She previously laid out the ways in which it functions oppressively in many Asian women's lives.

[27] Susan Brooks Thistlethwaite, *Sex, Race, and God: Christian Feminism in Black and White* (New York: Crossroad, 1989), 116-17.

[28] Grant, *White Women's Christ and Black Women's Jesus*, 219.

[29] Chung, *Struggle to Be the Sun Again*, 53-54, 56-57, recognizes aspects of Korean women's experience within this perspective. See also Johnson, *She Who Is*, 161.

[30] Chung, *Struggle to Be the Sun Again*, 54.

[31] Joanne Carlson Brown and Rebecca Parker, "For God So Loved the World?" in Brown and Bohn, *Christianity, Patriarchy, and Abuse*, 1-30.

[32] Brown and Parker, "God So Loved," 13.

[33] Margo G. Houts, "Atonement and Abuse: An Alternative View," *Daughters of Sarah* 18.3 (1992): 29-32; for a more critical feminist reclamation, see Carter Heyward, "Suffering, Redemption, and Christ: Shifting the Grounds of Feminist Christology," *Christianity and Crisis* 49 (1989): 381-86.

[34] Luce Irigaray, *Marine Lover of Friedrich Nietzsche*, trans. Gillian C. Gill (New York: Columbia University Press, 1991), 164. For a study of the theme of the immolation of the beloved son within Judaism and early Christianity, see Jon D. Levenson, *The Death and Resurrection of the Beloved Son: The Transformation of Child Sacrifice in Judaism and Christianity* (New Haven/London: Yale University Press, 1993).

[35] Here I have been influenced by Felski, *Beyond Feminist Aesthetics*, 66, who argues that a "theoretical model that is able to situate language in relation to social life by foregrounding its semantic and pragmatic functions allows a more differentiated analysis of women's communicative practices by moving away from the abstract dichotomy of 'masculine' versus 'feminine' speech."

[36] Mary Gerhart, "Imaging Christ in Art, Politics, Spirituality: An Overview," in *Imaging Christ: Politics, Art, Spirituality*, ed. Francis A. Eigo (Villanova: Villanova University Press, 1991), 4.

[37] Nelly Ritchie, "Women and Christology," in *Through Her Eyes: Women's Theology from Latin America*, ed. Elsa Tamez (Maryknoll, N.Y.: Orbis Books, 1989), 81-95.

[38] Chung, *Struggle to Be the Sun Again*, 62.

[39] Ruether, *Sexism and God-Talk*, 137-38.

[40] Daly, *Beyond God the Father*, 69.

[41] Daly, *Beyond God the Father*, 71. Irigaray, *Marine Lover*, 190, speaks too of "the universe already made flesh or capable of becoming flesh, and remaining in excess to the existing world."

[42] Daphne Hampson, *Theology and Feminism*, Signposts in Theology (Oxford: Basil Blackwell, 1990), 50-80.

[43] Heyward, *Speaking of Christ*, 22.

[44] Rita Nakashima Brock, "The Feminist Redemption of Christ," in *Christian Feminism: Visions of a New Humanity*, ed. Judith Weidman (San Francisco: Harper & Row, 1984), 57.

[45] Ruether, *Sexism and God-Talk*, 121.

[46] By way of example, see many of the essays in Barrett and Phillips, *Destabilizing Theory*, and in Nicholson, *Feminism/Postmodernism*.

[47] Braidotti, "Sexual Difference as a Nomadic Political Project," in *Nomadic Subjects*, 146-72.

[48] Chung, *Struggle to Be the Sun Again*, 65-66.

[49] Elizabeth Amoah and Mercy Amba Oduyoye, "The Christ for African Women," in Fabella and Oduyoye, *With Passion and Compassion*, 44. See also

Teresa M. Hinga, "Jesus Christ and the Liberation of Women in Africa," in *The Will to Arise: Women, Tradition and the Church in Africa*, ed. Mercy Amba Oduyoye and Musimbi R. A. Kanyoro (Maryknoll, N.Y.: Orbis Books, 1992), 183-94.

[50] See Doris Jean Dyke, *Crucified Woman* (Toronto: The United Church Publishing House, 1991).

[51] A reproduction of this painting, which depicts a female crucified figure against the backdrop of the Australian landscape, can be found in Rosemary Crumlin, *Images of Religion in Australian Art* (Kensington: Bay Books, 1988), 158-59.

[52] This piece was discovered by Rosemary Crumlin during her curation of an exhibition of the religious art of traditional Australian aboriginal artists during the bi-centenary of European settlement in Australia. A very beautiful photograph can be seen in *Aboriginal Art and Spirituality*, ed. Rosemary Crumlin and Anthony Knight (Melbourne: CollinsDove, 1991), 38.

[53] D'Angelo, "Re-membering Jesus," 206.

[54] Elisabeth Schüssler Fiorenza, "Toward a Feminist Biblical Hermeneutics: Biblical Interpretation and Liberation Theology," in *The Challenge of Liberation Theology*, ed. Brian Maher and L. Dale Richesin (Maryknoll, N.Y.: Orbis Books, 1981), 107.

[55] Schüssler Fiorenza, *In Memory of Her*, 105-59.

[56] Ruether, *Sexism and God-Talk*, 138.

[57] Elisabeth Moltmann-Wendel, "Beziehung—die vergessene Dimension der Christologie: Neutestamentliche Ansatspunkte feministischer Christologie," in Strahm and Strobel, *Vom Verlangen nach Heilwerden*, 100-111.

[58] Johnson, *She Who Is*, 72.

[59] Brock, *Journeys by Heart*, 66-70, 105-8. Graham Ward, "Divinity and Sexuality: Luce Irigaray and Christology," *Modern Theology* 12.2 (1996): 232, expresses a similar understanding—"Jesus is an historical figure in a Christological and on-going narrative. His divinity (and ours) is meaningless outside his relation to others and theirs to him. Without others his divinity is incomplete."

[60] In addition to the many voices already cited, see also Nelly Ritchie, "Women and Christology," 82, who links Jesus to the active call to people to participate in their own liberation.

[61] Donna Haraway, "Situated Knowledges: The Science Question in Feminism and the Privilege of Partial Perspective," *Feminist Studies* 14 (1988): 575-99.

[62] Ibid., 590.

[63] bell hooks develops this notion of "yearning" in her book by that title, noted above. Braidotti, *Nomadic Subjects*, 167, calls this an "intensive" reading of the feminist position, and she expresses it in terms of "someone who longs for, tends towards, is driven to feminism," employing the image of "nomadism."

## 2  WHAT YOU SEE AND HEAR—ENGENDERING READING

[1] Braidotti, *Patterns of Dissonance*, 216. See also Mohanty, "Feminist Encounters," 84, and her call for "uncovering alternative non-identical histories which challenge and disrupt the spatial and temporal location of a hegemonic history."

² In this regard, Schneiders, *The Revelatory Text*, 139, says that "texts, as language, not only say what they say but evoke a world of the unsaid that might well become articulate under different circumstances of interpretation. This unspoken range of meaning waits in the wings even as the spoken acts its part upon the stage of discourse. The cue for its appearance needs only to be whispered." See also Alicia Suskin Ostriker, *Feminist Revision and the Bible*, The Bucknell Lectures in Literary Theory (Oxford: Blackwell, 1993), 29, who suggests that in women's rewriting of myth the stories change or grow because "meanings latent in the story are recovered and foregrounded by a woman's perspective." Traditional understanding of scripture has named such potential for new meaning-making from the text the *sensus plenior* of scripture.

³ Schüssler Fiorenza has explored this twofold approach to feminist reading of biblical texts in great detail and within a broader framework in *Bread Not Stone: The Challenge of Feminist Biblical Interpretation* (Boston: Beacon Press, 1984), 1-22. She points to its rhetorical implications in *But She Said*, 131-32.

⁴ From a literary point of view, Shoshana Felman, *What Does a Woman Want? Reading and Sexual Difference* (Baltimore: Johns Hopkins University Press, 1993), 6, indicates that "literature . . . cannot simply be subsumed by the cultural prejudices that traverse it and by the ideologies its authors hold. . . . All great texts . . . are self-transgressive with respect to the conscious ideologies that inform them." She goes on to warn that care must be taken not to determine meaning in advance but to "*tune into the forms of resistance present in the text . . . to trace within each text its own resistance to itself*, its own specific literary, inadvertent *textual transgression of its male assumptions and prescriptions.*"

⁵ De Lauretis, *Technologies*, 2.

⁶ Haraway, "Situated Knowledges," 592. This project has been informed in its later stages by the work of Mikhail Bakhtin and his "dialogic imagination" (see *The Dialogic Imagination: Four Essays by M. M. Bakhtin*, ed. Michael Holquist and trans. Caryl Emerson and Michael Holquist [Austin: University of Texas Press, 1981]). I have found it of interest to note, however, that the feminist approach to reading is of itself dialogical.

⁷ Fulkerson, *Changing the Subject*, 142-47, recognizes these readings as a "multiplication of the text" from different subject positions; we might speak of the "text which is not one."

⁸ Schneiders, *The Revelatory Text*, 149, claims that the text is revelatory in the act of interpretation. I would want, however, to nuance this in a way that indicates that it is only in those acts of interpretation that are liberating of humanity for the fullness of God's dreaming that the text is, indeed, revelatory. Those interpretations that condemn humanity to oppressive structures and belief systems cannot be claimed to be revelatory of a liberating God or of Jesus as liberator. For Schüssler Fiorenza, the "revelatory canon" can only be formulated "in and through women's struggle for liberation." See *In Memory of Her*, 32.

⁹ Schneiders, *The Revelatory Text*, 137.

¹⁰ Charles Talbert, *What Is a Gospel? The Genre of the Canonical Gospels* (Philadelphia: Fortress, 1978). Grant R. Osborne, "Genre Criticism—Sensus Literalis," *Trinity Journal* 4 (1983): 1-27, offers a comprehensive discussion of this approach. While Osborne argues for the epistemological and ontological necessity of determining the "originally intended genre" and hence meaning, he has failed

to take account of the fact that decades of biblical scholarship have proposed an extraordinary variety of "originally intended" genres and meanings.

[11] Mary Gerhart, *Genre Choices, Gender Questions*, Oklahoma Project for Discourse and Theory (Norman: University of Oklahoma Press, 1992), 78, 163-66.

[12] Ibid., 29-43. See also F. Gerald Downing, "Contemporary Analogies to the Gospels and Acts: 'Genres' or 'Motifs,'" in *Synoptic Studies: The Ampleforth Conferences of 1982 and 1983*, ed. C. M. Tuckett, JSNTSS 7 (Sheffield: JSOT Press, 1984), 54, who questions the applicability of genre determination and focuses rather on the extensive use of items from what he calls a "common narrative 'vocabulary' of motifs."

[13] Gerhart, *Genre Choices, Gender Questions*, 20.

[14] Ibid., 164.

[15] Menakhem Perry, "Literary Dynamics: How the Order of a Text Creates Its Meaning," *Poetics Today* 1 (1979): 45.

[16] Sawicki, *Seeing the Lord*, 223, says in this regard that "the greater one's genre competence, the more different meanings one can make of a given text, because genre promotes variant readings."

[17] Gerhart, "Imaging Christ in Art," 30.

[18] See Gerhart, *Genre Choices, Gender Questions*, 79-83, who focuses particularly on the construction of gender.

[19] Ibid., 15.

[20] P. J. J. Botha, "Greco-Roman Literacy as Setting for New Testament Writings," *Neotestamentica* 26.1 (1992): 211.

[21] See Susan Guettel Cole, "Could Greek Women Read and Write?" in *Reflections of Women in Antiquity*, ed. Helene P. Foley (New York: Gordon and Breach Science, 1981), 219-45.

[22] Botha, "Greco-Roman Literacy," 210.

[23] Gerhart, *Genre Choices, Gender Questions*, 132.

[24] Thomas Docherty, *Reading (Absent) Character: Towards a Theory of Characterization in Fiction* (Oxford: Clarendon Press, 1983); B. Hochman, *Character in Literature* (Ithaca, N.Y.: Cornell University Press, 1985); James Phelan, *Reading People, Reading Plots: Character, Progression and the Interpretation of Narrative* (Chicago: University of Chicago Press, 1989); John A. Darr, *On Character Building: The Reader and the Rhetoric of Characterization in Luke-Acts*, Literary Currents in Biblical Interpretation (Louisville: Westminster/John Knox, 1992); and *Characterization in Biblical Literature*, Semeia 63, ed. Elizabeth Struthers Malbon and Adele Berlin (Atlanta: Scholars Press, 1993), to mention only a brief sampling.

[25] David Fishelov, "Types of Character, Characteristics of Types," *Style* 24.3 (1990): 425.

[26] Ibid.

[27] I note here that Darr's approach to characterization includes attention to "both the literary and social forces that conditioned reading in Greco-Roman times" and is "observant of the text's rhetoric." See Darr, *On Character Building*, 37.

[28] Ibid., 59

[29] Ulrich Luz, "The Son of Man in Matthew: Heavenly Judge or Human Christ," *JSNT* 48 (1992): 21, makes a statement in relation to the "Synoptic son

of man tradition" that is very relevant to this study; namely, that the fate of this tradition in the second century is "another example of the striking fact that the history of Jesus as a whole, as it is narrated in the Gospels, seems to be almost totally without effect in the next centuries." Close attention to the characterization of Jesus in the gospel text and especially from a feminist perspective may be one way in which the story of Jesus may be reread beyond prevailing theological claims from subsequent eras.

[30] Mary Doyle Springer, *A Rhetoric of Literary Character: Some Women of Henry James* (Chicago: University of Chicago Press, 1978), 14; Mieke Bal, *Narratology: Introduction to the Theory of Narrative*, trans. Christine van Boheemen (Toronto: University of Toronto Press, 1985), 86; and Uri Margolin, "Introducing and Sustaining Characters in Literary Narrative: A Set of Conditions," *Style* 21.1 (1987): 109.

[31] David McCracken, "Character in the Boundary: Bakhtin's Interdividuality in Biblical Narratives," *Semeia* 63 (1993): 29-42.

[32] Schneiders, *The Revelatory Text*, 101.

[33] Ibid., 100-101. Here Schneiders defines the "actual Jesus" as the ontic Jesus who lived an earthly life and is now the glorified Jesus who continues to live. The link with the historical Jesus seems, however, to be more specifically with the earthly Jesus, while the glorified Jesus of faith is more closely linked with the "proclaimed Jesus."

[34] The book of John Dominic Crossan, *The Historical Jesus: The Life of a Mediterranean Jewish Peasant* (San Francisco: Harper, 1991), follows this route. In his prologue, xxvii-xxxiv, he uses the term "historical Jesus" to refer to the actual Jesus of Galilee and establishes a sophisticated methodological approach for making claims regarding this Jesus of history. He is but one of a number of scholars whose recent works constitute a new "new quest" for the historical Jesus. See Schüssler Fiorenza's critique of this quest in terms of its participation in the Western "logic of identity" (*But She Said*, 141, and more extensively in *Jesus*, 82-88).

[35] Margolin, "Introducing and Sustaining Characters," 108.

[36] Bal, *Narratology*, 83.

[37] Schneiders, *The Revelatory Text*, 101.

[38] Haraway, "Ecce Homo," 90.

[39] See, for example Paul Ricoeur, *The Rule of Metaphor: Multi-Disciplinary Studies of the Creation of Meaning in Language*, trans. Robert Czerny with Kathleen McLaughlin and John Costello (Toronto: University of Toronto Press, 1981); Janet Martin Soskice, *Metaphor and Religious Language* (Oxford: Clarendon Press, 1985); and Mary Gerhart and Allan Melvin Russell, *Metaphoric Process: The Creation of Scientific and Religious Understanding* (Fort Worth: Texas Christian University Press, 1984).

[40] Soskice, *Metaphor*, 15.

[41] Note that Gerhart and Russell title their book *Metaphoric Process* in recognition of this process, using the phrase "knowledge-in-process" as a chapter designation, 61-81. The notion of metaphor as creative of new meaning previously unknown is also central to Soskice's theory of metaphor.

[42] Schneiders, *The Revelatory Text*, 105-8.

[43] See Soskice, *Metaphor*, 53, 130.

[44] Ibid., 150.

[45] Patricia Parker, *Literary Fat Ladies: Rhetoric, Gender, Property* (London: Methuen, 1987), 36-53.

[46] See Ricoeur, *Rule of Metaphor*, 216-56; Sallie McFague, *Metaphorical Theology: Models of God in Religious Language* (Philadelphia: Fortress, 1982), who develops Ricoeur's model in relation to religious language, especially the metaphor or model of father for God; and Bernard J. Lee, *Jesus and the Metaphors of God: The Christs of the New Testament*, Studies in Judaism and Christianity, Conversation on the Road Not Taken 2 (New York: Paulist, 1993), 14-16.

[47] Soskice, *Metaphor*, 86-90.

[48] Ibid., 118-61. In her final chapter Soskice explores the notion of "theological realism" in terms of a context of inquiry, noting that "it is not words but speakers using words who refer, and that speakers use words according to established patterns of investigation and interest."

[49] Sheila Davaney, "Review of Models of God: Theology for an Ecological, Nuclear Age," *RSR* 16 (1990): 36-40; Claudia V. Camp, "Metaphor in Feminist Biblical Interpretation: Theoretical Perspectives," *Semeia* 61 (1993): 30-34.

[50] Mieke Bal, "Metaphors He Lives By," *Semeia* 61 (1993): 205.

[51] Son of God is the image that Jack Dean Kingsbury has claimed is central to the Matthean gospel using both redaction criticism, *Matthew: Structure, Christology, Kingdom* (Philadelphia: Fortress, 1975), and narrative criticism, *Matthew as Story* (Philadelphia: Fortress, 1986). See also the literary critical debate in Jack Dean Kingsbury, "The Figure of Jesus in Matthew's Story: A Literary-Critical Probe," *JSNT* 21 (1984): 3-36, and David Hill, "The Figure of Jesus in Matthew's Story: A Response to Professor Kingsbury's Literary-Critical Probe," *JSNT* 21 (1984): 37-52.

[52] Methodologically, not only the traces of Sophia imagery in the Matthean text but also the intertextual approach within literary criticism opens the possibilities for such an alternative reading. For this approach, see Danna Nolan Fewell, ed., *Reading between Texts: Intertextuality and the Hebrew Bible*, Literary Currents in Biblical Interpretation (Louisville: Westminster/John Knox, 1992).

[53] A question similar to this last is raised by Caroline Walker Bynum, "Introduction: The Complexity of Symbols," in *Gender and Religion: On the Complexity of Symbols*, ed. Caroline Walker Bynum, Stevan Harrell, and Paula Richman (Boston: Beacon Press, 1986), 2. See also the comment of Janet Martin Soskice, "Blood and Defilement: Jesus, Gender and the Universality of Christ," *European Association for Catholic Theology Bulletin* 5 (1994): 234, who questions whether "gender symbolisms are always tied in fixed ways to the biological sexes."

[54] For a discussion of the reading process in relation to a gospel text, especially understood as the interactive process discussed here, see Darr, *On Character Building*, 16-36. For a feminist perspective on reader-oriented approaches, see Elizabeth Struthers Malbon and Janice Capel Anderson, "Literary-Critical Methods," in *Searching the Scriptures*, 1:248-51.

[55] Tzvetan Todorov, *Mikhail Bakhtin: The Dialogical Principle*, trans. Wlad Godzich, Theory and History of Literature 13 (Minneapolis: University of Minnesota Press, 1984), 60.

[56] Julia Kristeva, *Desire in Language: A Semiotic Approach to Literature and Art*, ed. Leon S. Roudiez and trans. Thomas Gora, Alice Jardine, and Leon S. Roudiez (New York: Columbia University Press, 1980), 66.

⁵⁷ Julia Kristeva, *Revolution in Poetic Language*, trans. Margaret Waller (New York: Columbia University Press, 1984), 59-60.

⁵⁸ Fulkerson, *Changing the Subject*, 142.

⁵⁹ Gary Phillips, "'What Is Written? How Are You Reading?' Gospel, Intertextuality and Doing Lukewise: A Writerly Reading of Lk 10:25-37 (and 38-42)," in *SBLSP* 31, ed. Eugene H. Lovering (Atlanta: Scholars Press, 1992), 287. For more extensive treatments of intertextuality in relation to biblical texts, see Fewell, *Reading between Texts* and *Intertextuality and the Bible*, Semeia 69/70, ed. George Aichele and Gary A. Phillips (Atlanta: Scholars Press, 1995).

⁶⁰ Ebert, *Patriarchy, Ideology, Subjectivity*, 26, discusses what she calls ideologically constituted "frames of intelligibility" that organize the production of significations in the reading process. Schüssler Fiorenza draws on Annette Kolodny's notion of reading paradigms or formations to point out the impossibility of determining the "true meaning of the text itself." She then undertakes a reading of Luke 13:10-17 according to different "frames of meaning" (see *But She Said*, 196-217).

⁶¹ Darr, *On Character Building*, 35.

⁶² The question of a feminist ethical reading of biblical texts is treated extensively by Elisabeth Schüssler Fiorenza, "The Ethics of Interpretation: De-Centring Biblical Scholarship," *JBL* 107 (1988): 3-17.

⁶³ Luz attempts to address this aspect of the interpretation of Matthew's gospel in his proposed multivolumed commentary. See Ulrich Luz, *Matthew 1-7: A Commentary*, trans. Wilhelm C. Linss (Edinburgh: T. & T. Clark, 1990).

⁶⁴ Fernando Segovia, "And They Began to Speak in Other Tongues: Competing Modes of Discourse in Biblical Interpretation," a paper delivered at the Episcopal Divinity School, 29 September 1993. This paper has been subsequently published under the same title as the introductory essay to Segovia and Tolbert, *Reading from This Place*, 1:1-32.

⁶⁵ Schüssler Fiorenza, *But She Said*, 101.

⁶⁶ For a discussion of this process of historical reconstruction, see Elaine Wainwright, *Towards a Feminist Critical Reading of the Gospel according to Matthew*, BZNW 60 (Berlin: de Gruyter, 1991), 51-54.

⁶⁷ Bal, *Narratology*, 81-82, says in this regard that "the description of a character is always strongly colored by the ideology of the investigators, who are usually unaware of their own ideological principles. Consequently, what is presented as description is an implicit value-judgment."

⁶⁸ Such a critique has been undertaken much more extensively than is possible here by Monika Fander, "Historical-Critical Methods," in Schüssler Fiorenza, *Searching the Scriptures*, 1:205-24; and Mary Ann Tolbert, "Social, Sociological, and Anthropological Methods," in Schüssler Fiorenza, *Searching the Scriptures*, 1:255-71.

⁶⁹ For an analysis of the differences among women, see Kathleen E. Corley, *Private Women, Public Meals: Social Conflict in the Synoptic Tradition* (Peabody: Hendrickson, 1993); for an analysis of the structuring of patriarchy, see Schüssler Fiorenza, *But She Said*, 114-18.

⁷⁰ Recent resources in this regard include Ross Shepard Kraemer's edited texts, *Maenads, Martyrs, Matrons, Monastics: A Sourcebook on Women's Religions in the Greco-Roman World* (Philadelphia: Fortress, 1988) and *Her Share of the Blessings: Women's Religions among Pagans, Jews, and Christians in the Greco-Roman World*

(New York: Oxford University Press, 1992); Corley, *Private Women*; Amy-Jill Levine, ed., *"Women Like This": New Perspectives on Jewish Women in the Greco-Roman World*, Early Judaism and Its Literature 1 (Atlanta: Scholars Press, 1991).

[71] Louis Montrose, "New Historicisms," in *Redrawing the Boundaries: The Transformation of English and American Literary Studies*, ed. Stephen Greenblatt and Giles Gunn (New York: Modern Language Association of America, 1992), 404.

[72] Paul Ricoeur, *Interpretation Theory: Discourse and the Surplus of Meaning* (Fort Worth: Texas Christian University Press, 1976). See also Schneiders, *The Revelatory Text*, 157-79.

[73] See especially Schüssler Fiorenza, *But She Said*.

[74] Schüssler Fiorenza, *But She Said*, 150-52, 157-58.

[75] Schneiders, *The Revelatory Text*, 167, suggests that "the ultimate objective of reading is enhanced subjectivity, an experience that belongs finally . . . to the sphere of spirituality." Schüssler Fiorenza, *But She Said*, 157, would ground a "logic of democracy" in "a spirituality of vision and imagination," and we could add that in the dialogical process of interpretation, new feminist readings can also function to be creative of such vision and imagination.

[76] Annette Kolodny, "Dancing through the Minefield: Some Observations on the Theory, Practice, and Politics of a Feminist Literary Criticism," *Feminist Studies* 6 (1980): 1-25, used the image of "dancing through the minefield" seventeen years ago to characterize doing feminist literary criticism within a mainstream discipline. Negotiating a feminist reading of Jesus that is focused primarily on the gospel text but is in the context of contemporary Christian faith and theology seems well characterized by that same metaphor today.

## 3 "FROM GALILEE AND THE DECAPOLIS"— A CONTEXT FOR READING

[1] Bakhtin, *Dialogic Imagination*, 253.

[2] As indicated earlier, it is an assumption of this work that the Matthean audience was primarily an oral/aural community and that the majority would have heard the gospel story rather than read it.

[3] Anthony J. Saldarini, *Matthew's Christian-Jewish Community* (Chicago: University of Chicago Press, 1994).

[4] Schüssler Fiorenza, *But She Said*, 81-88.

[5] Ibid., 84. See also, Schüssler Fiorenza, *In Memory of Her*, 68-95; and Bernadette J. Brooten, "Early Christian Women and Their Cultural Context: Issues on Method in Historical Reconstruction," in *Feminist Perspectives on Biblical Scholarship*, ed. Adela Yarbro Collins (Chico: Scholars Press, 1985), 65-91.

[6] Michael Crosby, *House of Disciples: Church, Economics, and Justice in Matthew* (Maryknoll, N.Y.: Orbis Books, 1988), 47-48, notes tensions around ethnic issues, economic issues, and leadership or authority.

[7] Bakhtin, *Dialogic Imagination*, 12.

[8] Ibid., 63.

[9] Dale M. Bauer and S. Jaret McKinstry, eds., *Feminism, Bakhtin, and the Dialogic* (Albany: State University of New York Press, 1991).

[10] Dale M. Bauer and S. Jaret McKinstry, "Introduction," in ibid., 3.

[11] Jay Clayton and Eric Rothstein, "Figures in the Corpus: Theories of Influence and Intertextuality," in *Influence and Intertextuality in Literary History*, ed. Jay Clayton and Eric Rothstein (Madison: University of Wisconsin Press, 1991), 27.

[12] Ibid.

[13] Michel Foucault, *The History of Sexuality*, Vol. 1: *Introduction*, trans. Robert Hurley (New York: Vintage, 1978), 95. Marianne Sawicki nuances the Foucauldian perspective, noting that "while negotiation for power can be an aspect of gender, gender systems can express many other kinds of quests as well." See Marianne Sawicki, "Spatial Management of Gender and Labor in Greco-Roman Galilee," 13, in *Archaeology and the World of Galilee: Texts and Contexts in the Roman and Byzantine Periods*, ed. Douglas R. Edwards and Thomas McCollough, forthcoming. This material was available to me only in draft form at the time of this publication.

[14] Hilde Lindemann Nelson, "Resistance and Insubordination," *Hypatia* 10.2 (1995): 23-40, provides a contemporary example of narratives of resistance while also undertaking a theoretical analysis of these.

[15] Sawicki, "Spatial Management," 21.

[16] Wainwright, *Feminist Reading*, 342.

[17] Wayne A. Meeks, *The Moral World of the First Christians*, Library of Early Christianity (Philadelphia: Westminster, 1986), 137.

[18] Crosby, *House of Disciples*, 279, n.83.

[19] This study recognizes that in the first-century world birth, land, and wealth were significant status markers and that the differences between status groups was quite stark because of a lack of a "middle class." As a result, some scholars speak of the difficulty of using the term *class* in relation to antiquity. I use it here not in the contemporary sense but as a marker for first-century status. Sawicki, *Seeing the Lord*, 12, draws attention to the use of Gerhard E. Lenski's *Power and Privilege: A Theory of Social Stratification* by John Dominic Crossan (and, one could add, by other social scientific biblical critics) in relation to classes within agrarian societies.

[20] Text criticism, based on copies of the Matthean gospel from the third, fourth, and later centuries, reconstructs as far as is possible the original text of the gospel. See *Novum Testamentum Graece*, 27th edition, ed. Barbara and Kurt Aland, Johannes Karavidopoulos, Carlo M. Martini, and Bruce M. Metzger (Stuttgart: Deutsche Bibelgesellschaft, 1993).

[21] Werner Kelber's *The Oral and the Written Gospel: The Hermeneutics of Speaking and Writing in the Synoptic Tradition, Mark, Paul and Q* (Philadelphia: Fortress, 1983), was one of the first studies in this area. Joanna Dewey in a recent article, "Textuality in an Oral Culture: A Survey of the Pauline Traditions," *Semeia* 65 (1995): 37-65, notes the formation of the "Bible in Ancient and Modern Media Group" of the Society of Biblical Literature by Thomas Boomershine around the same time. See also P. J. J. Botha, "Mark's Story as Oral Traditional Literature: Rethinking the Transmission of Some Traditions about Jesus," *Hervormde Teologiese Studies* 47 (1991): 304-31.

[22] For an extensive treatment of this, see William V. Harris, *Ancient Literacy* (Cambridge: Harvard University Press, 1989). The situation is summarized by Joanna Dewey, "Textuality in an Oral Culture," 39-47; and idem, "From

Storytelling to Written Text: The Loss of Early Christian Women's Voices," *BTB* 26.2 (1996): 73-78.

[23] Alex Scobie, "Storytellers, Storytelling, and the Novel in Graeco-Roman Antiquity," *Rheinishes Museum für Philologie* 122 (1979): 229-59, notes the presence of religious storytellers in antiquity who were attached to temples or synagogues (and, we might add, emerging house-churches that shared a close relationship to synagogues). The content of their stories was more religious than that of the secular storytellers, whose purpose was to entertain the listeners.

[24] The most generally held opinion regarding the provenance of the Matthean gospel is Antioch on the Orontes in Syria—see the articles in *Social History of the Matthean Community: Cross-Disciplinary Approaches*, ed. David L. Balch (Minneapolis: Fortress, 1991); and most recently, David C. Sim, *Apocalyptic Eschatology in the Gospel of Matthew*, SNTSMS 88 (Cambridge: Cambridge University Press, 1996), 205. Recent studies, however, that highlight the close relationship with Formative or Rabbinic Judaism, propose either Galilee (J. Andrew Overman, *Matthew's Gospel and Formative Judaism: The Social World of the Matthean Community* [Minneapolis: Fortress, 1990]), or Syria generally (Saldarini, *Matthew's Community*, 11, 26). Since it is extremely difficult to locate the Matthean provenance with any certainty, Alan F. Segal's suggestion of an arc between Galilee and Syrian Antioch, "Matthew's Jewish Voice," in Balch, *Social History*, 29, seems particularly appropriate, allowing for movement as a result of the Roman War as well as the continued missionary activity of the community as Matthew 10 and 28:18-20 would seem to indicate. Textually, Galilee as context for Jesus' ministry is in fulfillment of the scriptures (Mt 4:12-16). It is the place of Jesus' ministry (4:23; 17:22); the narrator specifically notes when Jesus leaves Galilee (19:1); and it is from a mountain in Galilee that the final commissioning of the disciples takes place (28:16).

[25] I have argued elsewhere (see *Feminist Reading*, 244-45; and "A Voice from the Margin: Reading Matthew 15:21-28 in an Australian Feminist Key," in *Reading from This Place*, Vol 2: *Social Location and Biblical Interpretation in Global Perspective*, ed. Fernando F. Segovia and Mary Ann Tolbert [Minneapolis: Fortress, 1995], 150-53), the significance of the house-church context for the development of varieties of gospel traditions. Dewey, "From Storytelling to Written Text," points to the further variety of locations for Christian storytelling. The public square may well have been the primary location for hearing the Christian story for many of the poorer and marginalized of the community whose lives were lived predominantly in the public arena. This means that the genderized public/ private dichotomy proposed by male social scientists was status-bound and was also much more permeable than their theories allow. See Louise Lamphere, "The Domestic Sphere of Women and the Public World of Men: The Strengths and Limitations of an Anthropological Dichotomy," in *Gender in Cross-Cultural Perspective*, ed. Caroline B. Brettell and Carolyn F. Sargent (Englewood Cliffs, N.J.: Prentice Hall, 1993), 67-76.

[26] Dewey, "Textuality in an Oral Culture," 46, who relies on Gideon Sjoberg, *The Preindustrial City: Past and Present* (New York: Macmillan Free Press, 1960).

[27] Wainwright, *Feminist Reading*, 183-91.

[28] Crosby, *House of Disciples*, argues for a community of reception of the Matthean gospel that is urbanized and relatively secure financially in a way that is

plausible, but he also recognizes that the gospel's call for justice toward the poor is in response to substantial numbers who are economically poor. Rodney Stark, "Antioch as the Social Situation for Matthew's Gospel," in Balch, *Social History*, 189-210, leaves the reader in no doubt about the conditions of life of large numbers of the poor in Greco-Roman cities.

[29] Dewey, "Textuality in an Oral Culture," 42. Sawicki, "Spatial Management," 4, states a similar point but from another perspective: "This literature . . . is a literature produced in accommodation to colonization, often by the collaborating class, growing out of the fissures in society and seeking to patch them over."

[30] This may well account for Antoinette Clark Wire's reading of the Matthean context as that of a scribal community, "Gender Roles in a Scribal Community," in Balch, *Social History*, 87-121. While what she suggests may characterize authorship, it does not necessarily characterize reception, especially not the "primary intended audience," as Wire claims.

[31] Wainwright, *Feminist Reading*.

[32] Mary R. Lefkowitz and Maureen B. Fant, eds., *Women's Lives in Greece and Rome: A Source Book in Translation*, 2d ed. (Baltimore: Johns Hopkins University Press, 1992), §216, 167; §219-20, 168-69; §223-24, 169. Mary R. Lefkowitz, "Did Ancient Women Write Novels?" in Levine, *"Women Like This,"* 199-219; and Ross S. Kraemer, "Women's Authorship of Jewish and Christian Literature in the Greco-Roman Period," in Levine, *"Women Like This,"* 221-45. See also Cole, "Could Greek Women Read and Write?" In Matthew's gospel, however, no woman is specifically characterized as a householder, as are Lydia and Mary (Acts 16:11-15; 12:12) and Martha (Lk 10:38) in other early Christian texts; there is little indication of women's wealth or status by comparison with the women of independent means in Luke 8:1-3 or Phoebe as *diakonos* and *prostatis* (Rom 16:1-2). Satoko Yamaguchi, *Re-visioning Martha and Mary: A Feminist Critical Reading of a Text in the Fourth Gospel*, unpublished Doctor of Ministry thesis, Episcopal Divinity School, Cambridge, Massachusetts, 1996, points out, however, that women householders and indeed many Christian households may have been located in the poor dwellings around a central courtyard rather than in the households of the more wealthy (see especially 88-90).

[33] This does not eliminate women from participation in the traditioning process, as Wire suggests. The traditioning of both the Canaanite woman, especially her voicing of the community's significant titles for Jesus, as well as the anointing woman and her recognition of and meaning-making around Jesus' impending death could be signs of women's role in making and interpreting tradition, contrary to the claim of Wire, "Gender Roles," 115.

[34] Loveday Alexander, "The Living Voice: Scepticism towards the Written Word in Early Christian and in Graeco-Roman Texts," in *The Bible in Three Dimensions: Essays in Celebration of Forty Years of Biblical Studies in the University of Sheffield*, ed. David J. A. Clines, Stephen E. Fowl, and Stanley E. Porter, *JSOTSS* 87 (Sheffield: JSOT Press, 1990), 244-45.

[35] Dewey demonstrates this in relation to women's stories in "Jesus' Healings of Women: Conformity and Non-Conformity to Dominant Cultural Values as Clues for Historical Reconstruction," *BTB* 24.3 (1994): 122-31. Although a similar study has not been undertaken from the perspective of other marginalized groups, we can presume that the results would be similar.

[36] One catches glimpses of this in those scenes in which the crowds listen to Jesus' teaching (Mt 5:1; 7:28; 13:1-3), follow him (14:13), and are fed by him in multitudes (14:13-21; 15:32-39). Richard A. Horsley and John S. Hanson, *Bandits, Prophets, and Messiahs: Popular Movements at the Time of Jesus* (San Francisco: Harper, 1985), document the presence of popular messianic movements within Galilee (and perhaps even in surrounding areas), at least prior to the Roman War.

[37] That the gospel contains perspectives of the more wealthy and cultural elite as well as those experiencing economic hardship and even crisis seems a more plausible explanation than that of Wire, "Gender Roles," 115-18, who seems constrained to choose a dominant community of reception.

[38] F. Gerald Downing, *Cynics and Christian Origins* (Edinburgh: T. & T. Clark, 1992), 127, 145.

[39] Later analyses will reveal that the early chapters of Exodus function intertextually in the shaping of the second chapter of the infancy narrative and that Wisdom 2:10-24 may well have provided a pattern for the passion narrative.

[40] See especially, Saldarini, *Matthew's Community*, and Overman, *Matthew's Gospel and Formative Judaism*.

[41] Overman, *Matthew's Gospel and Formative Judaism*, 8-19, discusses the sectarian nature of Judaism in the period 165 B.C.E.–100 C.E. See also, Overman, *Church and Community in Crisis: The Gospel according to Matthew*, The New Testament in Context (Valley Forge, Penn.: Trinity Press International, 1996), 10, and his reference to "Matthean Judaism." For an overview of the variety, see the articles in Robert A. Kraft and George W. E. Nickelsburg, eds., *Early Judaism and Its Modern Interpreters* (Philadelphia: Fortress, 1986).

[42] Saldarini, *Matthew's Community*, 84-123. See his discussion of the distinction between group and community, 85-87.

[43] Saldarini, *Matthew's Community*, 112.

[44] Ibid., 90-100.

[45] Leo G. Perdue, "The Wisdom Sayings of Jesus," *Forum* 2 (1986): 3-35; and Gary Tuttle, "The Sermon on the Mount: Its Wisdom Affinities and Their Relation to Its Structure," *JETS* 20 (1977): 213-30.

[46] See the analysis by Celia Deutsch, *Hidden Wisdom and the Easy Yoke: Wisdom, Torah, and Discipleship in Matthew 11.25-30*, JSNTSS 18 (Sheffield: JSOT Press, 1987).

[47] Saldarini, *Matthew's Community*, 104.

[48] This returns us to Bakhtin's understanding that "the living utterance, having taken meaning and shape at a particular historical moment in a socially specific environment, cannot fail to brush up against thousands of living dialogic threads, woven by socio-ideological consciousness around the given object of an utterance; it cannot fail to become an active participant in social dialogue. After all, the utterance arises out of this dialogue as a continuation of it and as a rejoinder to it—it does not approach the object from the sidelines." See Bakhtin, *Dialogic Imagination*, 276.

[49] Saldarini, *Matthew's Community*, 86, 112-16, 199.

[50] Jana Sawicki, *Disciplining Foucault: Feminism, Power, and the Body*, Thinking Gender (New York: Routledge, 1991), 10.

[51] Saldarini, *Matthew's Community*, 110, recognizes the operation of such power, but while his social scientific model of deviance locates the power distribu-

tion across different communities within a first-century Jewish context, the theories of Bakhtin and Foucault enable us to examine the power dynamics and the presence of a variety of voices within the Matthean context.

[52] Overman, *Matthew's Gospel and Formative Judaism,* and *Church and Community.*

[53] Segal, "Matthew's Jewish Voice," 3-37.

[54] Overman, *Church and Community,* 10.

[55] Ibid., 19-26.

[56] Segal, "Matthew's Jewish Voice," 32, uses the term *Pharisaism* as distinct from *Judaism* to characterize the Matthean opponent.

[57] Ibid., 35.

[58] Amy-Jill Levine, *The Social and Ethnic Dimensions of Matthean Salvation History: "Go Nowhere among the Gentiles . . . " (Matt. 10.5b),* Studies in the Bible and Early Christianity 14 (Lewiston: Edwin Mellen, 1988).

[59] Ibid., 2, 4.

[60] This is summarized in her introduction, ibid., 2-11, but it is demonstrated throughout the subsequent analysis.

[61] Ibid., 11.

[62] See Sim, *Apocalyptic Eschatology,* 181-221, for his comprehensive account of the Matthean social setting.

[63] Following Sim's indication, ibid., 198, I will dialogue with his more extensive treatment of this topic in "The Gospel of Matthew and the Gentiles," *JSNT* 57 (1995): 19-48.

[64] Ibid., 23, n. 10. Sim affirms Levine's recognition that gentile characters are not included among the disciples but fails to take account of the rest of her chapter, which analyzes the centrality of the Great Commission (28:16-20) and the gentile mission in the post-resurrection period.

[65] Sim, "Matthew and the Gentiles," 25-30.

[66] Bruce J. Malina and Jerome H. Neyrey, *Calling Jesus Names: The Social Value of Labels in Matthew* (Sonoma: Polebridge Press, 1988); and Bruce J. Malina, *The New Testament World: Insights from Cultural Anthropology,* rev. ed. (Louisville: Westminster/John Knox, 1993), 97.

[67] Levine, *Social and Ethnic Dimensions,* 32-37.

[68] Ibid., 34. Levine draws attention to this point.

[69] Corley, *Private Women,* 89-93.

[70] Sim, "Matthew and the Gentiles," 30.

[71] Many others have put forward arguments that the Matthean author was a gentile Christian, and hence that the community of reception was gentile; see W. D. Davies and Dale C. Allison, *A Critical and Exegetical Commentary on the Gospel according to Saint Matthew,* vol. 1 (Edinburgh: T. & T. Clark, 1988), 10-11, for a convenient list. It does not seem necessary at this point in my analysis to establish further the presence of gentile Christians either as householders or within households in the Matthean community context.

[72] Bruce J. Malina, "'Religion' in the World of Paul," *BTB* 16 (1986): 95.

[73] Wainwright, *Feminist Reading;* and Dewey, "Jesus' Healings of Women."

[74] Stuart Love, "The Household: A Major Social Component for Gender Analysis in the Gospel of Matthew," *BTB* 23 (1993): 21-31; and idem, "The Place of Women in Public Settings in Matthew's Gospel: A Sociological Inquiry," *BTB* 24.2 (1994): 52-65.

[75] Of particular significance is Wire, "Gender Roles."

[76] Note in particular D'Angelo, "Re-membering Jesus," and also Sawicki, *Seeing the Lord*, 149-81, for other examples within early Christianity of women's prophetic and traditioning roles.

[77] Love, "The Household," 22, with the major reliance being on Gerhard and Jean Lenski, *Human Societies: An Introduction to Macrosociology*, 5th ed. (New York: McGraw-Hill, 1987). See also Wire, "Gender Roles," 88. She also introduces another model, that of "scribal community," 89-94.

[78] Love, "Place of Women in Public Settings."

[79] Love, "The Household," 29.

[80] Marianne Sawicki, "Making the Best of Jesus," unpublished paper presented at the 1992 Society of Biblical Literature Meeting, San Francisco, 7.

[81] Judith Shapiro, "Anthropology and the Study of Gender," *Soundings* 64 (1981): 458.

[82] Margaret W. Conkey and Joan M. Gero, "Tensions, Pluralities, and Engendering Archaeology: An Introduction to Women and Prehistory," in *Engendering Archaeology: Women and Prehistory,* ed. Joan M. Gero and Margaret W. Conkey (Oxford: Blackwell, 1991), 9, 14. See also Alison Wylie, "Gender Theory and the Archaeological Record: Why Is There No Archaeology of Gender?" in Gero and Conkey, *Engendering Archaeology,* 36, who states that "it is a fundamental tenet of most feminist theorizing that gender . . . is a highly variable *social* construct which incorporates irreducibly symbolic and ideational components."

[83] Ross Kraemer, "Non-Literary Evidence for Jewish Women in Rome and Greece," in *Rescuing Creusa: New Methodological Approaches to Women in Antiquity,* ed. Marilyn Skinner (Lubbock: Texas Tech., 1987), 85-101; and idem, "Hellenistic Jewish Women: The Epigraphical Evidence," in *SBLSP* 25, ed. K. H. Richards (Atlanta: Scholars, 1986), 183-200, looks specifically at women in Asia Minor and Rome. Sarah B. Pomeroy's research is predominantly of women in Egypt; see, by way of example, *Women in Hellenistic Egypt from Alexander to Cleopatra* (New York: Schocken Books, 1984). Tal Ilan, *Jewish Women in Greco-Roman Palestine,* Texte und Studien zum Antiken Judentum 44 (Tübingen: Mohr, 1995), focuses very specifically on women in Palestine. See also the Babatha archives of the early second century, which point to the legal and socio-economic independence of a woman in southern Palestine—*The Documents from the Bar Kokhba Period in the Cave of Letters*, "Greek Papyri," ed. Naphtali Lewis, and "Aramaic and Nabatean Signatures and Subscriptions," ed. Jigael Yadin and Jonas C. Greenfield (Jerusalem: Israel Exploration Society, 1989); Naphtali Lewis, Ranon Katzoff, and Jonas C. Greenfield, "Papyrus Yadin 18," *IEJ* 37 (1987): 229-50; and Mordechai A. Friedman, "Babatha's *Ketubba*: Some Preliminary Observations," *IEJ* 46 (1996): 55-76.

[84] Luise Schottroff, *Lydia's Impatient Sisters: A Feminist Social History of Early Christianity*, trans. Barbara and Martin Rumscheidt (Louisville: Westminster/ John Knox, 1995), read in conjunction with Richard A. Horsley, *Galilee: History, Politics, and People* (Valley Forge, Penn.: Trinity Press International, 1995), points to the situation of the majority of women, who were poor.

[85] Ilan, *Women;* Bernadette J. Brooten, *Women Leaders in the Ancient Synagogue: Inscriptional Evidence and Background Issues*, Brown Judaic Studies 36 (Chico: Scholars Press, 1982); Kraemer's source book, *Maenads,* and her analysis, *Her Share of the Blessings.*

⁸⁶ Feminist critiques of this division abound. See, by way of example, Lamphere, "The Domestic Sphere," 69-76; and Cynthia Nelson, "Public and Private Politics: Women in the Middle Eastern World," in Brettel and Sargent, *Gender in Cross-Cultural Perspective*, 94-106.

⁸⁷ Contrary to both Love, "The Household," 26 (who considers the last woman from the point of view of the social deference given to Zebedee by way of his name); and Wire, "Gender Roles," 103 (who sees her "embedded in male relatives"), it would have to be argued that the narrative is little concerned with Zebedee. The woman reconstructs gender in that she addresses a significant male in the public arena and she is among the faithful women at the foot of the cross when her sons have fled (27:55-56; 26:56).

⁸⁸ Love, "The Household," 23. See Sarah B. Pomeroy, *Goddesses, Whores, Wives, and Slaves: Women in Classical Antiquity* (New York: Schocken Books, 1975), 199-202, for a more faithful representation of poor women's lives; and Schottroff, *Lydia's Impatient Sisters*, 93-97.

⁸⁹ Sawicki, *Seeing the Lord*, 149-81, is an excellent example, although the context she suggests is upper-class Hellenistic women in Jerusalem.

⁹⁰ Jill Dubish, "Introduction," in her edited volume, *Gender and Power in Rural Greece* (Princeton: Princeton University Press, 1986), 12; and Nelson, "Public and Private Politics," 98.

⁹¹ Love, "The Household," 21.

⁹² Sawicki, *Disciplining Foucault*, 21.

⁹³ Ibid., 23. Sawicki notes that resistance will be "carried out in local struggles against the many forms of power exercised at the everyday level of social relations." A more sinister possibility, perhaps a long-term outcome rather than local strategy, is that women's storytelling was coopted at the scribal stage for the purposes of the more patriarchal final narrative. There is a tendency in Wire's analysis that the use of the category of role and the blurring of distinctions between the community of writing and the communities of reception ("Gender Roles," 102-8) does not allow sufficiently for such "local struggles," which may provide an equally valid explanation of her data.

⁹⁴ Sawicki, *Disciplining Foucault*, 26.

## 4   OF RACHEL'S LINEAGE—
## ENDANGERED CHILD/LIBERATED LIBERATOR

¹ Overman, *Church and Community*, 33, draws attention to the association of gentile sympathizers with the synagogue within the Greco-Roman world, warning that the division Jews and gentiles belongs more to scholarly categories than to the experience of first-century citizens of the Empire. Frederick W. Danker, "God with Us: Hellenistic Christological Perspectives in Matthew," *CurTM* 19 (1992): 433-39, explores the impact of aspects of the gospel in a Greco-Roman matrix outside Judaism.

² Phyllis Bird, "'Male and Female He Created Them': Gen 1:27b in the Context of the Priestly Account of Creation," *HTR* 74 (1981): 129-59, raises a question in relation to Genesis 1:27, as to the understanding of the reference "male and female" by the Priestly Writer. One could raise a similar question in relation to the first-century Jewish reader of the Matthean gospel. For the contemporary

reader, however, it is evocative of difference—male and female subjectivity in humanity, and male and female imaging of divinity. See Elaine Wainwright, "What's in a Name? The Word Which Binds/The Word Which Frees," in Confoy, et al., *Freedom and Entrapment*, 100-120.

³ Peter Miscall, "Isaiah: New Heavens, New Earth, New Book," in Fewell, *Reading between Texts*, 45. In his conclusion, Miscall understands Isaiah to be seeking to close off a series of "creations" by positing this new book "precluding further figuration." One must ask whether the Matthean implied author reads/ writes in a similar way. Readers will, however, choose between textual potentialities.

⁴ Nelson, "Resistance and Insubordination," 23. This notion is further amplified by the image used by Fulkerson, *Changing the Subject*, 151-54, of the "graf(ph)t" that directs or stimulates the flow of sap or meaning in a new direction.

⁵ Overman, *Church and Community*, 31; and George MacRae, "Messiah and Gospel," in *Judaisms and Their Messiahs at the Turn of the Christian Era*, ed. Jacob Neusner, William S. Green, and Ernest Frerichs (Cambridge: Cambridge University Press, 1987), 179. Fred W. Burnett, "Characterization and Christology in Matthew: Jesus in the Gospel of Matthew," in *SBLSP* 28, ed. David J. Lull (Atlanta: Scholars Press, 1989), 591, considers it a title in apposition to the name Jesus.

⁶ Horsley and Hanson, *Bandits, Prophets, Messiahs*, 89-90. In relation to the third aspect, see Neusner, et al., *Judaisms and Their Messiahs*.

⁷ See Horsley and Hanson, *Bandits, Prophets, Messiahs*, 94-96.

⁸ Levine, *Social and Ethnic Dimensions*, 102, 89-106. It should also be noted here that her reading of the ethnic inclusiveness of the genealogy would mean that ethnicity was constructed inclusively along the social but not necessarily the temporal axis of the gospel.

⁹ For an extensive discussion of the various texts that intersect in the genealogy, see Raymond E. Brown, *The Birth of the Messiah: A Commentary on the Infancy Narratives in the Gospels of Matthew and Luke*, new updated ed. (New York: Doubleday, 1993), 74-84, and Davies and Allison, *Matthew*, 1:161-67.

¹⁰ Bruce J. Malina and Richard L. Rohrbaugh, *Social Science Commentary on the Synoptic Gospels* (Minneapolis: Fortress, 1992), 24-25.

¹¹ Lucretia B. Yaghjian, *How Shall We Read? A Preface to Matthew's Protocols of Reading*, unpublished manuscript, 1994, 5.

¹² Malina and Rohrbaugh, *Social Science Commentary*, 24-25. See also Marshall D. Johnson, *The Purpose of the Biblical Genealogies with Special Reference to the Setting of the Genealogies of Jesus* (Cambridge: Cambridge University Press, 1969).

¹³ Overman, *Church and Community*, 31.

¹⁴ David P. Moessner, "And Once Again, What Sort of 'Essence'?: A Response to Charles Talbert," *Semeia* 43 (1988): 76, asks whether the overriding question for the reader is "What sort of person is this?" or "Who is this person in light of God's dealings with Israel?"

¹⁵ Danker, "God with Us," 434, notes that Roman readers "would have been impressed by Matthew's tracing of Jesus' ancestry to Abraham," which would have caused them to interpret Jesus as "bigger than life."

¹⁶ For a comprehensive study of the intertextual possibilities of the titles Jesus Christ, son of David, son of Abraham, see Davies and Allison, *Matthew*, 1:149-60.

[17] Readers also would have noted the text-type or genre transgression that links the "book of the genealogy" not to the ancestor Abraham but to the final progeny, Jesus. Jesus *Christos* subverts expected patterns, at least textually, at this point in the opening of the narrative.

[18] In relation to such erasure, note the repeated reference to the daughters as well as sons in the genealogical narrative of Genesis 5:1-32 already pointed out above, and the stories of the matriarchs, Sarah, Rebecca, Rachel, and Leah, in subsequent chapters of Genesis. See J. Cheryl Exum, "The Mothers of Israel: The Patriarchal Narratives from a Feminist Perspective," *Bible Review* 2.1 (1986): 60-67, and Ilona N. Rashkow, "Daughters and Fathers in Genesis . . . Or, What Is Wrong with This Picture?" in *A Feminist Companion to Exodus to Deuteronomy*, ed. Athalya Brenner (Sheffield: Sheffield Academic Press, 1994), 22-36, which deal respectively with inclusion and erasure.

[19] The literature is extensive. See Wainwright, *Feminist Reading*, 63-67, for a summary of representative samples.

[20] Brown, *Birth*, 73-74, offers this reading as the most widely held among scholars today, but in his work, it is offered in supposedly value-neutral theological terms and not analyzed in relation to the support such theology proffers for the patriarchal structure of the narrative, and hence its rhetorical effect in terms of construction of readers.

[21] For a more comprehensive analysis of these women's stories and their inclusion into the Matthean text, see Wainwright, *Feminist Reading*, 60-69, 160-70. Both this reading and that of Jane Schaberg, *The Illegitimacy of Jesus: A Feminist Theological Interpretation of the Infancy Narratives* (San Francisco: Harper & Row, 1987), 33, recognize that the stories of each of these women are brought back under patriarchal control in their respective narratives.

[22] Note the title of Schüssler Fiorenza's book, *Jesus: Miriam's Child*.

[23] Ebert, *Patriarchy, Ideology, Subjectivity*, 66, points out that ideology is not a given but is continually being secured and reproduced by narratives, but that alternatively those same narratives can be the arena of ideological contradiction and social conflicts.

[24] David E. Aune, *The New Testament in Its Literary Environment*, Library of Early Christianity (Philadelphia: Westminster, 1987), 37-42.

[25] Philip L. Shuler, *A Genre for the Gospels: The Biographical Character of Matthew* (Philadelphia: Fortress, 1982), 13, recognizes that life-stories were told in less formal ways than classical literary biographies.

[26] See the interpretation given by Brian N. Nolan, *The Royal Son of God: The Christology of Matthew 1-2 in the Setting of the Gospel*, OBO 23 (Göttingen: Vandenhoeck & Ruprecht, 1979), 13.

[27] See Shuler, *A Genre*, 6-12, for a discussion of "folk" literature and its "small and often incoherently joined literary units." Mary Ann Tolbert, "The Gospel in Greco-Roman Culture," in *The Book and the Text: The Bible and Literary Theory*, ed. Regina M. Schwartz (Oxford: Blackwell, 1990), 267, calls for a more serious study of "popular culture"; and Alan Dundes, "The Hero Pattern and the Life of Jesus," in *In Quest of the Hero*, Otto Rank, Lord Raglan, and Alan Dundes (Princeton: Princeton University Press, 1990), 179-223, summarizes elements of the patterns in hero narratives.

[28] Talbert, *What Is a Gospel?*, 89-108, discusses the way in which stories of founders of movements, schools, and cities became the myth of origin for that

community, and he suggests that the gospels functioned in a similar way. Sandra A. Zagarell, "Narrative of Community: The Identification of a Genre," in *Revising the Word and the World: Essays in Feminist Literary Criticism*, ed. VèVè A. Clark, Ruth-Ellen B. Joeres, and Madelon Sprengnether (Chicago: University of Chicago Press, 1993), 249-78, identifies a particular genre that she calls "narrative of community," a terminology that captures elements of a genre possibility for the gospel narrative shifting the focus from the hero to the life of the community.

[29] It is not possible to develop this link in any detail here, but it is being suggested that the Jesus story can be and must be read today in dialogue with those who seek a new story in light of our ecological crisis—see Thomas Berry, *The Dream of the Earth* (San Francisco: Sierra Club Books, 1988); Sallie McFague, *Models of God: Theology for an Ecological, Nuclear Age* (Philadelphia: Fortress, 1987); idem, *The Body of God: An Ecological Theology* (Minneapolis: Fortress, 1993); and Carol J. Adams, ed., *Ecofeminism and the Sacred* (New York: Continuum, 1993), by way of example. The most recent and explicit example in relation to this study is Denis Edwards, *Jesus the Wisdom of God: An Ecological Theology* (Maryknoll, N.Y.: Orbis Books, 1995).

[30] This is the first example in Matthew's gospel of the use of the ancient rhetorical device of *sygkrisis*, or comparison, to characterize Jesus. See Graham N. Stanton, *A Gospel for a New People: Studies in Matthew* (Edinburgh: T. & T. Clark, 1992), 77-80.

[31] This distinction between instability and tension is developed by Phelan, *Reading People, Reading Plots*, 15: "The first (instabilities) are those occurring within the story, instabilities between characters, created by situations, and complicated and resolved through actions. The second are those created by the discourse, instabilities—of values, belief, opinion, knowledge, expectation—between authors and/or narrators, on the one hand, and the authorial audience on the other."

[32] In this regard, see Wainwright, *Feminist Reading*, 70-71, 172; and Schaberg, *Illegitimacy*, 42-62, for an extensive treatment of this perspective of the narrative.

[33] See, for example, W. D. Davies, "The Jewish Sources of Matthew's Messianism," in *The Messiah: Developments in Earliest Judaism and Christianity*, The First Princeton Symposium on Judaism and Christian Origins, ed. James H. Charlesworth (Minneapolis: Fortress, 1992), 494-95; and J. Nolland, "No Son-of-God Christology in Matthew 1:18-25," *JSNT* 62 (1996): 3-12.

[34] In the *Biblical Antiquities* of Pseudo-Philo, composed in Palestine toward the end of the first century C.E., Miriam, the sister of Moses, is visited by a divine messenger in a dream and is told regarding the child born of her parents: "By him will I do signs, and I will save my people" (LAB 9.10). See *The Biblical Antiquities of Philo*, trans. M. R. James (New York: KTAV, 1971) or *Pseudo-Philon—Les Antiquités Bibliques*, critical text and introduction by Daniel J. Harrington and translation by Jacques Cazeaux, Source Chrétiennes (Paris: Les Editions du Cerf, 1976). It is important to note that in this account the message comes through the female, Miriam, whereas in the Matthean account it is through the male, Joseph. Note Betty Halpern-Amaru's study, "Portraits of Women in Pseudo-Philo's *Biblical Antiquities*," in Levine, *"Women Like This,"* 83-106, in which she demonstrates that women are either instruments or agents of God in this text. Such intertextuality creates another fissure in the unified narrative.

[35] It is this reference that Jane Schaberg thinks may have alerted some readers to the intertextual links with Deuteronomy 22:23-27, laws in response to the seduction or rape of a young woman or virgin, the basis for her thesis that this narrative developed in response to claims of Jesus' illegitimacy.

[36] Danker, "God with Us," 435, notes that Greco-Romans would also have been impressed by the prophecies surrounding Jesus' birth, a sign of greatness in the future.

[37] For parallels with Moses, see, in particular, Dale C. Allison, *The New Moses: A Matthean Typology* (Minneapolis: Fortress, 1993), 144-51. He assumes, however, literary parallels rather than a popular prophetic tradition.

[38] For a lengthy discussion of the different types of prophecy in first-century Palestine and their links with earlier prophecy in Israel, see Horsley and Hanson, *Bandits, Prophets, Messiahs*, 135-89.

[39] John Dominic Crossan, *Jesus: A Revolutionary Biography* (San Francisco: Harper, 1994), 10-15, outlines the parallels in detail, as does Allison, *New Moses*, 140-65.

[40] See Eileen Schuller, "Women of the Exodus in Biblical Retellings of the Second Temple Period," in *Gender and Difference in Ancient Israel*, ed. Peggy L. Day (Minneapolis: Fortress, 1989), 178-94, for an analysis of the erasure of women in these retellings in a way similar to what we will see in the Matthean infancy narrative.

[41] Miriam and Jocabed are not named here in the narrative, being identified simply as the sister and the mother of the child, but the reader discovers their names later, in Exodus 6:20.

[42] For a study of the significance of their roles see J. Cheryl Exum, "'You Shall Let Every Daughter Live': A Study of Exodus 1:8-2:10," *Semeia* 28 (1983): 63-82; and Phyllis Trible, "Bringing Miriam out of the Shadows," *Bible Review* 5.1 (1989): 14-25, 34.

[43] J. Cheryl Exum, "Second Thoughts about Secondary Characters: Women in Exodus 1.8–2.10," in *A Feminist Companion to Exodus to Deuteronomy*, ed. Athalya Brenner (Sheffield: Sheffield Academic Press, 1994), 75-87.

[44] For further readings of Matthean geography in Matthew 2 as this affects the interpretation of Jesus, see Levine, *Social and Ethnic Dimensions*, 99-101.

[45] See Horsley and Hanson, *Bandits, Prophets, Messiahs*, 110-17, for a discussion of the use of the title king for leaders of popular resistance movements toward the end of Herodian rule. See Luz, *A Commentary*, 134-35, for a discussion of the East as the symbolic origin of religious wisdom. Luz also points out that the word *Ioudaios* is used only on the lips of gentiles in Matthew (27:11, 29, 37), except in 28:15, when it is used by the narrator.

[46] For a discussion of the wisdom trajectory as "reflective mythology," see Elisabeth Schüssler Fiorenza, "Wisdom Mythology and the Christological Hymns of the New Testament," in *Aspects of Wisdom in Judaism and Early Christianity*, ed. Robert L. Wilken (Notre Dame, Ind.: University of Notre Dame Press, 1975), 26-33.

[47] Silvia Schroer, "Weise Frauen und Ratgeberinnen in Israel—Vorbilder der personifizierten Chokmah," in *Auf den Spuren der Weisheit: Sophia—Wegweiserin für ein neues Gottesbild*, ed. Verena Wodtke (Freiburg: Herder, 1991), 9-23; and Claudia V. Camp, *Wisdom and the Feminine in the Book of Proverbs*, Bible and Literature Series 11 (Sheffield: Almond Press, 1985).

[48] For a discussion of both the problems and potentialities of such a reading from a feminist perspective, see Schüssler Fiorenza, *Jesus*, 155-62.

[49] Danker, "God with Us," 435.

[50] Richard A. Horsley, *The Liberation of Christmas: The Infancy Narratives in Social Context* (New York: Crossroad, 1989), 39-60; and Overman, *Church and Community*, 43-45.

[51] Horsley, *Liberation of Christmas*, 59.

[52] Crosby, *House of Disciples*, 38-48.

[53] Contemporary readers may interpret them as maternal or paternal as a result of shifting socio-cultural role definitions within the human community and of more inclusive imaging of divinity.

[54] Overman, *Church and Community*, 49-51.

[55] Phyllis Trible, *God and the Rhetoric of Sexuality*, Overtures to Biblical Theology (Philadelphia: Fortress, 1978), 45.

[56] This text is evocative of many meanings, as has been indicated by its various translations (*The New American Bible* gives at least three in a footnote to the verse). A number of scholars consider the text "secondary" or a later addition, but, with Trible, I affirm that it belongs to the final form of the poem in the MT (Trible, *God and the Rhetoric*, 59, n. 39). The LXX has paraphrased the text. Gleason L. Archer and G. C. Chirichigno, *Old Testament Quotations in the New Testament: A Complete Survey* (Chicago: Moody Press, 1983), 137, suggest that the Matthean text "is closer (especially in word order) to the MT than the LXX." William L. Holladay, *Jeremiah 2: A Commentary on the Book of the Prophet Jeremiah Chapters 26-52*, Hermeneia (Minneapolis: Fortress, 1989), 195, proposes both a sexual and a military sense to the use of the verb translated as "surround" or "encircle, enfold."

[57] For a more extended discussion see Trible, *God and the Rhetoric*, 49 and 59, n. 44; and Mieke Bal, *Death and Dissymmetry: The Politics of Coherence in the Book of Judges* (Chicago: University of Chicago Press, 1988), who demonstrates the centrality of the image of the *gibbor [geber]* or warrior within the symbolic world of the book of Judges.

## 5   WISDOM IS JUSTIFIED—
### DOING HER DEEDS AND BEARING HER YOKE

[1] D'Angelo, "Re-membering Jesus," 209, where she brings to a climax the previous developments of her essay with this claim: "The gospels give us reason to see the companions of Jesus as prophets with him, to see the movement rather than the person of Jesus as the locus of the spirit."

[2] Ulrich Luz, "The Disciples in the Gospel according to Matthew," in *Interpretation of Matthew*, ed. Graham Stanton, Issues in Religion and Theology 3 (Philadelphia: Fortress, 1983), 110-14, says of the character group of disciples that they are "transparent for the present situation."

[3] Elisabeth Schüssler Fiorenza, "The Twelve," in *Women Priests: A Catholic Commentary on the Vatican Declaration*, ed. Leonard and Arlene Swidler (New York: Paulist, 1977), 117. See also Wainwright, *Feminist Reading*, 331-36, for a more comprehensive treatment of the development of the tradition.

[4] Fred W. Burnett, "*Paliggenesia* in Matt. 19:28: A Window on the Matthean Community?" *JSNT* 17 (1983): 64-65.

⁵ Shuler, *A Genre*, 99, points to the thematically organized materials as characteristic of the "bios" form into which he sees the traditions of Jesus being organized.

⁶ M. Jack Suggs, *Wisdom, Christology, and Law in Matthew's Gospel* (Cambridge: Harvard University Press, 1970), 37, suggests that "the deeds of Jesus" would have been the more expected expression.

⁷ See Davies and Allison, *Matthew*, 1:312-14, for a comprehensive discussion of possible meanings and intertextualities.

⁸ Overman, *Church and Community*, 162-65.

⁹ W. D. Davies and Dale C. Allison, *A Critical and Exegetical Commentary on the Gospel according to Saint Matthew*, vol. 2 (Edinburgh: T. & T. Clark, 1991), 242; John P. Meier, *A Marginal Jew: Rethinking the Historical Jesus*, Vol. 2: *Mentor, Message and Miracles*, Anchor Bible Reference Library (New York: Doubleday, 1994), 134; and Sharon H. Ringe, *Jesus, Liberation, and the Biblical Jubilee*, Overtures to Biblical Theology (Philadelphia: Fortress, 1989), 45.

¹⁰ Ringe, *Jesus, Liberation, and the Biblical Jubilee*, 44.

¹¹ Crosby, *House of Disciples*, 210.

¹² Schüssler Fiorenza, *But She Said*, 150-51, 157-58, discusses the difference between a "logic of identity," which seeks a unified center, and the "logic of democracy," which is engaged toward a vision of democracy and hence needs to be open to change and movement.

¹³ Crosby, *House of Disciples*. Crosby's entire book explores this theme.

¹⁴ Stephenson Humphries-Brooks, "Indicators of Social Organization and Status in Matthew's Gospel," in *SBLSP* 30, ed. Eugene H. Lovering (Atlanta: Scholars, 1991), 31-49.

¹⁵ Patricia Cox, *Biography in Late Antiquity: A Quest for the Holy Man* (Berkeley and Los Angeles: University of California Press, 1983), 17-44.

¹⁶ Ibid., 21.

¹⁷ Ibid., 34, 44.

¹⁸ Gerhart, *Genre Choices, Gender Questions*, 187.

¹⁹ Cox, *Biography*, 38.

²⁰ Meier, *Marginal Jew*, 2:135.

²¹ John Meier entitles his multivolume work on the historical Jesus *A Marginal Jew*.

²² David McCracken, "Character in the Boundary," *Semeia* 63 (1993): 39-40.

²³ Nelson, "Resistance and Insubordination," 37, notes that "resistance and insubordination are of course an ongoing process, as will be the storytelling that fuels it, but if a counter-story is to be effective, its telling will have to achieve a temporary stopping-point that permits the community to act." This stopping-point, however, must be "momentary," and this study stands as a challenge to the experience within the Christian *poiesis* of Jesus that has become fixed and stationary, halting the ongoing process.

²⁴ Wendy J. Cotter, "Children Sitting in the Agora: Q (Luke) 7:31-35," *Forum* 5.2 (1989): 78.

²⁵ Darr, *On Character Building*, 66.

²⁶ Schüssler Fiorenza, *Jesus*, 142.

²⁷ Malina and Neyrey, *Calling Jesus Names*, for a more extensive study of labeling, deviance, and prominence-making in the Matthean context.

[28] Gerd Theissen, "Jünger als Gewalttäter (Mt 11,12f.; Lk 16,16): Der Stürmerspruch als Selbststigmatisierung einer Minorität," *ST* 49 (1995): 183-200.

[29] Rod Doyle, "Matthew 11:12—A Challenge to the Evangelist's Community," *Colloquium* 18 (1985): 26.

[30] Ibid., 26-27.

[31] These two possible meanings generally characterize the range of scholarly opinion in relation to these verses.

[32] Meier, *Marginal Jew*, 2:146.

[33] Cotter, "Children Sitting," 67-68. See also idem, "The Parable of the Children in the Market-Place, Q (Lk) 7:31-35: An Examination of the Parable's Image and Significance," *NovT* 29 (1987): 289-304.

[34] Cotter, "Children Sitting," 71-74, demonstrates that while the ascetic lifestyle may have been considered deviant within a Hellenistic audience, it would not have been so among those of Jewish heritage and traditions.

[35] This is so regardless of whether one considers such actions as belonging to the actual Jesus of Galilee or whether it was a labeling device as suggested by Corley, *Private Women*, 130-33, 152-54.

[36] Luz, "The Son of Man," 6, points out—rightly, I think—that "'Son of Man' is not a title."

[37] For an extensive discussion of this interpretation of the phrase within recent scholarship, see Delbert Burkett, "The Nontitular Son of Man: A History and Critique," *NTS* 40 (1994): 504-21.

[38] Meier, *Marginal Jew*, 2:152.

[39] See Jack Dean Kingsbury, "The Title 'Son of Man' in Matthew's Gospel," *CBQ* 37 (1975): 196-202, in which he considers this title as public by comparison with "Son of God" as a confessional title. He considers the saying "titular" and his claim to its "public" nature seems to miss its subtlety within its narrative context. See Luz, "The Son of Man," 12, n. 21, for a critique similar to mine.

[40] Cotter, "The Parable," 303.

[41] This is the imagery coined by Elisabeth Schüssler Fiorenza, *In Memory of Her*, 130-40.

[42] Schüssler Fiorenza, *Jesus*, 139-43; and Martin Hengel, "Jesus as Messianic Teacher of Wisdom and the Beginnings of Christology," in Martin Hengel, *Studies in Early Christology* (Edinburgh: T. & T. Clark, 1995), 73-117.

[43] The literature on this topic is extensive. See in particular Claudia V. Camp, "Woman Wisdom as Root Metaphor: A Theological Consideration," in *The Listening Heart: Essays in Wisdom and the Psalms in Honor of Roland E. Murphy*, ed. Kenneth G. Hoglund, et al., *JSOTSS* 58 (Sheffield: JSOT Press, 1987), 45-76; Celia Deutsch, "Wisdom in Matthew: Transformation of a Symbol," *NovT* 32 (1990): 17-31; and Bernhard Lang, *Wisdom and the Book of Proverbs: A Hebrew Goddess Redefined* (New York: Pilgrim Press, 1986).

[44] The scholars who make this identification are quite numerous. See, in particular, Deutsch, "Wisdom in Matthew," 46-47; Suggs, *Wisdom*, 55; and Schüssler Fiorenza, *Jesus*, 151-52, to name but a few. A counter opinion is expressed by Marshall D. Johnson, "Reflections on a Wisdom Approach to Matthew's Christology," *JBL* 36 (1974): 44-64, who fails to recognize that readers steeped in the sapiential traditions could have heard the gospel traditions in a way that differed greatly from what he presents in relation to a scribal author from a different trajectory within Israel's traditions.

[45] For this aspect, which cannot be further developed here, see Edwards, *Jesus the Wisdom of God*.

[46] Luise Schottroff, "Itinerant Prophetesses: A Feminist Analysis of the Sayings Source Q," in *Occasional Papers of the Institute for Antiquity and Christianity* 21 (Claremont, 1991), 1-16.

[47] Camp, *Wisdom and the Feminine*, places the social location of Proverbs 1–9 in the more egalitarian period of reconstruction subsequent to the Babylonian exile, a time in which women participated with men in the rebuilding of the nation and the shaping of its traditions. It would seem that wisdom traditions, even when they move into the court or the school, still retain their links with folk tradition.

[48] Silvia Schroer, "Jesus Sophia: Erträge der feministischen Forschung zu einer frühchristlichen Deutung der Praxis und des Schicksals Jesu von Nazaret," in Strahm and Strobel, *Vom Verlangen nach Heilwerden*, 121-22.

[49] Overman, *Church and Community*, 171.

[50] The most extensive is Deutsch, *Hidden Wisdom*.

[51] Mary Rose D'Angelo, "*Abba* and 'Father': Imperial Theology and the Jesus Traditions," *JBL* 111 (1992): 611-30; and Eileen Schuller, "4Q372 1: A Text about Joseph," *RevQ* 14 (1990): 343-76; and idem, "The Psalm of 4Q372 1 within the Context of Second Temple Prayer," *CBQ* 54 (1992): 67-79.

[52] D'Angelo, "*Abba*," 621.

[53] Ibid., 623-26; see Schüssler Fiorenza, *But She Said*, 114-18, for a discussion of Greek and Roman kyriarchal structures.

[54] Wainwright, *Feminist Reading*, whose overall perspective makes this point. D'Angelo, "*Abba*," 629, points out, however, that the rejection of patriarchal organization in the community is at the expense of the "absolute patriarchal claim of God."

[55] Deutsch, *Hidden Wisdom*, 57.

[56] Ibid., 108. Here Deutsch suggests that "babes" is being used as part of the Matthean language of discipleship.

[57] See m'Abot 1.1-18.

[58] Schüssler Fiorenza, *Jesus*, 144. We see here also the characteristic of the divine sage as "son of God," occupying "sacred territory, which is inaccessible to others" (see Cox, *Biography*, 38).

[59] For extensive treatment of this aspect, see Allison, *New Moses*, 218-33.

[60] Deutsch, *Hidden Wisdom*, 133, makes the point that there is no reference in Second Temple or Tannaitic Judaism to a teacher's yoke.

[61] It is not possible here to pick up the threads common to Matthew 3–4 and 11:25-30. How households and readers interpreted "Son of God" references and the calling of disciples in those earlier chapters would certainly have intratextually shaped meaning-making in this segment of the gospel.

[62] Overman, *Church and Community*, 172-73.

[63] Ibid., 173.

## 6  AS SHE DESIRED AND HE CONFESSED

[1] Gail R. O'Day, "Surprised by Faith: Jesus and the Canaanite Woman," *Listening* 24 (1989): 294.

[2] Schüssler Fiorenza pointed out in *But She Said*, 100, that the third- and fourth-century Jewish-Christian Pseudo-Clementine Homilies gave the woman of this story a name, Justa. Even though the Matthean gospel does not name her, I will use "Justa" throughout so as not to continue the ancient practice that renders women more invisible because of the absence of their names in their stories.

[3] O'Day, "Surprised by Faith"; Schüssler Fiorenza, *But She Said*, 11-14, 96-101; Levine, *Social and Ethnic Dimensions*, 131-64; and Wainwright, *Feminist Reading*, 102-18, 217-47, and "A Voice from the Margin," 132-53.

[4] One of the firm conclusions I have drawn from previous study of this story is that it was a site of contention within the Matthean group around issues of women's leadership within the community, especially in a ritual or liturgical context, and that the different households' understanding of Jesus shaped its traditioning. See Wainwright, *Feminist Reading*, 244-47, and my imaginative reconstruction of this process in "A Voice from the Margin," 150-53.

[5] For a comprehensive bibliography, see Davies and Allison, *Matthew*, 2:643-47.

[6] I do not wish to enter discussion here as to the variety of ways this section of the narrative could be divided. It seems that whether one reads the structure according to the five-discourse format, the chiastic structure, the three part "from that time . . . " division, or the more recent narrative structuring, the two pericopes under consideration belong together. See Donald P. Senior, *What Are They Saying about Matthew?*, rev. and exp. ed. (New York: Paulist, 1996), 25-37, for a summary of the various positions.

[7] Wainwright, *Feminist Reading*, 100.

[8] For a very clear diagram of the challenge and response model, see Dennis C. Duling, "Matthew's Plurisignificant 'Son of David' in Social Science Perspective: Kinship, Kingship, Magic, and Miracle," *BTB* 22 (1992): 107.

[9] Wainwright, *Feminist Reading*, 245.

[10] Levine, *Social and Ethnic Dimensions*, 137, and Davies and Allison, *Matthew*, 2:546, both note the ambiguity in the text at this point.

[11] McCracken, "Character in the Boundary," will be a significant dialogue partner in the discussion of this pericope, which is characterized by the boundary motif.

[12] It is generally Jesus who is understood and characterized in this way by contemporary interpreters (see ibid., 34).

[13] Jean-Yves Thériault, "Le Maître maîtrisé! Mathieu 15,21-28," in *De Jésus et des Femmes: Lectures sémiotiques. Suivies d'un entretien avec A. J. Greimas*, ed. Adèle Chené, et al., Recherches Nouvelle Série 14 (Montreal: Les Editions Bellarmin, 1987), 26.

[14] O'Day, "Surprised by Faith," 294.

[15] Wainwright, *Feminist Reading*, 237-38.

[16] See ibid., 243, for a more extensive explanation of this connection within the Matthean narrative. Also, the narrator has earlier, by way of intertextuality, characterized Jesus' mission in terms of "justice to the Gentiles" and his name as one in which the Gentiles will hope (12:15-21).

[17] It is also possible that some readers would have recognized intertextually the relationship between the vision that Justa proposes and the Jewish tradition of the poor and the non-Jewish alien having access to the remnants (Lv 19: 9-10; Dt

24:19). I was alerted to this insight in P. Pokorn'y, "From a Puppy to the Child: Some Problems of Contemporary Biblical Exegesis Demonstrated from Mark 7.24-30/Matt 15.21-8," *NTS* 41 (1995): 329.

[18] D'Angelo, "Re-membering Jesus," points to the prophetic but not necessarily the sapiential ministry of the communities shaping the Jesus tradition.

[19] McCracken, "Character in the Boundary," 34.

[20] Levine, *Social and Ethnic Dimensions*, 137 and elsewhere within this section of her study, claims that the temporal axis of the Matthean narrative consistently separates Jesus from a gentile mission. While her case is argued convincingly, it does not allow sufficiently for alternative voices in the narrative as indicated above or the possibility of alternative readings within the Matthean communities of reception.

[21] In the Middle East dogs were generally considered scavengers and even those more domesticated, which the diminutive of the noun might indicate in this text, would be found in the courtyard or on the street rather than in the house.

[22] This is the social axis that Levine, *Social and Ethnic Dimensions*, 132, 152, 156, sees as equally significant in this story.

[23] Bal, "Metaphors," 205.

[24] Duling, "Matthew's Plurisignificant 'Son of David.'"

[25] McCracken, "Character in the Boundary," 38, who draws on Mikhail Bakhtin, *Problems of Dostoevsky's Poetics*, ed. and trans. Caryl Emerson (Minneapolis: University of Minneapolis Press, 1984), 135-56.

[26] Supplementary to McCracken, who suggests that Justa's story continues from the threshold through response to the "eccentric," to "faith in an eccentric world (the kingdom of God)" (ibid.), I have suggested in this reading that by way of cross-characterization Jesus too moves from the threshold by way of encounter with the eccentric or the *skandalon* to a new and expansive faith in and understanding of the reign of God.

[27] John P. Meier, "Matthew 15:21-28," *Int* 40 (1986): 399, like many other scholars, focuses the story in Jesus. If Jesus is key protagonist, it seems necessary to understand that he has "led this woman up four steps to the heights of faith."

[28] O'Day, "Surprised by Faith," 298, talks of Justa's "spirit of defiant resistance to despair, and bold faith in God's promises."

[29] Overman, *Church and Community*, 237; and Davies and Allison, *Matthew*, 2:616. For a more extensive discussion of the impact of Herodian cities on the Galilean countryside, see Horsley, *Galilee*, 158-81.

[30] Levine, *Ethnic and Social Dimensions*, 7.

[31] Horsley, *Galilee*, 158-81.

[32] I do not intend here any link between the gender-bias of this text and its specifically Jewish character. It has already been more than amply demonstrated that kyriarchy and androcentrism cross most ethnic boundaries. See Schüssler Fiorenza, *Jesus*, 67-96, for an extensive discussion of the Christian anti-Judaism that has constituted so much christology.

[33] Malina and Rohrbaugh, *Social Science Commentary*, 112.

[34] This is the phrase traditionally translated as "Son of Man."

[35] Overman, *Church and Community*, 237.

[36] Davies and Allison, *Matthew*, 2:617, for a list of possible meanings.

[37] Donald J. Verseput, "The Faith of the Reader and the Narrative of Matthew 13.53-16.20," *JSNT* 46 (1992): 12.

[38] For a detailed study of the Jeremian tradition in Matthew, see David J. Zucker, "Jesus and Jeremiah in the Matthean Tradition," *JES* 27 (1990): 288-305.

[39] Horsley and Hanson, *Bandits, Prophets, Messiahs*, 135-89.

[40] Kingsbury, in both *Matthew*, 67, and "The Figure of Jesus," 3, 11-14, argues that Peter's confession is "pivotal" or a "culmination" in the development of what he considers the central Matthean title for Jesus—Son of God. For a more extensive study of this title beyond the Kingsbury/Hill debate and the confines of this study, see Donald J. Verseput, "The Role and Meaning of the 'Son of God' Title in Matthew's Gospel," *NTS* 33 (1987): 532-56; and Dale C. Allison, "The Son of God as Israel: A Note on Matthean Christology," *IBS* 9 (1987): 74-81.

[41] Horsley and Hanson, *Bandits, Prophets, Messiahs*, 88-127.

[42] Sawicki, *Seeing the Lord*, 119-48, reconstructs a political *poiesis* around Jesus' identity and other community issues in relation to Matthew 4:1-11, undertaken in a context of struggle, which draws on a more extensive intertextuality than do many other interpreters. See also Allison, *New Moses*, 165-72, and Birger Gerhardsson, *The Testing of God's Son (Matt 4:1-11 & Par): An Analysis of an Early Christian Midrash* (Lund: Gleerup, 1966), for alternatives.

[43] M. Eugene Boring, Klaus Berger, and Carsten Colpe, eds., *Hellenistic Commentary to the New Testament* (Nashville: Abingdon, 1995), 104-5, point to the practice of commending great ones with divine titles and the reticence that sometimes surrounded such commendations. Danker, "God with Us," demonstrates convincingly though briefly how Jesus, Son of God, would have been interpreted within a Greco-Roman matrix.

[44] Crosby, *House of Disciples*, 51, notes that "'Son' is essentially a house-connected word; the line of house-based authority was extended from the head of the house through the sons."

[45] Johnson, *She Who Is*, and Catherine Mowry LaCugna, *God for Us: The Trinity and Christian Life* (San Francisco: Harper, 1991), both open up the potentialities of trinitarian theology in a way that invites the theological *poiesis* of contemporary women.

[46] Malina and Rohrbaugh, *Social Science Commentary*, 112.

[47] For a discussion of *ekklesia* in the Greco-Roman and Matthean settings, see Crosby, *House of Disciples*, 33-35, 49-54.

[48] See Schüssler Fiorenza, *But She Said*, 114-20, for an excellent discussion of this system from a feminist perspective. She demonstrates that it is a system of multiplicative oppressions and domination.

[49] For a more detailed discussion, see Augustine Stock, "Is Matthew's Presentation of Peter Ironic?" *BTB* 17.2 (1987): 66-67.

[50] This aspect of the gospel has already been discussed earlier in this chapter and in the previous one.

[51] Bernard P. Robinson, "Peter and His Successors: Tradition and Redaction in Matthew 16.17-19," *JSNT* 21 (1984): 87.

[52] J. A. Emerton, "Binding and Loosing—Forgiving and Retaining," *JTS* 13 (1962): 325-31; J. Duncan M. Derrett, "Binding and Loosing (Matt 16:19; 18:18; John 20:23)," *JBL* 102 (1983): 112-17; Richard H. Hiers, "'Binding' and 'Loos-

ing': The Matthean Authorizations," *JBL* 104 (1985): 233-50; Herbert W. Basser, "Derrett's 'Binding' Reopened," *JBL* 104 (1985): 297-300; and Dennis C. Duling, "Binding and Loosing: Matthew 16:19; Matthew 18:18; John 20:23," *Forum* 3.4 (1987): 3-31, suggest intertextual meaning-making for this phrase, some of which may not have been actualized within the Matthean reading communities.

[53] See the claim of Paul de Man quoted in Wallace W. Bubar, "Killing Two Birds with One Stone: The Utter De(con)struction of Matthew and His Church," *Biblical Interpretation* 3 (1995): 146.

[54] Stephen D. Moore, *Literary Criticism and the Gospels: The Theoretical Challenge* (New Haven: Yale University Press, 1989), 167.

[55] Stock, "Matthew's Presentation."

[56] Arlo J. Nau, *Peter in Matthew: Discipleship, Diplomacy, and Dispraise ... with an Assessment of Power and Privilege in the Petrine Office*, Good News Studies 36 (Collegeville, Minn.: Liturgical Press, 1992), especially 122-33 for conclusions.

[57] Bubar, "Killing Two Birds," 155.


## 7   THE LIBERATOR LIBERATED, THE CRUCIFIED ONE RAISED

[1] Schüssler Fiorenza, *Jesus*, 120-21 (emphasis added).

[2] For a detailed account of this history generally, see Raymond E. Brown, *The Death of the Messiah: A Commentary on the Passion Narratives in the Four Gospels*, 2 vols., Anchor Bible Reference Library (New York: Doubleday, 1993); and within the Matthean context, Donald P. Senior, *The Passion Narrative according to Matthew: A Redactional Study*, BEThL 39 (Leuven: University Press, 1982) and *The Passion of Jesus in the Gospel of Matthew*, The Passion Series 1 (Wilmington: Michael Glazier, 1985).

[3] Sawicki, *Seeing the Lord*, 267-73. See also 149-81 for her reconstruction of women's traditioning of the story of the anointing of Jesus at Bethany and its link to interpretations of the death of the Messiah.

[4] Kathleen E. Corley, "He Was Buried, On the Third Day He Was Raised: Women and the Crucifixion and Burial of Jesus," unpublished paper presented to the Jesus Seminar, Fall 1995, 42.

[5] Schüssler Fiorenza, *Jesus*, 122.

[6] Wainwright, *Feminist Reading*, 314-16.

[7] See ibid., 122-23, for an outline of the intricate weave of the passion and resurrection accounts in the Matthean narrative.

[8] Matthew 27:35 recounts the crucifixion in a participial phrase; 27:46 and 50 make reference to the cry of Jesus, and his death is passed over in the phrase "he handed over his spirit" (27:50).

[9] Crossan, *Historical Jesus*, 379.

[10] Ibid., 389, 376-91.

[11] Overman, *Church and Community*, 384-91, raises questions regarding the historicity of the trials of Jesus, suggesting that a small coalition of local and Roman officials very readily gained Roman military approval without any formalities.

[12] See ibid., 389-91.

[13] Schüssler Fiorenza, *Jesus*, 67-73.

[14] Crossan, *Historical Jesus*, 385-87, names this layer of traditioning "innocence rescued," and it is clearly central to the Matthean characterization of the death of Jesus.

[15] A similar argument pertains to the religious title "King of Israel" on the lips of the chief priests, scribes, and elders, which appears only in 27:42.

[16] John Paul Heil, *The Death and Resurrection of Jesus: A Narrative-Critical Reading of Matthew 26-28* (Minneapolis: Fortress, 1991), 81, is representative of the reading for coherence among Christian interpreters—"Jesus proves he is worthy of belief as the true King of Israel with power to save himself and all others by remaining on the cross and refusing to save himself from the death that is *God's will*" (emphasis added).

[17] Burnett, "Characterization and Christology," 591.

[18] Senior, *Passion of Jesus*, 133, says that "the word 'save' has deep and comprehensive meaning in Matthew's Gospel; it refers to the total transformation and redemption of the human person, body and spirit."

[19] Schüssler Fiorenza, *Jesus*, 104, 106.

[20] Burnett, "Characterization and Christology," 593, suggests that the semantic relationship between Jesus and Emmanuel in 1:23 continually raises the question for the reader, "Is God present when Jesus is present?" See also Schüssler Fiorenza, *Jesus*, 110-11, for a further elaboration of the *basileia* symbol within the meaning-making of the death of Jesus.

[21] Brown, *Death of the Messiah*, 2:999, says of Jesus on the cross that "he is a solitary righteous man closely surrounded on all sides by enemies."

[22] Malina and Neyrey, *Calling Jesus Names*, 69-131.

[23] Ibid., 96. Note also McCracken, "Character in the Boundary," 34, who observes that Jesus as *skandalon* is either sign of offense or object of faith. The challenge of the chief priests that if Jesus removed the offense and came down from the cross they would be persuaded (27:42) should be read in light of this.

[24] Malina and Neyrey, *Calling Jesus Names*, 79. They recognize a twofold process of claims to deviance responded to by those so named with claims to prominence, a process that they suggest shaped the telling of the Jesus story over decades, beginning in the life of Jesus.

[25] Ibid., 97.

[26] For examples of cosmic phenomena that accompanied the deaths of emperors and other Roman heroes, see Boring, et al., *Hellenistic Commentary*, §212, 160; §213, 160-61; and §221, 166-67.

[27] See in particular, Plutarch, *Parallel Lives*, "Agis and Cleomenes," in ibid., 160.

[28] Brown, *Death of the Messiah*, 2:1207-11.

[29] Corley, "He Was Buried," 1.

[30] Ibid., 36-43.

[31] Ibid., 42.

[32] Brown, *Death of the Messiah*, 2:1159.

[33] Heil, *Death and Resurrection*, 92. Raymond E. Brown, "The Resurrection in Matthew (27:62-28:20)," *Worship* 64 (1990): 164, also calls the women "passive." In his interpretation of their "looking on from afar," he fails to recognize, however, the possible shaping of their positioning by the intertexual echo of Psalm 38:11.

[34] Brown, *Death of the Messiah*, 2:1224.

[35] Wainwright, *Feminist Reading*, 140-43, 288-99.

[36] There is also potential for intertextual exploration in the cosmic phenomena that surround the death of Jesus, pointing to God's judgment against unjust suffering.

[37] Senior, *Passion of Jesus*, 129. See also Pierre Bonnard, *L'Evangile selon Saint Matthieu*, Commentaire du Nouveau Testament, Deuxième Série 1 (Genève: Labor et Fides, 1982), 402.

[38] The references to the Psalms will be to the English version of the NRSV. The numbering in the LXX differs from these.

[39] Malina and Neyrey, *Calling Jesus Names*, 127, suggest that Jesus would have been seen as a "typical righteous sufferer who prayed to God in his distress." Crossan, *Historical Jesus*, 156, suggests a model of "rescued innocence" in the intertextual spaces of the narrative, although his study is based more on historical origins.

[40] Richard J. Dillon, "The Psalms of the Suffering Just in the Accounts of Jesus' Passion," *Worship* 61 (1987): 430-40, develops the two aspects of this intertextuality.

[41] There is a combination in the Psalms of the two verbs "to save" (Mt 27:40, 42, 49) and "to deliver" (27:43).

[42] Malina and Neyrey, *Calling Jesus Names*, 127-28.

[43] See Joel Marcus, "The Old Testament and the Death of Jesus: The Role of Scripture in the Gospel Passion Narratives," in *The Death of Jesus in Early Christianity*, ed. John T. Carroll and Joel B. Green (Peabody: Hendrickson, 1995), 209, who typically reads Jesus' death as "divine necessity, since it was foretold in the Scriptures." Likewise Margaret Davies, *Matthew*, Readings: A New Biblical Commentary (Sheffield: JSOT Press, 1993), 197, says that the psalm "reminds readers that God allowed the sufferings of the innocent," a sentiment foreign to the gospel as far as I can reconstruct its meaning-making potential.

[44] Carolyn Osiek, "The Women at the Tomb: What Are They Doing There?" *Ex Auditu* 9 (1993): 102-4, and Wainwright, *Feminist Reading*, 314-16, while recognizing the possibility of women's contribution to the tradition of women's presence at the tomb, share with Schüssler Fiorenza, *Jesus*, 125, the awareness of the difficulty of making these claims with any degree of certainty.

[45] Schüssler Fiorenza, *Jesus*, 121; Sawicki, *Seeing the Lord*, 79.

[46] Brown, *Death of the Messiah*, 2:1126; and Danker, "God with Us," 437-38. Boring, et al., *Hellenistic Commentary*, §215, 161-62, and §221, 166-67, offer instances of cosmic phenomena surrounding the death of a hero or significant one.

[47] Reginald H. Fuller, *The Formation of the Resurrection Narratives* (Philadelphia: Fortress, 1971), 83, contrary to Jack Dean Kingsbury, "The Composition and Christology of Matt 28:16-20," *JBL* 93 (1974): 581-84, who argues that affinity with other parts of the gospel in which "Son of God" christology is prominent leads to the assumption that Jesus in Matthew 28:16-20 must be understood as raised and exalted as "Son of God." Jane Schaberg, *The Father, the Son and the Holy Spirit: The Triadic Phrase in Matthew 28:19b*, SBLDS 61 (Atlanta: Scholars, 1982), on the other hand, suggests an apocalyptic matrix for an understanding of the triadic formula of 20:19b and hence "Son of man" connections for Jesus. While this study has demonstrated the significance of both intratextuality and intertextuality in readers' meaning-making, perhaps the very simplicity of the text, in this instance, belies such *poiesis*.

[48] Schüssler Fiorenza, *Jesus*, 125.

[49] I have chosen in this study, not to address Matthew 28:11-15, as its meaning potential belongs within another stream of tradition within the final segments of the gospel story.

[50] Ibid., 123-25.

[51] In terms of the development of the narrative, we may see here what Ebert, *Patriarchy, Ideology, Subjectivity*, 66, has observed; namely, that ideological positions need to be constantly reestablished and reiterated narratively, especially when they are perceived to be under threat.

[52] As an example of this see Brown's interpretation of these two accounts, "Resurrection in Matthew," 164-70, in which what has been identified as the "open road" tradition associated with women is called a "popular" tradition that "may have been of great interest and have received narrative development" but is compared unfavorably with "church-founding appearances" associated with "official preaching." I think it is extremely difficult to argue for such a distinction within the Matthean text and would contend that such an interpretation is through the lens of later kyriarchal perspectives on authority and power.

[53] The same verb is used in the commission given by the angel to the women (28:7) and by Jesus to the Eleven (28:19). A different verb is used by Jesus to the women (28:10), but the meaning is the same.

[54] Schüssler Fiorenza, *Jesus*, 111.

[55] Crossan, *A Revolutionary Biography*, 166.

[56] Ibid., 169.

[57] See Levine, *Social and Ethnic Dimensions*, 165-92, 193-204, for a discussion of this commission and a dialogue with the breadth and diversity of scholarly literature.

[58] See the conclusion to chapter 4 for a similar discussion in relation to the beginning of the narrative.

[59] For one of the most extensive explorations of the triadic formulation, see Schaberg, *Father*.

[60] Sawicki, *Seeing the Lord*, 79.

# Select Bibliography

*This bibliography does not contain citations of individual articles drawn from a collection of essays when a number of essays from that collection have informed the study. Only when a single article from such a collection has been consulted will it be cited under its author rather than the editors of the collection.*

Abraham, Dulcie, et al., eds. *Asian Women Doing Theology: Report from Singapore Conference, November 20-29, 1987*. Kowloon: Asian Women's Resource Centre for Culture and Theology, 1989.

Adams, Carol J., ed. *Ecofeminism and the Sacred*. New York: Continuum, 1993.

Aichele, George, and Gary A. Phillips, eds. *Intertextuality and the Bible. Semeia 69/70*. Atlanta: Scholars Press, 1995.

Aland, Barbara, Kurt Aland, Johannes Karavidopoulos, Carlo M. Martini, and Bruce M. Metzger, eds. *Novum Testamentum Graece*. 27th edition. Stuttgart: Deutsche Bibelgesellschaft, 1993.

Alexander, Loveday. "The Living Voice: Scepticism towards the Written Word in Early Christian and in Graeco-Roman Texts." In *The Bible in Three Dimensions: Essays in Celebration of Forty Years of Biblical Studies in the University of Sheffield*. Edited by David J. A. Clines, Stephen E. Fowl, and Stanley E. Porter, 221-47. *JSOTSS* 87. Sheffield: JSOT Press, 1990.

Allison, Dale C. *The New Moses: A Matthean Typology*. Minneapolis: Fortress, 1993.

———. "The Son of God as Israel: A Note on Matthean Christology." *IBS* 9 (1987): 74-81.

Aune, David E. *The New Testament in Its Literary Environment*. Library of Early Christianity. Philadelphia: Westminster, 1987.

Bakhtin, Mikhail M. *The Dialogic Imagination: Four Essays by M. M. Bakhtin*. Edited by Michael Holquist. Translated by Caryl Emerson and Michael Holquist. Austin: University of Texas Press, 1981.

Bal, Mieke. *Death and Dissymmetry: The Politics of Coherence in the Book of Judges*. Chicago: University of Chicago Press, 1988.

———. "Metaphors He Lives By." *Semeia* 61 (1993): 185-207.

———. *Narratology: Introduction to the Theory of Narrative*. Translated by Christine van Boheemen. Toronto: University of Toronto Press, 1985.

Balch, David L., ed. *Social History of the Matthean Community: Cross-Disciplinary Approaches*. Minneapolis: Fortress, 1991.

Barrett, Michèle, and Anne Phillips, eds. *Destabilizing Theory: Contemporary Feminist Debates*. Stanford: Stanford University Press, 1992.

Basser, Herbert W. "Derrett's 'Binding' Reopened." *JBL* 104 (1985): 297-300.

Bauer, Dale M., and S. Jaret McKinstry, eds. *Feminism, Bahktin and the Dialogic*. Albany: State University of New York Press, 1991.

Benhabib, Seyla, and Drucilla Cornell, eds. *Feminism as Critique*. Minneapolis: University of Minnesota Press, 1987.

Berry, Thomas. *The Dream of the Earth*. San Francisco: Sierra Club Books, 1988.

*The Biblical Antiquities of Philo*. Translated by M. R. James. New York: KTAV, 1971.

Bird, Phyllis. "'Male and Female He Created Them': Gen 1:27b in the Context of the Priestly Account of Creation." *HTR* 74 (1981): 129-59.

Bonnard, Pierre. *L'Evangile selon Saint Matthieu*. Commentaire du Nouveau Testament. Deuxième Série 1. Genève: Labor et Fides, 1982.

Boring, M. Eugene, Klaus Berger, and Carsten Colpe, eds. *Hellenistic Commentary to the New Testament*. Nashville: Abingdon, 1995.

Botha, P. J. J. "Greco-Roman Literacy as Setting for New Testament Writings." *Neotestamentica* 26.1 (1992): 195-215.

———. "Mark's Story as Oral Traditional Literature: Rethinking the Transmission of Some Traditions about Jesus." *Hervormde Teologiese Studies* 47 (1991): 304-31.

Braidotti, Rosi. *Nomadic Subjects: Embodiment and Sexual Difference in Contemporary Feminist Theory*. Gender and Culture. New York: Columbia University Press, 1994.

———. *Patterns of Dissonance: A Study of Women in Contemporary Philosophy*. Translated by Elizabeth Guild. Cambridge: Polity Press, 1991.

Brenner, Athalya, and Fokkelien van Dijk-Hemmes. *On Gendering Texts: Female and Male Voices in the Hebrew Bible*. Leiden: Brill, 1993.

Brettell, Caroline B., and Carolyn F. Sargent, eds. *Gender in Cross-Cultural Perspective*. Englewood Cliffs: Prentice-Hall, 1993.

Brock, Rita Nakashima. "The Feminist Redemption of Christ." In *Christian Feminism: Visions of a New Humanity*. Edited by Judith Weidman, 55-74. San Francisco: Harper & Row, 1984.

———. *Journeys by Heart: A Christology of Erotic Power*. New York: Crossroad, 1988.

Brooten, Bernadette J. "Early Christian Women and Their Cultural Context: Issues on Method in Historical Reconstruction." In *Feminist Perspectives on Biblical Scholarship*. Edited by Adela Yarbro Collins, 65-91. Chico: Scholars Press, 1985.

———. *Women Leaders in the Ancient Synagogue: Inscriptional Evidence and Background Issues*. Brown Judaic Studies 36. Chico: Scholars Press, 1982.

Brown, Joanne Carlson, and Carole R. Bohn, eds. *Christianity, Patriarchy and Abuse: A Feminist Critique*. New York: Pilgrim Press, 1989.

Brown, Raymond E. *The Birth of the Messiah: A Commentary on the Infancy Narratives in the Gospels of Matthew and Luke*. New updated edition. New York: Doubleday, 1993.

———. *The Death of the Messiah: A Commentary on the Passion Narratives in the Four Gospels*. 2 vols. Anchor Bible Reference Library. New York: Doubleday, 1993.

———. "The Resurrection in Matthew (27:62-28:20)." *Worship* 64 (1990): 157-70.

Bubar, Wallace W. "Killing Two Birds with One Stone: The Utter De(con)struction of Matthew and His Church." *Biblical Interpretation* 3 (1995): 144-57.

Burkett, Delbert. "The Nontitular Son of Man: A History and Critique." *NTS* 40 (1994): 504-21.

Burnett, Fred W. "Characterization and Christology in Matthew: Jesus in the Gospel of Matthew." In *SBLSP* 28. Edited by David J. Lull, 588-603. Atlanta: Scholars Press, 1989.

————. "*Paliggenesia* in Matt. 19:28: A Window on the Matthean Community?" *JSNT* 17 (1983): 60-72.

Butler, Judith, and Joan W. Scott, eds. *Feminists Theorize the Political*. New York: Routledge, 1992.

Bynum, Caroline Walker, Stevan Harrell, and Paula Richman, eds. *Gender and Religion: On the Complexity of Symbols*. Boston: Beacon Press, 1986.

Camp, Claudia V. "Metaphor in Feminist Biblical Interpretation: Theoretical Perspectives." *Semeia* 61 (1993): 3-36.

————. *Wisdom and the Feminine in the Book of Proverbs*. Bible and Literature Series 11. Sheffield: Almond Press, 1985.

————. "Woman Wisdom as Root Metaphor: A Theological Consideration." In *The Listening Heart: Essays in Wisdom and the Psalms in Honor of Roland E. Murphy*. Edited by Kenneth G. Hoglund, et al., 45-76. *JSOTSS* 58. Sheffield: JSOT Press, 1987.

Carr, Anne. "Feminist Views of Christology." *Chicago Studies* 35 (1996): 128-40.

Carroll, John T., and Joel B. Green, eds. *The Death of Jesus in Early Christianity*. Peabody: Hendrickson, 1995.

Chung, Hyun Kyung. *Struggle to Be the Sun Again: Introducing Asian Women's Theology*. Maryknoll, N.Y.: Orbis Books, 1990.

Clayton, Jay, and Eric Rothstein, eds. *Influence and Intertextuality in Literary History*. Madison: University of Wisconsin Press, 1991.

Cole, Susan Guettel. "Could Greek Women Read and Write?" In *Reflections of Women in Antiquity*. Edited by Helene P. Foley, 219-45. New York: Gordon and Breach Science, 1981.

Confoy, Maryanne, Dorothy Lee, and Joan Nowotny, eds. *Freedom and Entrapment: Women Thinking Theology*. North Blackburn, Vic.: Dove, 1995.

Corley, Kathleen E. "He Was Buried, On the Third Day He Was Raised: Women and the Crucifixion and Burial of Jesus." Unpublished paper presented to the Jesus Seminar. Fall 1995.

————. *Private Women, Public Meals: Social Conflict in the Synoptic Tradition*. Peabody: Hendrickson, 1993.

Cotter, Wendy J. "Children Sitting in the Agora: Q (Luke) 7:31-35." *Forum* 5.2 (1989): 63-82.

————. "The Parable of the Children in the Market-Place, Q (Lk) 7:31-35: An Examination of the Parable's Image and Significance." *NovT* 29 (1987): 289-304.

Cox, Patricia. *Biography in Late Antiquity: A Quest for the Holy Man*. Berkeley and Los Angeles: University of California Press, 1983.

Crosby, Michael. *House of Disciples: Church, Economics, and Justice in Matthew*. Maryknoll, N.Y.: Orbis Books, 1988.

Crossan, John Dominic. *The Historical Jesus: The Life of a Mediterranean Jewish Peasant*. San Francisco: Harper, 1991.

————. *Jesus: A Revolutionary Biography*. San Francisco: Harper, 1994.

Crumlin, Rosemary. *Images of Religion in Australian Art*. Kensington, NSW.: Bay Books, 1988.

Crumlin, Rosemary, and Anthony Knight, eds. *Aboriginal Art and Spirituality*. Melbourne: CollinsDove, 1991.

Daly, Mary. *Beyond God the Father: Toward a Philosophy of Women's Liberation*. Boston: Beacon Press, 1973.

D'Angelo, Mary Rose. "*Abba* and 'Father': Imperial Theology and the Jesus Traditions." *JBL* 111 (1992): 611-30.

———. "Re-membering Jesus: Women, Prophecy, and Resistance in the Memory of the Early Churches." *Horizons* 19 (1992): 199-218.

Danker, Frederick W. "God with Us: Hellenistic Christological Perspectives in Matthew." *CurTM* 19 (1992): 433-39.

Darr, John A. *On Character Building: The Reader and the Rhetoric of Characterization in Luke-Acts.* Literary Currents in Biblical Interpretation. Louisville: Westminster/John Knox, 1992.

Davaney, Sheila. "Review of Models of God: Theology for an Ecological Nuclear Age." *RSR* 16 (1990): 36-40.

Davies, Margaret. *Matthew.* Readings: A New Biblical Commentary. Sheffield: JSOT Press, 1993.

Davies, W. D. "The Jewish Sources of Matthew's Messianism." In *The Messiah: Developments in Earliest Judaism and Christianity.* The First Princeton Symposium on Judaism and Christian Origins. Edited by James H. Charlesworth, 494-511. Minneapolis: Fortress, 1992.

Davies, W. D., and Dale C. Allison. *A Critical and Exegetical Commentary on the Gospel according to Saint Matthew.* Volume 1. Edinburgh: T. & T. Clark, 1988.

———. *A Critical and Exegetical Commentary on the Gospel according to Saint Matthew.* Volume 2. Edinburgh: T. & T. Clark, 1991.

de Lauretis, Teresa. *Technologies of Gender: Essays on Theory, Film and Fiction.* Theories of Representation and Difference. Bloomington: Indiana University Press, 1986.

Derrett, J. Duncan M. "Binding and Loosing (Matt 16:19; 18:18; John 20:23)." *JBL* 102 (1983): 112-17.

Deutsch, Celia. *Hidden Wisdom and the Easy Yoke: Wisdom, Torah and Discipleship in Matthew 11.25-30.* JSNTSS 18. Sheffield: JSOT Press, 1987.

———. "Wisdom in Matthew: Transformation of a Symbol." *NovT* 32 (1990): 13-47.

Dewey, Joanna. "Jesus' Healings of Women: Conformity and Non-Conformity to Dominant Cultural Values as Clues for Historical Reconstruction." *BTB* 24.3 (1994): 122-31.

———. "From Storytelling to Written Text: The Loss of Early Christian Women's Voices." *BTB* 26.2 (1996): 73-78.

———. "Textuality in an Oral Culture: A Survey of the Pauline Traditions." *Semeia* 65 (1995): 37-65.

van Dijk-Hemmes, Fokkelien, and Athalya Brenner, eds. *Reflections on Theology and Gender.* Kampen: Kok Pharos, 1994.

Dillon, Richard J. "The Psalms of the Suffering Just in the Accounts of Jesus' Passion." *Worship* 61 (1987): 430-40.

Docherty, Thomas. *Reading (Absent) Character: Towards a Theory of Characterization in Fiction.* Oxford: Clarendon Press, 1983.

Downing, F. Gerald. "Contemporary Analogies to the Gospels and Acts: 'Genres' or 'Motifs.'" In *Synoptic Studies: The Ampleforth Conferences of 1982 and 1983.* Edited by C. M. Tuckett, 51-65. JSNTSS 7. Sheffield: JSOT Press 1984.

———. *Cynics and Christian Origins.* Edinburgh: T. & T. Clark, 1992.

Doyle, Rod. "Matthew 11:12—A Challenge to the Evangelist's Community." *Colloquium* 18 (1985): 20-30.

Dubish, Jill, ed. *Gender and Power in Rural Greece.* Princeton: Princeton University Press, 1986.

Duling, Dennis C. "Binding and Loosing: Matthew 16:19; Matthew 18:18; John 20:23." *Forum* 3.4 (1987): 3-31.

———. "Matthew's Plurisignificant 'Son of David' in Social Science Perspective: Kinship, Kingship, Magic, and Miracle." *BTB* 22 (1992): 99-116.

Dyke, Doris Jean. *Crucified Woman.* Toronto: The United Church Publishing House, 1991.

Ebert, Teresa Lynn. *Patriarchy, Ideology, Subjectivity: Towards A Theory of Feminist Critical Cultural Studies.* Ph.D. thesis submitted to the University of Minnesota, Minneapolis, 1988.

Edwards, Denis. *Jesus the Wisdom of God: An Ecological Theology.* Maryknoll, N.Y.: Orbis Books, 1995.

Emerton, J. A. "Binding and Loosing—Forgiving and Retaining." *JTS* 13 (1962): 325-31.

Exum, J. Cheryl. "The Mothers of Israel: The Patriarchal Narratives from a Feminist Perspective." *Bible Review* 2.1 (1986): 60-67.

———. "Second Thoughts about Secondary Characters: Women in Exodus 1.8-2.10." In *A Feminist Companion to Exodus to Deuteronomy.* Edited by Athalya Brenner, 75-87. Sheffield: Sheffield Academic Press, 1994.

———. "'You Shall Let Every Daughter Live': A Study of Exodus 1:8–2:10." *Semeia* 28 (1983): 63-82.

Fabella, Virginia, and Mercy Amba Oduyoye, eds. *With Passion and Compassion: Third World Women Doing Theology—Reflections from the Women's Commission of the Ecumenical Association of Third World Theologians.* Maryknoll, N.Y.: Orbis Books, 1988.

Felman, Shoshana. *What Does a Woman Want? Reading and Sexual Difference.* Baltimore: Johns Hopkins University Press, 1993.

Felski, Rita. *Beyond Feminist Aesthetics: Feminist Literary and Social Change.* Cambridge: Harvard University Press, 1989.

Fewell, Danna Nolan, ed. *Reading between Texts: Intertextuality and the Hebrew Bible.* Literary Currents in Biblical Interpretation. Louisville: Westminster/John Knox, 1992.

Fishelov, David. "Types of Character, Characteristics of Types." *Style* 24.3 (1990): 422-39.

Flax, Jane. "Postmodernism and Gender-Relations in Feminist Theory." *Signs* 12.4 (1987): 621-43.

Foucault, Michel. *The History of Sexuality.* Volume 1: *Introduction.* Translated by Robert Hurley. New York: Vintage, 1978.

Friedman, Mordechai A. "Babatha's *Ketubba*: Some Preliminary Observations." *IEJ* 46 (1996): 55-76.

Fulkerson, Mary McClintock. *Changing the Subject: Women's Discourses and Feminist Theology.* Minneapolis: Fortress, 1994.

Fuller, Reginald H. *The Formation of the Resurrection Narratives.* Philadelphia: Fortress, 1971.

Fuss, Diana. *Essentially Speaking: Feminism, Nature and Difference.* New York: Routledge, 1989.

Gerhardsson, Birger. *The Testing of God's Son (Matt 4:1-11 & Par): An Analysis of an Early Christian Midrash.* Lund: Gleerup, 1966.

Gerhart, Mary. *Genre Choices, Gender Questions.* Oklahoma Project for Discourse and Theory. Norman: University of Oklahoma Press, 1992.

———. "Imaging Christ in Art, Politics, Spirituality: An Overview." In *Imaging Christ: Politics, Art, Spirituality.* Edited by Francis A. Eigo, 1-43. Villanova: Villanova University Press, 1991.

Gerhart, Mary, and Allan Melvin Russell. *Metaphoric Process: The Creation of Scientific and Religious Understanding.* Fort Worth: Texas Christian University Press, 1984.

Gero, Joan M., and Margaret W. Conkey, eds. *Engendering Archaeology: Women and Prehistory.* Oxford: Blackwell, 1991.

Graff, Ann O'Hara, ed. *In the Embrace of God: Feminist Approaches to Theological Anthropology.* Maryknoll, N.Y.: Orbis Books, 1995.

Grant, Jacquelyn. *White Women's Christ and Black Women's Jesus: Feminist Christology and Womanist Response.* AARAS 64. Atlanta: Scholars Press, 1989.

Grassi, Joseph A. "Matthew's Gospel as Live Performance." *BibT* 27 (1989): 225-32.

Hampson, Daphne. *Theology and Feminism.* Signposts in Theology. Oxford: Basil Blackwell, 1990.

Haraway, Donna. "Situated Knowledges: The Science Question in Feminism and the Privilege of Partial Perspective." *Feminist Studies* 14 (1988): 575-99.

Harris, William V. *Ancient Literacy.* Cambridge: Harvard University Press, 1989.

Heil, John Paul. *The Death and Resurrection of Jesus: A Narrative-Critical Reading of Matthew 26-28.* Minneapolis: Fortress, 1991.

Hengel, Martin. *Studies in Early Christology.* Edinburgh: T. & T. Clark, 1995.

Heyward, Carter. *Speaking of Christ: A Lesbian Feminist Voice.* Edited by Ellen C. Davis. New York: Pilgrim Press, 1989.

———. "Suffering, Redemption, and Christ: Shifting the Grounds of Feminist Christology." *Christianity and Crisis* 49 (1989): 381-86.

Hiers, Richard H. "'Binding' and 'Loosing': The Matthean Authorizations." *JBL* 104 (1985): 233-50.

Hill, David. "The Figure of Jesus in Matthew's Story: A Response to Professor Kingsbury's Literary-Critical Probe." *JSNT* 21 (1984): 37-52.

Hochman, B. *Character in Literature.* Ithaca: Cornell University Press, 1985.

Holladay, William L. *Jeremiah 2: A Commentary on the Book of the Prophet Jeremiah Chapters 26-52.* Hermeneia. Minneapolis: Fortress, 1989.

hooks, bell. *Ain't I a Woman: Black Women and Feminism.* Boston: South End Press, 1981.

———. *Yearning: Race, Gender, and Cultural Politics.* Boston: South End Press, 1990.

Horsley, Richard A. *Galilee: History, Politics, and People.* Valley Forge, Penn.: Trinity Press International, 1995.

———. *The Liberation of Christmas: The Infancy Narratives in Social Context.* New York: Crossroad, 1989.

Horsley, Richard A., and John S. Hanson. *Bandits, Prophets, and Messiahs: Popular Movements at the Time of Jesus.* San Francisco: Harper, 1985.

Houts, Margo G. "Atonement and Abuse: An Alternative View." *Daughters of Sarah* 18.3 (1992): 29-32.

Humphries-Brooks, Stephenson. "Indicators of Social Organization and Status in Matthew's Gospel." In *SBLSP* 30. Edited by Eugene H. Lovering, 31-49. Atlanta: Scholars Press, 1991.

Ilan, Tal. *Jewish Women in Greco-Roman Palestine: An Inquiry into Image and Status*. Texte und Studien zum Antiken Judentum 44. Tübingen: Mohr, 1995.

Irigaray, Luce. *Marine Lover of Friedrich Nietzsche*. Translated by Gillian C. Gill. New York: Columbia University Press, 1991.

———. *Sexes and Genealogies*. Translated by Gillian C. Gill. New York: Columbia University Press, 1993.

Johnson, Elizabeth A. *She Who Is: The Mystery of God in Feminist Theological Discourse*. New York: Crossroad, 1992.

Johnson, Marshall D. *The Purpose of the Biblical Genealogies with Special Reference to the Setting of the Genealogies of Jesus*. Cambridge: Cambridge University Press, 1969.

———. "Reflections on a Wisdom Approach to Matthew's Christology." *JBL* 36 (1974): 44-64.

Kelber, Werner. *The Oral and the Written Gospel: The Hermeneutics of Speaking and Writing in the Synoptic Tradition, Mark, Paul and Q*. Philadelphia: Fortress, 1983.

Kingsbury, Jack Dean. "The Composition and Christology of Matt 28:16-20." *JBL* 93 (1974): 573-84.

———. "The Figure of Jesus in Matthew's Story: A Literary-Critical Probe." *JSNT* 21 (1984): 3-36.

———. *Matthew as Story*. Philadelphia: Fortress, 1986.

———. *Matthew: Structure, Christology, Kingdom*. Philadelphia: Fortress, 1975.

———. "The Title 'Son of Man' in Matthew's Gospel." *CBQ* 37 (1975): 193-202.

Kolodny, Annette. "Dancing through the Minefield: Some Observations on the Theory, Practice, and Politics of a Feminist Literary Criticism." *Feminist Studies* 6 (1980): 1-25.

Kraemer, Ross S. "Hellenistic Jewish Women: The Epigraphical Evidence." In *SBLSP* 25. Edited by K. H. Richards, 183-200. Atlanta: Scholars Press, 1986.

———. *Her Share of the Blessings: Women's Religions among Pagans, Jews, and Christians in the Greco-Roman World*. New York: Oxford University Press, 1992.

———. "Non-Literary Evidence for Jewish Women in Rome and Greece." In *Rescuing Creusa: New Methodological Approaches to Women in Antiquity*. Edited by Marilyn Skinner, 85-101. Lubbock: Texas Tech., 1987.

———, ed. *Maenads, Martyrs, Matrons, Monastics: A Sourcebook on Women's Religions in the Greco-Roman World*. Philadelphia: Fortress, 1988.

Kraft, Robert A., and George W. E. Nickelsburg, eds. *Early Judaism and Its Modern Interpreters*. Philadelphia: Fortress, 1986.

Kristeva, Julia. *Desire in Language: A Semiotic Approach to Literature and Art*. Edited by Leon S. Roudiez. Translated by Thomas Gora, Alice Jardine, and Leon S. Roudiez. New York: Columbia University Press, 1980.

———. *Revolution in Poetic Language*. Translated by Margaret Waller. New York: Columbia University Press, 1984.

LaCugna, Catherine Mowry, ed. *Freeing Theology: The Essentials of Theology in Feminist Perspective*. San Francisco: Harper, 1993.

———. *God for Us: The Trinity and Christian Life* . San Francisco: Harper, 1991.

Lang, Bernhard. *Wisdom and the Book of Proverbs: A Hebrew Goddess Redefined.* New York: Pilgrim Press, 1986.

Lee, Bernard J. *Jesus and the Metaphors of God: The Christs of the New Testament.* Studies in Judaism and Christianity. Conversation on the Road Not Taken 2. New York: Paulist, 1993.

Lefkowitz Mary R., and Maureen B. Fant, eds. *Women's Lives in Greece and Rome: A Source Book in Translation.* 2d ed. Baltimore: Johns Hopkins University Press, 1992.

Levenson, Jon D. *The Death and Resurrection of the Beloved Son: The Transformation of Child Sacrifice in Judaism and Christianity.* New Haven: Yale University Press, 1993.

Levine, Amy-Jill. *The Social and Ethnic Dimensions of Matthean Salvation History: "Go Nowhere among the Gentiles . . . " (Matt. 10.5b).* Studies in the Bible and Early Christianity 14. Lewiston: Edwin Mellen, 1988.

———, ed. *"Women Like This": New Perspectives on Jewish Women in the Greco-Roman World.* Early Judaism and Its Literature 1. Atlanta: Scholars Press, 1991.

Lewis, Naphtali, et al., eds. *The Documents from the Bar Kokhba Period in the Cave of Letters.* Jerusalem: Israel Exploration Society, 1989.

———. "Papyrus Yadin 18." *IEJ* 37 (1987): 229-50.

Lorde, Audre. *Sister Outsider: Essays and Speeches.* New York: The Crossing Press, 1984.

Love, Stuart. "The Household: A Major Social Component for Gender Analysis in the Gospel of Matthew." *BTB* 23 (1993): 21-31.

———. "The Place of Women in Public Settings in Matthew's Gospel: A Sociological Inquiry." *BTB* 24.2 (1994): 52-65.

Luz, Ulrich. "The Disciples in the Gospel according to Matthew." In *Interpretation of Matthew.* Edited by Graham Stanton, 98-128. Issues in Religion and Theology 3. Philadelphia: Fortress, 1983.

———. *Matthew 1–7: A Commentary.* Translated by Wilhelm C. Linss. Edinburgh: T. & T. Clark, 1990.

———. "The Son of Man in Matthew: Heavenly Judge or Human Christ." *JSNT* 48 (1992): 3-21.

McCracken, David. "Character in the Boundary: Bakhtin's Interdividuality in Biblical Narratives." *Semeia* 63 (1993): 29-42.

McFague, Sallie. *The Body of God: An Ecological Theology.* Minneapolis: Fortress, 1993.

———. *Metaphorical Theology: Models of God in Religious Language.* Philadelphia: Fortress, 1982.

———. *Models of God: Theology for an Ecological, Nuclear Age.* Philadelphia: Fortress, 1987.

Malbon, Elizabeth Struthers, and Adele Berlin, eds. *Characterization in Biblical Literature. Semeia* 63. Atlanta: Scholars Press, 1993.

Malina, Bruce J. *The New Testament World: Insights from Cultural Anthropology.* Rev. ed. Louisville: Westminster/John Knox, 1993.

———. "'Religion' in the World of Paul." *BTB* 16 (1986): 92-101.

Malina, Bruce J., and Jerome H. Neyrey. *Calling Jesus Names: The Social Value of Labels in Matthew.* Sonoma: Polebridge Press, 1988.

Malina, Bruce J., and Richard L. Rohrbaugh. *Social Science Commentary on the Synoptic Gospels.* Minneapolis: Fortress, 1992.

Margolin, Uri. "Introducing and Sustaining Characters in Literary Narrative: A Set of Conditions." *Style* 21.1 (1987): 107-24.

Masian, Sennie. "The Profile of Filipino Women—Not Read, Seen, or Heard." In *National Women's Conference 1990 Proceedings*, 182-84. Canberra: Write People, 1990.

Meeks, Wayne A. *The Moral World of the First Christians.* Library of Early Christianity. Philadelphia: Westminster, 1986.

Meier, John P. *A Marginal Jew: Rethinking the Historical Jesus.* Volume 2: *Mentor, Message and Miracles.* Anchor Bible Reference Library. New York: Doubleday, 1994.

———. "Matthew 15:21-28." *Int* 40 (1986): 397-402.

Miller, Nancy K., ed. *The Poetics of Gender.* New York: Columbia University Press, 1986.

Moessner, David P. "And Once Again, What Sort of 'Essence?': A Response to Charles Talbert." *Semeia* 43 (1988): 75-84.

Mohanty, Chandra Talpade, Anne Russo, and Lourdes Torres, eds. *Third World Women and The Politics of Feminism.* Bloomington: Indiana University Press, 1991.

Montrose, Louis. "New Historicisms." In *Redrawing the Boundaries: The Transformation of English and American Literary Studies.* Edited by Stephen Greenblatt and Giles Gunn, 392-418. New York: Modern Language Association of America, 1992.

Moore, Stephen D. *Literary Criticism and the Gospels: The Theoretical Challenge.* New Haven: Yale University Press, 1989.

Nau, Arlo J. *Peter in Matthew: Discipleship, Diplomacy, and Dispraise . . . with an Assessment of Power and Privilege in the Petrine Office.* Good News Studies 36. Collegeville, Minn.: Liturgical Press, 1992.

Nelson, Hilde Lindemann. "Resistance and Insubordination." *Hypatia* 10.2 (1995): 23-40.

Neusner, Jacob, William S. Green, and Ernest Frerichs, eds. *Judaisms and Their Messiahs at the Turn of the Christian Era.* Cambridge: Cambridge University Press, 1987.

Nicholson, Linda J., ed. *Feminism/Postmodernism.* New York: Routledge, 1990.

Nolan, Brian N. *The Royal Son of God: The Christology of Matthew 1–2 in the Setting of the Gospel.* OBO 23. Göttingen: Vandenhoeck & Ruprecht, 1979.

Nolland, J. "No Son-of-God Christology in Matthew 1:18-25." *JSNT* 62 (1996): 3-12.

O'Day, Gail R. "Surprised by Faith: Jesus and the Canaanite Woman." *Listening* 24 (1989): 290-301.

Oduyoye, Mercy Amba, and Musimbi R. A. Kanyoro, eds. *The Will to Arise: Women, Tradition, and the Church in Africa.* Maryknoll, N.Y.: Orbis Books, 1992.

Osborne, Grant R. "Genre Criticism—Sensus Literalis." *Trinity Journal* 4 (1983): 1-27.

Osiek, Carolyn. "The Women at the Tomb: What Are They Doing There?" *Ex Auditu* 9 (1993): 97-107.

Ostriker, Alicia Suskin. *Feminist Revision and the Bible.* The Bucknell Lectures in Literary Theory. Oxford: Blackwell, 1993.

Overman, J. Andrew. *Church and Community in Crisis: The Gospel according to Matthew*. The New Testament in Context. Valley Forge, Penn.: Trinity Press International, 1996.

———. *Matthew's Gospel and Formative Judaism: The Social World of the Matthean Community*. Minneapolis: Fortress, 1990.

Parker, Patricia. *Literary Fat Ladies: Rhetoric, Gender, Property*. London: Methuen, 1987.

Pattel-Gray, Anne. *Through Aboriginal Eyes: The Cry from the Wilderness*. Geneva: WCC Publications, 1991.

Perdue, Leo G. "The Wisdom Sayings of Jesus." *Forum* 2 (1986): 3-35.

Perry, Menakhem. "Literary Dynamics: How the Order of a Text Creates Its Meaning." *Poetics Today* 1 (1979): 35-64.

Phelan, James. *Reading People, Reading Plots: Character, Progression, and the Interpretation of Narrative*. Chicago: University of Chicago Press, 1989.

Phillips, Gary. "'What Is Written? How Are You Reading?' Gospel, Intertextuality and Doing Lukewise: A Writerly Reading of Lk 10:25-37 (and 38-42)." In *SBLSP* 31. Edited by Eugene H. Lovering, 266-301. Atlanta: Scholars Press, 1992.

Pomeroy, Sarah B. *Goddesses, Whores, Wives, and Slaves: Women in Classical Antiquity*. New York: Schocken Books, 1975.

———. *Women in Hellenistic Egypt from Alexander to Cleopatra*. New York: Schocken Books, 1984.

Pokorn'y, P. "From a Puppy to the Child: Some Problems of Contemporary Biblical Exegesis Demonstrated from Mark 7.24-30/Matt 15.21-8." *NTS* 41 (1995): 321-37.

*Pseudo-Philon—Les Antiquités Bibliques*. Critical Text and Introduction by Daniel J. Harrington. Translation by Jacques Cazeaux. Source Chrétiennes. Paris: Les Editions du Cerf, 1976.

Rank, Otto, Lord Raglan, and Alan Dundes. *In Quest of the Hero*. Princeton: Princeton University Press, 1990.

Rashkow, Ilona N. "Daughters and Fathers in Genesis . . . Or, What Is Wrong with This Picture?" In *A Feminist Companion to Exodus to Deuteronomy*. Edited by Athalya Brenner, 22-36. Sheffield: Sheffield Academic Press, 1994.

Ricoeur, Paul. *Interpretation Theory: Discourse and the Surplus of Meaning*. Fort Worth: Texas Christian University Press, 1976.

———. *The Rule of Metaphor: Multi-Disciplinary Studies of the Creation of Meaning in Language*. Translated by Robert Czerny with Kathleen McLaughlin and John Costello. Toronto: University of Toronto Press, 1981.

Ringe, Sharon H. *Jesus, Liberation, and the Biblical Jubilee*. Overtures to Biblical Theology. Philadelphia: Fortress, 1989.

Ritchie, Nelly. "Women and Christology." In *Through Her Eyes: Women's Theology from Latin America*. Edited by Elsa Tamez, 81-95. Maryknoll, N.Y.: Orbis Books, 1989.

Robinson, Bernard P. "Peter and His Successors: Tradition and Redaction in Matthew 16.17-19." *JSNT* 21 (1984): 85-104.

Ruether, Rosemary Radford. *Sexism and God Talk: Toward a Feminist Theology*. Boston: Beacon Press, 1983.

Saldarini, Anthony J. *Matthew's Christian-Jewish Community*. Chicago: University of Chicago Press, 1994.

Sawicki, Jana. *Disciplining Foucault: Feminism, Power, and the Body.* Thinking Gender. New York: Routledge, 1991.

Sawicki, Marianne. "Making the Best of Jesus." Unpublished paper presented at the Society of Biblical Literature Meeting, San Francisco, 1992.

———. *Seeing the Lord: Resurrection and Early Christian Practices.* Minneapolis: Fortress, 1994.

———. "Spatial Management of Gender and Labor in Greco-Roman Galilee." In *Archaeology and the World of Galilee: Texts and Contexts in the Roman and Byzantine Periods.* Edited by Douglas R. Edwards and Thomas McCollough. Forthcoming.

Schaberg, Jane. *The Father, the Son, and the Holy Spirit: The Triadic Phrase in Matthew 28:19b.* SBLDS 61. Atlanta: Scholars Press, 1982.

———. *The Illegitimacy of Jesus: A Feminist Theological Interpretation of the Infancy Narratives.* San Francisco: Harper & Row, 1987.

Schneiders, Sandra M. *The Revelatory Text: Interpreting the New Testament as Sacred Scripture.* San Francisco: Harper, 1991.

———. *Women and the Word: The Gender of God in the New Testament and the Spirituality of Women.* 1986 Madeleva Lecture in Spirituality. New York: Paulist, 1986.

Schottroff, Luise. "Itinerant Prophetesses: A Feminist Analysis of the Sayings Source Q." In *Occasional Papers of the Institute for Antiquity and Christianity* 21, 1-16. Claremont, 1991.

———. *Lydia's Impatient Sisters: A Feminist Social History of Early Christianity.* Translated by Barbara and Martin Rumscheidt. Louisville: Westminster/John Knox, 1995.

Schroer, Silvia. "Jesus Sophia: Erträge der feministischen Forschung zu einer frühchristlichen Deutung der Praxis und des Schicksals Jesu von Nazaret." In *Vom Verlangen nach Heilwerden: Christologie in feministisch-theologischer Sicht.* Edited by Doris Strahm and Regula Strobel, 112-28. Fribourg: Edition Exodus, 1991.

———. "Weise Frauen und Ratgeberinnen in Israel—Vorbilder der personifizierten Chokmah." In *Auf den Spuren der Weisheit: Sophia—Wegweiserin für ein neues Gottesbild.* Edited by Verena Wodtke, 9-23. Freiburg: Herder, 1991.

Schuller, Eileen. "4Q372 1: A Text about Joseph." *RevQ* 14 (1990): 343-76.

———. "The Psalm of 4Q372 1 within the Context of Second Temple Prayer." *CBQ* 54 (1992): 67-79.

———. "Women of the Exodus in Biblical Retellings of the Second Temple Period." In *Gender and Difference in Ancient Israel.* Edited by Peggy L. Day, 178-94. Minneapolis: Fortress, 1989.

Schüssler Fiorenza, Elisabeth. *Bread Not Stone: The Challenge of Feminist Biblical Interpretation.* Boston: Beacon Press, 1984.

———. *But She Said: Feminist Practices of Biblical Interpretation.* Boston: Beacon Press, 1992.

———. *Discipleship of Equals: A Critical Feminist Ekklesia-logy of Liberation.* New York: Crossroad, 1993.

———. "The Ethics of Interpretation: De-Centering Biblical Scholarship." *JBL* 107 (1988): 3-17.

———. *Jesus: Miriam's Child, Sophia's Prophet: Critical Issues in Feminist Christology.* New York: Continuum, 1994.

————. *In Memory of Her: A Feminist Theological Reconstruction of Christian Origins.* New York: Crossroad, 1983.

————. "Toward a Feminist Biblical Hermeneutics: Biblical Interpretation and Liberation Theology." In *The Challenge of Liberation Theology.* Edited by Brian Maher and L. Dale Richesin, 91-112. Maryknoll, N.Y.: Orbis Books, 1981.

————. "The Twelve." In *Women Priests: A Catholic Commentary on the Vatican Declaration.* Edited by Leonard and Arlene Swidler, 114-22. New York: Paulist, 1977.

————. "Wisdom Mythology and the Christological Hymns of the New Testament." In *Aspects of Wisdom in Judaism and Early Christianity.* Edited by Robert L. Wilken, 17-41. Notre Dame, Ind.: University of Notre Dame Press, 1975.

————, ed. *Searching the Scriptures,* Volume 1: *A Feminist Introduction.* New York: Crossroad, 1993.

Scobie, Alex. "Storytellers, Storytelling, and the Novel in Graeco-Roman Antiquity." *Rheinishes Museum für Philologie* 122 (1979): 229-59.

Scott, Joan W. "Gender: A Useful Category of Historical Analysis." In *Coming to Terms: Feminism, Theory, Politics.* Edited by Elizabeth Weed, 81-100. New York: Routledge, 1989.

Segovia, Fernando F., and Mary Ann Tolbert, eds. *Reading from This Place.* Volume 1: *Social Location and Biblical Interpretation in the United States.* Minneapolis: Fortress, 1995.

————. *Reading from This Place.* Volume 2: *Social Location and Biblical Interpretation in Global Perspective.* Minneapolis: Fortress, 1995.

Senior, Donald P. *The Passion Narrative according to Matthew: A Redactional Study.* BEThL 39. Leuven: University Press, 1982.

————. *The Passion of Jesus in the Gospel of Matthew.* The Passion Series 1. Wilmington, Del.: Michael Glazier, 1985.

————. *What Are They Saying about Matthew?* Revised and expanded edition. New York: Paulist, 1996.

Shapiro, Judith. "Anthropology and the Study of Gender." *Soundings* 64 (1981): 446-65.

Shuler, Philip L. *A Genre for the Gospels: The Biographical Character of Matthew.* Philadelphia: Fortress, 1982.

Sim, David C. *Apocalyptic Eschatology in the Gospel of Matthew.* SNTSMS 88. Cambridge: Cambridge University Press, 1996.

————. "The Gospel of Matthew and the Gentiles." *JSNT* 57 (1995): 19-48.

Sobrino, Jon. *Christology at the Crossroads: A Latin American Approach.* Maryknoll, N.Y.: Orbis Books, 1978.

Soskice, Janet Martin. "Blood and Defilement: Jesus, Gender, and the Universality of Christ." *European Association for Catholic Theology Bulletin* 5 (1994): 230-41.

————. *Metaphor and Religious Language.* Oxford: Clarendon Press, 1985.

Springer, Mary Doyle. *A Rhetoric of Literary Character: Some Women of Henry James.* Chicago: University of Chicago Press, 1978.

Stanton, Graham N. *A Gospel for a New People: Studies in Matthew.* Edinburgh: T. & T. Clark, 1992.

Stock, Augustine. "Is Matthew's Presentation of Peter Ironic?" *BTB* 17.2 (1987): 64-69.

Strahm, Doris, and Regula Strobel, eds. *Vom Verlangen nach Heilwerden: Christologie in feministisch-theologischer Sicht.* Fribourg: Edition Exodus, 1991.

Suggs, M. Jack. *Wisdom, Christology, and Law in Matthew's Gospel.* Cambridge: Harvard University Press, 1970.

Talbert, Charles H. *What Is a Gospel? The Genre of the Canonical Gospels.* London: SPCK, 1978.

Tamez, Elsa, ed. *Through Her Eyes: Women's Theology from Latin America.* Maryknoll, N.Y.: Orbis Books, 1989.

Theissen, Gerd. "Jünger als Gewalttäter (Matthew 11,12f.; Lk 16,16): Der Stürmerspruch als Selbststigmatisierung einer Minorität." *ST* 49 (1995): 183-200.

Thériault, Jean-Yves. "Le Maître maîtrisé! Mathieu 15,21-28." In *De Jésus et des Femmes: Lectures sémiotiques. Suivies d'un entretien avec A. J. Greimas.* Edited by Adèle Chené, et al., 19-34. Recherches Nouvelle Série 14. Montreal: Les Editions Bellarmin, 1987.

Thistlethwaite, Susan Brooks. *Sex, Race, and God: Christian Feminism in Black and White.* New York: Crossroad, 1989.

Thistlethwaite, Susan Brooks, and P. Engel, eds. *Lift Every Voice: Constructing Christian Theologies from the Underside.* San Francisco: Harper & Row, 1990.

Todorov, Tzvetan. *Mikhail Bakhtin: The Dialogical Principle.* Translated by Wlad Godzich. Theory and History of Literature 13. Minneapolis: University of Minnesota Press, 1984.

Tolbert, Mary Ann. "The Gospel in Greco-Roman Culture." In *The Book and the Text: The Bible and Literary Theory.* Edited by Regina M. Schwartz, 258-75. Oxford: Blackwell, 1990.

Trible, Phyllis. "Bringing Miriam out of the Shadows." *Bible Review* 5.1 (1989): 14-25, 34.

———. *God and the Rhetoric of Sexuality.* Overtures to Biblical Theology. Philadelphia: Fortress, 1978.

Tuttle, Gary. "The Sermon on the Mount: Its Wisdom Affinities and Their Relation to Its Structure." *JETS* 20 (1977): 213-30.

Verseput, Donald J. "The Faith of the Reader and the Narrative of Matthew 13.53-16.20." *JSNT* 46 (1992): 3-24.

———. "The Role and Meaning of the 'Son of God' Title in Matthew's Gospel." *NTS* 33 (1987): 532-56.

Wainwright, Elaine Mary. *Towards a Feminist Critical Reading of the Gospel according to Matthew.* BZNW 60. Berlin: de Gruyter, 1991.

Ward, Graham. "Divinity and Sexuality: Luce Irigaray and Christology." *Modern Theology* 12.2 (1996): 221-37.

Yaghjian, Lucretia B. *How Shall We Read? A Preface to Matthew's Protocols of Reading.* Unpublished manuscript, 1994.

Yamaguchi, Satoko. *Re-visioning Martha and Mary: A Feminist Critical Reading of a Text in the Fourth Gospel.* Unpublished Doctor of Ministry thesis, Episcopal Divinity School, Cambridge, Massachusetts, 1996.

Zagarell, Sandra A. "Narrative of Community: The Identification of a Genre." In *Revising the Word and the World: Essays in Feminist Literary Criticism.* Edited by VèVè A. Clark, Ruth-Ellen B. Joeres, and Madelon Sprengnether, 249-78. Chicago: University of Chicago Press, 1993.

Zucker, David J. "Jesus and Jeremiah in the Matthean Tradition." *JES* 27 (1990): 288-305.

# Index

African-American women, 13. *See also* women: of color

African women, 16. *See also* women: of color

Allison, Dale C., 81, 93, 144n.37, 144n.39

Amoah, Elizabeth, 16

androcentricity: Caesarea Philippi and, 93; as crossing most ethnic boundaries, 150n.32; and early interpretations of Jesus' death, 105; of the first-century household, 91–92; Jesus/Sophia metaphor as read in a context of, 77

anthropology, 12, 46

anti-Judaism, 103, 122n.8

archaeology, 41

Archer, Gleason L., 145n.56

Asian women, 10, 125n.26

Bakhtin, Mikhail, 29, 36–37, 91, 128n.6, 137n.48, 138n.51

Bal, Mieke, 25, 27, 132n.67, 145n.57

baptismal liturgy, 112

Bathsheba, 56

Bauer, Dale M., 37

biography, 57, 70, 91, 102

Bird, Phyllis, 140n.1

Botha, P. J. J., 22

Boyd, Arthur, 17

Braidotti, Rosi, 2, 3, 16, 19, 121n.1, 127n.63

bread, 85, 87, 88, 98

Brock, Rita Nakashima, 12–13, 15, 16, 17, 125n.25

Brooten, Bernadette, 36

Brown, Joanne Carlson, 13

Brown, Raymond E., 101, 109–10, 113, 142n.20, 153n.21, 153n.33, 154n.46, 155n.52

Bubar, Wallace, 100

Burnett, Fred, 68, 104, 153n.20

Butler, Judith, 11

Bynum, Caroline Walker, 131n.53

Camp, Claudia, 27, 148n.47

Canaanite woman, the. *See* Justa (the Canaanite woman)

catechesis, 112, 117, 118

characterization: a feminist reading of the, of Jesus, 11–12, 130n.29; literary and social forces and, 129n.27; and the poetics of engendered reading, 23–26

children, 12–13, 89, 98

Chirichigno, G. C., 145n.56

Choi Man Ja, 11, 16, 125n.26

christology: Elisabeth Schüssler Fiorenza on, 123n.5, 124n.11, 125n.22; feminist critiques of, 10–18, 124n.8; the Jesus/Sophia metaphor and, 77; new efforts in feminist, 3; privileging of the terms "Son of Man" and "Lord" by contemporary, 75; "from the side," 107; "Son of God," 154n.47

*Christos:* background of term, 54; as embedded in a people and family, 60; John's use of the term, 69; the Magi and, 62; the Petrine confession and, 95, 96, 97; Sophia and, 76–77; and the subversion of the political power of the crucifixion, 104